HE FRIGHTENED ME . . .

Then on Wednesday, June 22, one of Nicole's 911 calls was released to the media. I wasn't shocked that Nicole had called 911; I wasn't even shocked by what she said. . . .

But listening to that tape for the first time shook me up. I had never heard my uncle so much as raise his voice to anybody; if anything, I thought he backed down too often with Nicole. The voice on the tape, though, was not the voice of the man I knew. Oh, I recognized it, all right; I never thought the tape was a fake. But the rage, the yelling, the cusswords thundering in the background—this wasn't the uncle I was used to seeing. It frightened me, *he* frightened me. I kept thinking that if someone were yelling at me like that, I'd be terrified. A vision flashed into my head of a man on a football field, a man big and heavy-handed enough to inflict real damage on the other players. A man that seemed to be out of control. I shivered.

I'M NOT DANCING ANYMORE

TERRI BAKER
WITH KENNETH ROSS
AND MARY JANE ROSS

Pinnacle Books
Kensington Publishing Corp.

http://www.pinnaclebooks.com

DEDICATION

To my Higher Power, who gives me wisdom,
courage, serenity, and love.
To my entire family, especially our youngest generation.
The most beautiful flowers come from
the strongest roots.

ACKNOWLEDGMENTS

Mom and Dad, there are no words to express all you've given me and continue to give me. You will always have my deepest gratitude for your unconditional love, support, and guidance.

Thanks to my sisters, Tracy, Toni, Gyne, Khadi, and Cynthia. Who needs friends when we've got each other.

My Grandmother, my aunts, uncles, cousins and extended family whose presence continues to enrich all of our lives and keeps this family strong.

My brother, Benny, thanks for showing me how to turn lemons into lemonade.

Thanks to Dr. Monika Goodman-Korn, for her example and professional consultation in family dynamics, and for her support and encouragement as a friend and mentor.

Glenda girl, thanks, we did it. All those tears on the beach have turned into laughs.

Lex, of all your accomplishments the most incredible thing for me is that you still value our friendship so much. How lucky can I be.

Jerri, and her husband Frank Churchill, my bestest married friend. Who would ever think our lives would take so many turns 16 years ago. May God continue to bless your marriage and children. If you receive a fraction of all you give, your lives will overflow with blessings.

Leslie, Daisy, Richard, Kathy, Vincent, Carole, and Kelvin—just to name a few—I am so bad about staying in touch. Thanks for being so patient.

Dr. Heffner and the staff of Orange County Community Hospital. Without their compassionate professionalism I wouldn't be here today.

Ken Ross and Mary Jane, for finding the words (and time) to write my complex thoughts and feelings. You two are angels who performed a miracle.

Alan Nevins and the team at Renaissance, thanks for watching my back and believing in this project from the start.

Paul Dinas and the staff at Kensington Publishing, thanks for giving me the opportunity to write this book and the support to see it through. Nobody works harder than you, Paul. I appreciate your tireless hours.

CONTENTS

PROLOGUE

AWAKENINGS

I woke up slowly that morning. It had been a restless night filled with vague nightmares, fragmented images, and a nameless anxiety that clung to me still. As the gray light filtered through the blinds at Rockingham, I fought my way to consciousness. For a minute I couldn't remember where I was; then, I saw Kato, still sound asleep, curled up on the carpet near the couch where I lay. Suddenly it hit me: I was in the TV room at Uncle O.J.'s house, and today was the wake for his wife, Nicole Brown Simpson. My first impulse was to turn over and go back to sleep, but I knew that wasn't possible. I could hear my mother's voice in the distance, and I knew it was time to get up and stake out a bathroom. I sat up on the edge of the couch and tried to stretch out the kinks from my cramped night on the sofa. I could already hear the drone of media helicopters hovering over the roof.

By now Kato was beginning to stir, too, nudged into consciousness by my movements.

"Terri?" he said.

"Yeah."

"What time do we leave?"

"I don't know. I'm going to take a shower," I said, stepping over him as I rummaged around for my overnight bag.

"Terri? Can I ride in the limo with you?"

"Sure. I guess," I mumbled as I went on safari around the room, searching for the things I'd dumped there the night before.

Kato was sitting up by now, looking even sadder and more confused than I felt. Since my Uncle O.J. had left on Tuesday, and we hadn't seen him since, Kato had been left with a houseful of strangers who eyed him with skepticism. When he'd driven me home the night before to pick up my dress for the wake, my father had been immediately suspicious.

"Where were you?" Dad had asked me when I got back, as if I were thirteen instead of thirty. "We don't know that guy. You shouldn't be alone with him."

Kato Kaelin was the least of my problems that morning. Locating the plain black dress I'd picked up from home the night before, I went in search of a free bathroom. God knows there were enough of them at Uncle O.J.'s place, but with the whole Simpson clan in residence, space was already at a premium.

As I stood in the shower letting the warm water run over my body, I tried not to think of what lay ahead. I'd never been to a wake before. The only funerals I'd been to were those of my grandparents, and they'd died at a peaceful old age. I couldn't fathom going to a funeral for someone only a few years older than I was. What did people do at a wake, anyway? Surely there wouldn't be an open casket. Brief images of Nicole's body under its drape in the blood-spattered Bundy walkway flitted through my mind. I'd avoided those images on the news. Surely the Browns wouldn't want people to see their daughter like that. Shaking off the thought, I turned off the water.

A few minutes later, neatly dressed like the good Baptist girl my mother had raised, I returned to the TV room. Kato was fully awake by now, dressed in his stylishly rumpled clothes. I went on into the kitchen where the rest of my family was gathered. Gigi, my uncle's housekeeper, had made sure there was plenty of food laid out for us, but no one could eat. The helicopters hovering overhead made the grounds sound like a war zone. It didn't make for much conversation, not that anyone wanted to talk. The blinds, tightly closed against the lenses prying through every window, gave the whole house a ghostly dimness. The entire scene had an air of unreality.

Family members had been rushing around for nearly half an hour, careful to avoid the windows' prying eyes. With the hour of departure at hand, we began lining up at the front door. We were all there: Grandma in her wheelchair; my cousins Jason and Arnelle; my father; my mother Shirley, standing straight and her head held high; my sisters Tracy and Toni; my aunt Como and Uncle Charles. We were all going, except Justin and Sydney, who would be staying at the Browns' house with A.C. Cowlings during the wake. My family believed in being there for each other, and no one was missing that morning—no one but Uncle O.J., that is. We stood together in the hall, a congregation of black people, in black clothes, getting ready to file outside to three black limos, an unusual sight at a house where the usual crowd was predominantly white.

Kato's pale face was an anomaly as he tagged along behind me and fell into line.

"Can I ride in the limo with you?" Kato asked me once again, this time plaintively. His car was parked on the other side of the gate, in the midst of the media sharks, and I knew he didn't want to fight his way through them.

An army surrounded the house. Hordes of satellite trucks, TV cameras, bright lights, platforms, and boom microphones rose above the ivy-covered walls. Dozens of eyes waited for us on the other side of that door—hungry reporters, pushy photographers, indifferent technicians on portable platforms, aluminum ladders, and van roofs. It was a damn circus, with us as the freak show. Getting through them the night before had been like parting the Red Sea, and I knew Kato dreaded a repeat. Where was Moses when you needed him?

This time my mother answered Kato's question for me. "Oh no, no, the limo's just for family." There was a firmness in her voice that left no room for discussion.

Kato looked even more agitated. Turning to me again, he begged, "Terri, can I drive *your* car then?" My weather-beaten VW convertible was parked safely inside the compound.

"Sure," I started to say, but once again my mother preempted me.

"If he's going to go, he needs to drive his own car," she replied in third person, as if Kato weren't even there.

I looked at Kato and shrugged my shoulders helplessly. "Sorry," I whispered. One glance at my mother silenced any objections he might have had. Looking faintly desperate, he sighed and pushed open the front door. Edging gingerly out, he pressed through the gate out front and ran the gauntlet to his little car as the press descended on him like a flock of vultures. My family filed out behind him in a more dignified manner.

The horde of reporters surged in on us as we moved through the faded sunlight toward the black limos. The black faces of my family, somber above the black dresses of the women and the white collars of the men, filed toward the doors of the limos, held open by chauffeurs in black suits. The cries of the press and the roaring blades of the helicopters blended together. I adopted a blank, stoical expression as a refuge from the eyes boring into us from every side. I felt numb, detached. Psychologists call it dissociation. For me, it was just survival.

Once inside the refuge of the limos, we leaned back in silence. The gates opened, and the first limo made its way out, bearing Grandma, my parents, and Aunt Como and Uncle Charles. I was in the second limo with my two sisters, Tracy and Toni, and Jason and Arnelle. Safe inside the limo, we stared out the tinted windows as the car wound down to Sunset Boulevard, and turned east toward the 405 freeway. Looking out the rear window, I could see a brown mist hanging bleakly over the coast, making it difficult to tell where the ocean stopped and the horizon began. I could also see Kato in his little car, clinging to the train of limos like a small caboose, and behind him a stream of media vans and cars. Overhead were the helicopters, trailing us like we were escaped criminals. I just kept thinking how bizarre it all was.

Once on the 405 freeway, we relaxed a little bit. It was a good hour's drive to the mortuary in Orange County where the wake would be held. We were all exhausted from the chaos of the week and the mad dash to get everyone ready that morning. In the relative silence I wondered vaguely where Uncle O.J. was. I turned around to see if Kato was still behind us. He was. I hoped he wouldn't get separated from the limos. He didn't even know where the mortuary was. No one had bothered to give him the address. The wake was supposed to be limited to close friends and family. We weren't quite sure whether Kato fit into either category. As far as we were concerned, he was just a friend of Nicole's.

Nicole. Once again her image came floating back to me from the news reports. I wondered who the friend was that had been found with her. I thought again about the wake and promptly pushed the image out of my mind.

I lost track of time as our limo wound down the smoggy freeway. I could still hear the helicopters overhead. It worried me. Our destination was supposed to be a secret. It hadn't yet dawned on me that nothing in our lives was a secret anymore. It must have been over an hour later when we passed the line into Orange County. Our driver exited the freeway behind the other limo. Ahead of us lay the circular driveway of the mortuary.

I needn't have worried about the surveillance helicopters trailing behind. As soon as we pulled in the driveway, it was clear that our destination was anything but secret. Dozens of reporters and camera crews were already set up outside the mortuary complex. Someone had obviously tipped them off to both the time and the place of the wake. I felt a surge of anger at whoever they'd pressured or bribed into leaking the information. I was glad Sydney and Justin weren't there. My God, didn't these people have any sensitivity to what was happening? The limo drivers got us as close as possible to the door of the chapel, and we all hustled out of the limos and into the mortuary as quickly as possible, ignoring the assaults of yet another arsenal of cameras as we passed.

Once inside, we found ourselves in a lobby that opened into a corridor. To the left of the corridor was a chapel.

On the right was a viewing room. Out of the corner of my eye, I caught a glimpse of Nicole's casket inside the viewing room.

I could see the Browns standing in the lobby at the head of the corridor, greeting people as they arrived. I fidgeted nervously. The Browns made me uncomfortable during the best of times, much less now. It had been a long time since I'd seen them. One by one we filed in and greeted them as I stood with my own loved ones. There we all were, paying our respects, and in front of us stood Lou and Juditha, Nicole's parents, and her sisters Denise and Minnie, my old roommate. Their faces were rigid with shock and grief. I avoided their eyes. The rumor was already circulating that my uncle was a suspect in their daughter's murder. I wondered what they would do when they saw us. *Oh God,* I thought. *What must they be thinking?* They greeted us civilly, solemnly. There would be no scenes that day.

Uncle O.J. was already there, in the corridor near the Browns. I watched him anxiously as he stood in the doorway of the viewing room, staring in to where the coffin lay on a gurney on the far side. The Browns had already been in to see Nicole. We all waited so Uncle O.J. could go in and have some time alone with her. He walked in with my mother and father, disappearing from my sight. I stepped into the room with my sisters and got ready to pay my own respects.

The room that lay before me looked as much like a photographer's studio as a mortuary. On easels all around stood huge, poster-size color photos of Nicole, surrounded by garlands of flowers in festive colors of red, yellow, and orange. The photos were old modeling shots of Nicole, pictures of her with Sydney and Justin, and one photo of her in her white Ferrari convertible with the top down, surrounded by her children and friends. Uncle O.J. was conspicuously absent from all of the photographs. The room was silent except for the ubiquitous hum of the helicopters outside. The only jarring note was the coffin lying in the middle of all the stylish splendor. The lid was open, and I began to feel queasy.

Next to the coffin, in a chair by the wall, sat my uncle O.J. He was staring at the casket, his face a mask of pain. My parents sat on either side of him. Not wanting to intrude, my sisters and I crept quietly over to the corner of the room, opposite the coffin. Uncle O.J. broke down and sobbed. My mother held his hand, while my father put his arm around his shoulders for comfort. I had never seen my uncle cry. It unnerved me.

By now others were filtering in, milling around in the silence. The mourners spoke in muted voices if they spoke at all. There were about twenty people there altogether, mostly family. Bob Kardashian was there, solemn-faced, his hands shoved in his pockets, and a small group of Nicole's friends stood off to the side in a quiet circle. Kato had found his way in and was loitering uncomfortably in the background. Every now and then someone would walk through Uncle O.J.'s line of vision and he would acknowledge them, but for the most part he stared straight ahead, lost in his grief. The Browns came back into the room. My cousin Jason walked up to the coffin, looked down inside, and turned away, sobbing uncontrollably. My mom rose to comfort him as Arnelle went to his side and put her arms around him, leading him from the room.

Everyone was crying, most people silently, but every now and then the silence would be punctuated by the sobs of the Browns and of my uncle O.J. I felt paralyzed inside, sick with pain for my uncle and cousins, horrified at the manner of my aunt's death, but unable to grieve for Nicole.

Guilt rose up in my throat and choked me. Our two families said little to one another, as polarized in Nicole's death as they had been in her life. Another study in black and white. Only the still figure in the coffin united us—that and the two small people who waited at the Browns' house for their grandparents to return.

Finally it was my turn to pay my respects to my uncle's wife. My sisters and I made our way slowly to the coffin. Gathering my courage, I looked down at the woman with whom I'd had such a painful relationship. Nothing had prepared me for I saw.

Nicole lay inside a plain wooden coffin that was lined with white silk. Nothing about her looked familiar in that horrible moment. Her hands lay white and still, with long acrylic nails and clear polish. I remembered how hard she'd tried to grow long nails when I'd lived with her ten years before. She never succeeded. Always nervous, she invariably bit them off before they were long enough to file. Nicole always had tomboy nails. I didn't recognize the waxlike hands with the long nails lying on the white silk in front of me.

It was her face, though, that arrested me. I had often thought that Nicole would look old before her time because she'd always suntanned way too much, and up close, her face was prematurely lined with wrinkles. She'd looked much older than her thirty-six years when I'd seen her two months earlier. As she lay before me now, her skin looked old and dry. Her cheeks were red, her face swollen and grisly. No amount of effort on the part of the mortician had been able to erase the marks of her final moments of life.

Her face wasn't the worst part. As I looked down at the still form before me, I was struck by the notion that something was horribly wrong, but for a moment I couldn't figure out what. The coroner hadn't released the details of the autopsy yet, and for a moment I was startled and confused by her misshapen torso. Her head was bent forward, and it dawned on me that I couldn't see where her neck was. Instead, there was just her chin between her head and torso. It looked as if the mortician had placed her head directly onto her shoulders. It appeared as though there was no neck to hold it in place. It was horrible.

I turned away, unable to look at her any longer. My sisters and I shook our heads and shuddered. We couldn't believe how bad she looked. I touched her cold hand. I thought of my uncle O.J. and of Sydney and Justin, and felt sick for them. I thought of Lou and Juditha Brown and grieved for what they must be feeling at that moment. As I walked away from the still form lying behind me, I overheard Juditha telling someone how beautiful Nicole looked. I looked at my sisters in disbelief. Beautiful? My God. What did the lifeless figure lying in that casket have to do with the striking young woman I remembered? The embalmer's art could not conceal the fact of her death.

A few minutes later we all left the room and went into the chapel so the Browns could say their final good-byes to Nicole. Huddled together across the corridor, we could hear them crying. Uncle O.J. and Bob Kardashian went out the back where the media couldn't follow. We didn't ask him where he was going. We didn't want to intrude. We were there to support him, not to interrogate him.

Getting back out to the limousines half an hour later was even worse than our arrival, for the media crowd had grown to moblike proportions. They surged around the limos as we stepped out into the June afternoon, made suddenly bright by dozens of high-powered lights shining into our eyes. My parents were going over to the Browns' for a small gathering, but my sisters and I chose to go home to Rockingham. We'd had as much as we could take for one day. As we sank into the seats of the limo once again, our driver pulled slowly into the crowd, resisting the urge to run down the reporters blocking our path.

By the time we got back to Rockingham, it was nearly evening. Exhausted, we filed out of the limo and back into the house, settling into chairs around the living room. In spite of our day-long fast, no one wanted to eat. No one wanted to talk, either. In morbid fascination, we turned on the TV sets to watch the news coverage of Nicole's murder with the rest of America. Uncle O.J. had three televisions in his living room, and we turned on all three of them, tuning each to a different station. We watched them simultaneously, all three sets lined up next to each other along the living-room wall. Someone went in the kitchen and turned on the TV in there, too. Without comment we watched ourselves file in and out of the limo, over and over again, in living color. Station after station reported that Uncle O.J. had returned to the house with us and was hiding inside. He wasn't. We didn't know where he was—any place but the fortress at Rockingham, which now trapped as well as protected us.

Kato had returned with us, still trailing behind our limo, and was pacing nervously around the house. Uncle O.J.'s attorney had called him, and asked him to come by the office. As if it were a bizarre form of stereo, we listened to the helicopters humming simultaneously above the roof and on the screens lined up in front of us. It was better than silence. Too many rooms lay empty around us.

Forty-eight hours later my uncle would be arrested for murder, and the most painful and bizarre episode of our lives would begin. Lying on the same couch in the TV room at Rockingham later that night, dark images floated once more through my mind. How had it all gone wrong?

How had the beautiful blond woman on my uncle's arm turned into the still, sad figure stretched inside that wooden box? My father had once said about Nicole and Uncle O.J., "Those two need to leave each other alone." He had always advised me and my sisters not to play with men's emotions. Someone might get hurt. Lying there in the dark, my mind began to drift to the past, before Uncle O.J. married Nicole, to the days when they were young lovers and I was just a kid, eager to please them both.

CHAPTER 1

ROOTS

Mine is the story of a family. My family. Until June of 1994 no one in America outside our own family circle had ever given us a second thought. Then my uncle, O.J. Simpson, hurtled overnight into the media glare of a murder trial that became a national obsession, and we were thrust into the spotlight with him, a row of solemn black faces on television screens all over America. Along the way we lost anonymity, our peace of mind, and in the eyes of many, our good name. I want to tell you the story of my family. It's a painful story, but one America needs to hear.

The Simpson family I know is proud, loving, and fiercely loyal. We hold tight to our roots. And our roots go deep. Before you can understand our family, you have to understand where we came from. My maternal great-grandparents, Dennis Durden and Patsy Henden, lived in Rodessa, Louisiana, in the years when the South was still rigidly segregated. In spite of the difficulties, they made a decent living for themselves and their children off the land they owned. I've visited that home; one of my great-uncles still lives there, and the land my great-grandparents once farmed still supports itself through cattle grazing and oil wells. Once a year we have a big family reunion there. We live all over the country now, but we all still try to make the reunion if we can.

My grandmother, Eunice Durton Simpson, was born there in 1922, one of nine children. She was the rebel in the family; life on a Louisiana farm didn't satisfy her. She met my grandfather Jimmy when she was a teenager in Rodessa and shortly after he finished his service in World War II in 1944, they married and moved to San Francisco in search of a better life. They'd heard from others in the black community that there were jobs at the naval yard there, and the promise of a better job and more freedom than they could find in rural Lousiana was appealing. My grandfather had always loved to cook, and not long after they arrived in San Francisco, he found work as a chef, a profession he followed until the end of his life. My grandmother found work as an orderly in the Psychiatric Division at San Francisco General Hospital. Both my grandparents were deeply religious and immediately became involved with Evergreen Baptist Church, there in Hunter's Point. Fifty years later, my grandma and my mother still belong to that same church. Two of my grandmother's sisters came West, too, and soon we'd established a new family outpost in California.

Grandma and Grandpa Simpson had five children. My mother, Shirley, was their first child, born the year they moved to San Francisco. Uncle Truman, the first son, was born a year later, and two years after that, my uncle O.J., and then Aunt Como (her given name is Carmelita) was born a year later, in 1948. It was a lot of children, and a lot of responsibility for my grandparents. Years later my grandparents separated permanently, but my grandfather remained a part of his children's lives. He helped support them financially, and he helped discipline them as well. Instead of moving out of the neighborhood, as so often happens in cases of divorce, he stayed in San Francisco, where he could still attend church, come for holidays and other family functions. He remained a part of his children's lives, but still, it was hard. The breakup of a family is never easy.

With Grandpa out of the house and Grandma working nights, a lot of responsibility fell on my mother. She was only ten years old when her dad left, but she quickly began taking on the role of "mother" to her younger brothers and sister when Grandma was out of the house. Even when my aunt Ruth (Grandma's sister) moved in to help out, my mother felt a special sense of responsibility and authority among her siblings. When Grandma wasn't there, Mom ruled the roost. My mother also developed a special bond with my grandmother during this period of time. She came to think of herself as her mother's special helper, the one who was responsible to make sure my grandmother was all right. She still is. By sticking together, they managed to provide a pretty good home for all five of them.

Life wasn't easy for any of them. My grandmother's night work in the mental ward was exhausting and stressful. She would come home tired and tense, and my mother would try to make her feel better by taking more and more responsibility off her hands. By the time they were teenagers, Uncle Truman had become a problem child. He was gifted athletically, even more than Uncle O.J. when they were kids, but he didn't have the role models or mentors Uncle O.J. found. He nicknamed Uncle Truman "L.J." for

Lemon Juice, a callous reference to his inferiority to Uncle O.J.

In the projects where they grew up, it was hard for a young man without a father to stick to the straight and narrow. Uncle Truman never got into serious trouble, but somehow he could never seem to get his life together. He grew up working odd jobs and eventually got a job as a doorman at the famous Clift Hotel in San Francisco, where everybody knew him. Life was hard for him. And it didn't help that his little brother O.J. had become so rich and famous.

Uncle O.J. was born Orenthal James, a name he hated from the beginning. My aunt Johnnie May (another one of Grandma's sisters) had suggested the name because an organist she admired from her church was named Orenthal. He nicknamed himself "O.J." and eventually became "the Juice" when O.J. became slang for orange juice. He and Uncle Truman were Orange Juice and Lemon Juice, a family joke that pretty much says it all. Uncle O.J. had a tough time as a kid. He developed rickets at age two that left him skinny and bowlegged. He became "the little crippled boy." My grandmother couldn't afford the braces he really needed, so she put together a series of homemade "braces" that were really just iron bars rigged to his shoes. He couldn't play like the other kids, and everybody teased him about his crippled legs and his big head, which the other children called "Waterhead." Having his father move out of the house when Uncle O.J. was five only made things harder.

Starting school was also traumatic because besides the problems with his legs, he was dyslexic (what they called "slow" at the time), and learning to read was a struggle. I think my mother developed a special protectiveness toward her baby brother during those years. Eventually, though, his legs straightened out and got strong, and Uncle O.J. had the good fortune to meet people who wanted to help him develop his athletic talent. Grandma worked hard to get Uncle O.J. an athletic scholarship to Galileo High School, an upscale school across town. She was always reaching for something better for her children. It was in high school that Uncle O.J. switched from track to football, and the rest, as they say, is history.

In spite of the hardships—or maybe even because of them—the family stayed close through the tough times. Mom and Uncle O.J. both adored Grandma; as far as they were concerned, the world revolved around her. And they weren't the only ones who thought so. Grandma's house became home to their friends, too. Uncle O.J.'s best friends, Joe Bell and A.C. Cowlings, practically moved in with him. The three of them had been together since they started grade school. A.C. stuttered as a kid, so he and Uncle O.J. had banded together for protection and support—the two "crippled kids." A.C. ate at Grandma's house more than he did at home; he became Uncle O.J.'s unofficial brother. The bond was strong and lasting. When Uncle O.J. got transferred to the new high school, he managed to get A.C. and Joe Bell scholarships, too. Years later, when he was recruited for USC, Uncle O.J. made it clear that A.C. would be coming, too. They were a team. Luckily, the SC recruiter agreed, and the two boys from the projects went off to college together.

My dad's parents were Joshua and Edna Baker. Both of them were born in northern California. My grandfather, Joshua Baker, died just a year after I was born, so I don't remember him, but I've heard about him all my life. He was a very handsome man, and a real trailblazer for African-Americans of his generation. Grandpa Baker was the very first black Boy Scout leader in America. He was also the first black man to be hired as a garbage collector by the city of Sacramento. That may not sound like much now, but in the 1920s it was a huge step forward for a black man to break the color barrier and get a good government job in a state capital. My grandfather's courage and industry gave my father the self-esteem that has seen him through the pain of permanent disability. Grandpa Baker met my grandmother Edna in Sacramento in the early part of the century. She was as beautiful as Grandpa was handsome, and she had a string of suitors as a young woman. She'd had polio as a child, and though she recovered, she'd gotten used to being the center of attention. My dad says she was a real coquette when she was a girl— a regular heartbreaker. They had three children: Uncle Don, Aunt Barbara, and my father Ben in 1935. When my dad was fourteen, his parents also divorced.

Daddy is nearly ten years older than my mom, and he'd been married once before when he met Mom. He'd married a woman I know as "Aunt Gloria" some years before and had two children, my oldest sister Cindy (who's now a minister) and my only brother, Ben Jr. They were divorced in 1959, and my dad became involved in a relationship with Bonni, a Korean woman. Bonni gave birth to my sister Khadi a couple of years later. Khadi has remained an ongoing part of our lives.

Finally, in 1962, he met and married my mother. I always thought that my parents enhanced each other—the girl from the ghetto and the son of the Scout leader. She brought strength to the marriage, and he brought dignity. I came along a year later, my mother's first child and a seventh-generation Californian. My sister Tracy followed shortly after, and my baby sister Toni was born in 1968 on my fifth birthday. Somewhere between Tracy and Toni my adopted sister Gyne entered the family. Gyne's actually

Canadian by birth, but her father died, and her mother was gone on business most of the time, so a few years after she and her mother moved down to our neighborhood in San Francisco, Gyne became a permanent member of our family.

In a way, Gyne became my sister almost the same way A.C. became my uncle O.J.'s brother. They both needed a family, and Mom followed my grandmother's example when she welcomed Gyne into our home. Altogether I have one brother and five sisters. We're quite a collection of siblings—three of us are full siblings, three are half siblings, and one is no blood relation at all. Yet the funny thing is that I never think about the differences between us. My brother is my brother, and my sisters are my sisters. Not exactly the Brady Bunch, but not far off. In spite of the differences, all seven of us have remained close. As my parents look at it, family is family.

Our family was extremely close when I was growing up. Joined at the hip, I guess you could say. We were the ultimate middle-class American family. We lived in a nice house in Westborough, a largely white area of San Francisco. On Saturdays we'd visit Grandma Simpson and clean her house, and on Sundays we all went to the church together. Once a week my parents would get us all dressed up, and we'd go out for a nice dinner at a midpriced steak house like the Hungry Hunter. My parents would get us all Shirley Temples, the 7UP and grenadine drinks with the cherries and the little umbrellas, and we would think that was incredibly special and grown-up. We were always in clubs—Tracy was a Brownie, and I was a Bluebird— and of course, Mom was usually the club mother. We'd go to the meetings after school. Sometimes we'd take my Bluebird troop out to a place called the Coastside Corral and ride horses. We had two horses of our own named

Donnie and Stony for a while, and we'd go riding on Saturday afternoons. Every year we took family vacations, and every summer I'd go East to stay with my great aunt Sammy and uncle Buddy.

There was one way we weren't altogether traditional. In our family my mother worked for most of our lives. Nobody planned it that way, but when I was small, my dad broke his back in an accident and had to have a series of surgeries to try to correct the damage. As a result, he wasn't able to go back to work full-time and had to go on pension. As we children each turned sixteen, we got part-time jobs of our own. We were always encouraged to work. One of the jobs we had later was a team effort. My sisters and I delivered the New York Times seven days a week. We had to pick up the papers every night at nine or nine-thirty, wrap and rubber-band them, and put them in the car to deliver the next morning at five-thirty A.M. My dad would sometimes meet us at Hunt's Donut Shop at the crack of dawn, and bought donuts hot out of the grease—freshest donuts in town. It became my special time with my father. I treasure those memories.

When we weren't working or going to school, we were usually doing volunteer work. Grandma did volunteer work at the Senior Citizen's Center in Portrero Hill. My mother is the ultimate volunteer; she was always the bedrock of the PTA and every organization my sisters and I joined. We also volunteered to help out with the kids at the Special Olympics every year, and we worked at several community fund-raisers. Twice we drove over to Oakland to help with the sickle cell anemia fund-raisers. There was always something that needed doing, and whenever someone needed help, we were there, together. Nobody would have thought about not going. We were family. When one of us helped, we all helped.

We didn't see too much of Uncle Truman during those years; he showed up for major holidays, like Thanksgiving and Christmas. But Aunt Como was like a second mom to us, and Grandma and Grandpa Simpson were always there, along with an assortment of aunts, uncles, and cousins. All told, we were quite a crowd. The only family member who really wasn't around was my uncle O.J. He'd been recruited to USC when I was still a toddler, and by my fifth birthday he'd already won the Heisman Trophy and been drafted for the Buffalo Bills. So to me, he was Mom's celebrity brother, the uncle I knew I had but almost never saw. He was never around for family holidays, and even after he moved back to California from Buffalo, we only saw him if we went down to L.A.

As a matter of fact, most of what I heard about him came from the news. People who knew I was his niece were always asking me about something they'd heard on the news about Uncle O.J., and I was always embarrassed because I never knew anything about it. Still, there were advantages to having a celebrity uncle, even one you never saw. When my parents first bought their house in a predominantly white community, the neighbors were suspicious until they found out Mom was Uncle O.J.'s sister. Once they knew that, we became sort of celebrities by extension, and they welcomed us. I knew my mother was vastly proud of him, too. Her little brother had gone from being the little crippled boy in the projects to being the number one NFL draft choice in the nation, and soon he became a celebrity commentator and endorser, too. My mom had always watched out for him when they were kids, and now she vicariously enjoyed every minute of his success.

Not that she ever took advantage of it, though. Everybody, my parents believed, wanted to take advantage of Uncle O.J. now that he was famous, now that he had money.

Everybody wanted something from him. My parents were determined not to be a part of that process. Uncle O.J. had bought Grandma a house when he started making money, but otherwise we were pretty much on our own financially. Mom preferred it that way. Even when he started playing for our hometown team, the San Francisco 49ers, my parents never asked him for tickets. When he did send tickets, though, we were always there. In junior high and high school the last thing I wanted to do was sit in the stands all Saturday or Sunday and watch football, but my parents insisted we all go to support him.

The year after he left, when the 49ers were still winning every game and headed for the Super Bowl, all my friends thought we were so lucky because we could get tickets to the games. But the reality was, we didn't. Instead we'd camp out in the parking lot in line for the ticket office with everyone else and wait to buy our tickets. When the play-offs came along, we'd take turns camping out with our sleeping bags for up to three days so we could get our tickets. Dad would stay there alone while we kids were at school. We'd build little campfires right there in line and roast hot dogs and marshmallows at night. People thought it was hilarious that O.J. Simpson was our uncle, and here we were camping in the parking lot with everybody else. But it was fun, really. The memory of those times is precious.

Once Uncle O.J. started doing so many endorsements, he would get piles of free clothes from the various companies he represented. Then every year he'd clean out his closet and get rid of the things he didn't want. Most of them were new. He'd call my dad to say he was getting rid of them, and Daddy and Uncle Truman would drive down to Los Angeles and pick everything up, then drive straight back that night. It became an annual pilgrimage. They were always so excited to get the clothes; they were like little kids. My dad would spend hours laying all the clothes out carefully on the beds, and then we'd all crowd around to see them. It was so exciting. Then Dad and Uncle Truman would each choose what they wanted. My father was proud to be wearing Uncle O.J.'s beautiful new things.

Every now and then Dad would let me have one of the shirts, and I would be so proud to wear it. A lot of them even had Uncle O.J.'s name embroidered inside, and I'd show them off to friends. To this day I still have one of Uncle O.J.'s old tuxedos in a box under my bed. I always planned to have it tailored down to fit me, so I could wear it someday. When Uncle O.J. sold his house in Buffalo and wanted to get rid of some of the furniture, he gave my parents some pieces. They were thrilled. For us, that was the sign that we really were part of his family. My uncle's castoffs became a symbol of our connection.

Even though there was so little direct contact with Uncle O.J., our family did get a certain amount of special treatment because we were related to him. People who knew always thought it was very exciting, and Grandma became something of a celebrity in the community. When Uncle O.J. offered to buy her a house all those years ago, she didn't want to move far out of the neighborhood, so he bought her a little two-bedroom home not far from the projects. She still spends more time in the old neighborhood than anywhere else. She's comfortable there, and revered as O.J. Simpson's mother, which she really loves.

To this day she still buys groceries at the same place, a little corner market on the block where my mother grew up. She just pulls up in front of the market in her car, honks the horn, and waits for the owner to come out. And he always comes running out to her car to see what she wants. She gives him a list or just tells him what she wants, and he goes inside and packs it all up for her. Then he brings it out, puts it all in the back of Grandma's car, and tells her how much the groceries add up to. She'll tell him how much cash she wants, usually $100 or so, and then write a check for the correct amount. He gives her whatever cash she needs and then goes back inside while she drives off. She never even has to get out of the car. It's really a scream. I guess she thinks that if she went through all the trouble of raising Uncle O.J., she might as well enjoy the benefits.

Probably the high point of Grandma's life in the last twenty-five years was the time she got to do the TV commercial. That was when they'd been running all the television ads showing Uncle O.J. racing through the airport. Somehow Uncle O.J. set up a deal to put Grandma in one of the commercials. They dressed her up to look like an old lady and then had her racing through the airport just like Uncle O.J. did in the other ads. The commercial was very popular. Everyone loved it, and we were all so proud and thrilled for Grandma. She got paid $20,000 for doing it, and that was a fortune for our family. So with the money Grandma had the whole house redone. The renovators painted the walls, laid new carpet, removed the kitchen cabinets and put in new ones, and put in a new stove and refrigerator. Grandma's house was beautiful by the time they got done.

Everyone in the family talked about how wonderful it was of Uncle O.J. to set this up for her, and I guess it was, but then I found out later that he kept part of the money himself since he'd made the deal. What did Uncle O.J. need with the extra money? He was already wealthier than most people ever dream of being. I couldn't understand why he hadn't just let Grandma keep the whole fee.

Being related to Uncle O.J. meant the world to my parents, but as the years went by, it came to mean less and less to me. People were always expecting me to have all kinds of perks and inside information from him, and since we hardly ever saw him, it got embarrassing after a while. I'd barely seen his home in L.A. By the time I was a teenager, I'd realized that it was usually better not to tell people I was O.J.'s niece. It just caused more problems than it was worth.

I think I first began to question our relationship with Uncle O.J. when we went to visit him in Buffalo the summer I was twelve. That was the year Dad got the camper so we could all take a cross-country trip. The idea was to stop in Buffalo when we got to New York so we could spend time with Uncle O.J., and then drive home the long way, through the South, and visit our relatives there on the way back to California. It was my parents' version of an educational family vacation. We could learn about other states and have fun at the same time. So we piled everybody into the mobile home and made the long journey from San Francisco to New York. My parents had phoned ahead to Uncle O.J. so he'd know when to expect us. The plan was for us to meet him at the training camp, we could all go to lunch.

When we finally got to the training camp, Dad parked the mobile home and went inside to get Uncle O.J. while we waited in the camper. It was a blistering hot day, and we were all tired and hungry. We waited and waited in that camper. Finally, nearly two hours later, he came back. We asked him, "What happened? What took you so long? Where's Uncle O.J.?" Dad said that Uncle O.J. had decided to have lunch inside with the team, and it had taken longer than Dad had expected. Uncle O.J. would be out after a while. I remember thinking, *His family comes three thousand miles to see him, he has lunch with the team?* I wouldn't have been that rude to a stranger.

We stayed at his house for a couple of days, but it was uncomfortable. He was training most of the time, and when he was there, I couldn't help but notice how different he was from the rest of us. For one thing, everyone—including my parents—was always catering to him, and he did nearly all the talking. He didn't seem to have any interest in my parents' lives. Then the second evening we were there, the doorbell rang, and there were two cute little white teenage girls on the doorstep asking to see him. He went to the front door and signed autographs, while they gushed all over. Twelve-year-old that I was, I found the whole incident nauseating. Why was everybody always falling all over him? I didn't even think he was that handsome. *My father,* I thought, *is handsomer than Uncle O.J.*

The most troubling part of the journey, though, came when it was time to leave. My sister Gyne had met us in the Midwest and was going on the rest of the trip with us. She was just seventeen years old at the time, pretty, and anxious to prove how grown-up she was. She was especially anxious to impress our Uncle O.J., who hadn't seen her since she was a skinny little kid. So the whole time we were in Buffalo, she wore makeup and did her hair up so Uncle O.J. would be impressed by how pretty she'd grown up to be.

Then on the morning we were leaving, as we were all gathering downstairs to say our good-byes, Gyne came down to meet us looking very cute in a pair of shorts. For the first time, Uncle O.J. seemed to notice her. He went over to where she was standing on the stairs and made a comment about how pretty she was, and how he'd like to get to know her better. And then he leaned over and gave her a sensual kiss on her neck. Gyne was mortified.

All the way back to California in the camper, my mother was mad at Gyne. Gyne felt that she was getting the blame for what had happened. Her little burst of teenage vanity had turned out to have a price attached to it. But I knew it wasn't Gyne's fault. Uncle O.J. was over thirty years old. I was very disillusioned.

That was only the beginning of my gradual disillusionment. I saw how much my mother loved and admired her baby brother, and as a result, I tried hard not to be critical of him. I searched for excuses for his behavior, and for his neglect of the sister who was so devoted to him. Sometimes it was little things. Once he came up north for a rare appearance at a family function, and when he walked into the living room at Grandma's house, all the seats were already taken. As soon as everyone realized who it was, though, they all jumped out of their chairs at once, saying, "Let O.J. sit down. Come on, now. Somebody move those kids out of here; they're making noise." We were right in the middle of a television program, but immediately everyone began saying, "Do you like this program, O.J.? You want to watch this? Maybe you'd rather watch something else?" I couldn't believe it. It was unimaginable that anyone else in the family would ever have been treated that way.

Every one of his rare visits somehow turned into a celebrity appearance. The minute he appeared, all eyes turned to him, and everyone else in the room seemed to disappear. A classic example was actually years later, when Uncle O.J. flew up for a big seventieth birthday party we were giving Grandma in the reception hall. As soon as he walked in, he became the focus. It was supposed to be her big moment, but instead, it became an O.J. sighting. Even though he hadn't done anything to help plan the party, he was immediately given the seat of honor next to Grandma at the center table. People crowded around him, shaking his hand and asking for his autograph. He spent most of Grandma's party signing memorabilia and posing for photographs with the guests.

Of course, even these "celebrity appearances" were extremely rare. If you look at photos taken over the last thirty-five years of family holidays, you'll see everybody else in the family at nearly all of them, but you won't see Uncle O.J. In fact, I can't find a single picture of him at any family function during the entire time I was growing up. As far as I know, the only family functions he attended during three decades were Aunt Como's wedding, Uncle Truman's second wedding, and Grandma's seventieth birthday. That's it. When I was little, I took his absence for granted, but as I got older, I began to ask my parents questions. "How come Uncle O.J. never comes up for Mother's Day, Christmas or any holidays? How come he just sends flowers?" When he phoned, he usually called Grandma. As far as that goes, my parents didn't call him directly. If they wanted to get in touch with him, they'd call his secretary, Kathy Randa, and ask her to have Uncle O.J. get in touch with them. Somehow we all had the feeling that calling him at home would be presumptuous, because he was such a busy man. He was special, it became clear to me. We shouldn't bother him.

It was also his secretary's job, I discovered, to send the flowers and other tokens that did arrive on special occasions. Kathy Randa had a calendar, and on every major holiday, and on Grandma's birthday, she d see that flowers were sent to the people on her list in Uncle O.J.'s name. Every now and then she'd send flowers on Mom's or Aunt Como's birthday, but most years they didn't hear anything. At Christmastime the family would get Honey Baked hams. It was always such a big deal when the hams came: "I got my ham. Did you get yours?" they'd ask excitedly. Then they'd debate about whether to freeze it for later or enjoy it over the holiday. Aside from their expense, those hams seemed to taste even more special because they came from Uncle O.J. We often planned our Christmas dinner around them. Years later I remember how disillusioned I felt when I discovered that he routinely had Kathy Randa send hams to the gardener, the housekeeper, and anyone else he felt obligated to acknowledge. And here my family was, so excited that he'd sent them "something special."

The high point for my father was the year Uncle O.J. had a gift sent for my father's birthday. It was a bottle of Dom Pérignon, and my father was so proud and thrilled that he'd been remembered. He'd been around for so many years helping out with the family by then, but his birthday had never really been acknowledged. He was just Ben, Shirley's husband. But after that one year, his birthday was never acknowledged again. He never said a word, but I always felt sad to see him overlooked again.

I think that of all the things that hurt me, though, the thing that hurt me most was not how Uncle O.J. treated everybody, but the way they treated him, especially my parents. My dad, always so proud and dignified, slunk into the background when Uncle O.J. was around. Even my mother, the strong matriarch who had once spanked her baby brother's bottom, seemed to shrivel in his presence. I was used to seeing my mother as the person in charge; she never just belonged to the PTA, she was always *president* of it. She was always the one running the show, and everyone in our lives respected her. Shirley Baker was a woman to be taken seriously. But when it came to Uncle O.J., both of my parents changed. They became passive, subservient, like "good darkies" in the Old South. Even the mention of Uncle O.J.'s name seemed to transform them into people I hardly knew. It disappointed me. Why did they seem to feel so inferior to Uncle O.J.? Because he was rich? They'd never seemed to care about money, and they didn't seem to want Uncle O.J.'s. Because he was a celebrity? So he played football and made a few commercials. Big deal. I mean, it was nice, but it wasn't like he'd invented a cure for cancer. I couldn't understand it.

One thing was certain. I might not understand my parents' feelings, but I'd better accept them. There was no questioning anything my uncle did, as far as my mother and father were concerned. We learned to meet his needs and not make demands. My sisters and I all knew not to ask Uncle O.J. for anything. We shouldn't bother him with our little problems or take up his valuable time. Other people were always asking him for things because he was a celebrity, my parents taught us we shouldn't. We were his family. He deserved to be with people who weren't always wanting things from him.

The catch was, if he really was "just family," why didn't we treat him that way? We didn't relate to him like we did to anyone else we knew. Instead we put him up on a pedestal, like a living Heisman Trophy, and then erected a sign saying, "Don't touch." O.J. Simpson had become the family deity. In their heart of hearts, I came to believe my parents were afraid Uncle O.J. would shut us out of his life. Somewhere along the way, the self-esteem of my entire family had become inextricably tied to my uncle's success. Without Uncle O.J., we feared, the Simpsons would just be another bunch of nobodies from the projects.

CHAPTER 2

GAMES PEOPLE PLAY

I first met Nicole Brown at a football game in the fall of 1979. Uncle O.J. was playing for the 49ers by then, and Mom and Dad had taken us all to the game that afternoon. I was fifteen years old, just starting high school, and I thought spending Saturday watching my uncle play football was pretty boring. My parents wanted us all there, though, so we went. Uncle O.J. had gotten us seats near the sidelines, and during halftime Nicole and her sister Denise came down from one of the reserved boxes up above and introduced herself to us as a friend of Uncle O.J.'s. She was twenty years old but seemed older, and self-assured. We knew who she was—the rumor had gone the rounds of the family that Uncle O.J. had been "keeping" a young white girlfriend on the side for more than two years—but only my dad had met her. Everybody was polite, pleasant; clearly, this was someone important to Uncle O.J. But I guess you could say that we weren't overjoyed to make her acquaintance. Not because she was white but because Uncle O.J. was still married to my aunt Marguerite at the time.

We loved Aunt Marguerite. She was from the neighborhood; Uncle O.J. had met her when they were both in high school, and they'd married before he came down to play football at USC. So Aunt Marguerite had been there from the beginning, before all the fame and the changes that divided my uncle from us socially and geographically. Actually, Aunt Marguerite had been A.C.'s girlfriend when they first started high school, but Uncle O.J. had charmed her away, and A.C. had accepted it good-naturedly enough. Aunt Marguerite was like the rest of us: a hometown girl, very traditional, very religious, very close to her mother. She fit right into the family, and she and Mom got along great. We didn't get to see her as much as we liked, since she'd lived in Los Angeles from the time she and Uncle O.J. married. Still, she felt like family to us. There was a sense of connection.

She and Uncle O.J. had three children together—my cousins Arnelle, Jason, and Aaren. The marriage had been difficult; Uncle O.J. traveled constantly after he graduated from USC, and there were rumors of other women. During his years with the Bills, he and Aunt Marguerite lived on separate coasts part of the time because of the children. Aunt Marguerite wanted the kids to have some continuity in their lives, to stay in the same school and the same neighborhood. The house at Rockingham had been purchased in 1977, when Aunt Marguerite was pregnant with Aaren, as sort of a last-ditch effort to bring some stability to their lives. Not coincidentally, that was the same summer Uncle O.J. met Nicole. Tragically, when Aaren was eighteen months old, she toddled into the pool at Rockingham and drowned. The pain of losing Aaren seemed to overwhelm everyone. We knew there were problems in the marriage. When they divorced in 1980, nobody was really surprised.

Nicole moved in at Rockingham not long after Aunt Marguerite moved out. Uncle O.J. had already been supporting her in an apartment in L.A. He wasn't interested in remarrying at that point; he was still in the middle of a divorce, and he thought Nicole was too young for marriage yet, anyway. But it was clear from the beginning that the relationship was serious. Nicole wasn't just another football groupie; she was there to stay. And it was clear that it was up to us to accept her if we wanted to have any kind of relationship with Uncle O.J. Later, when we learned that Juditha Brown had met Lou two years before he divorced his first wife and married her, the whole picture seemed to fit.

About a year after Nicole moved into Rockingham, my family came down to Los Angeles to visit. My sister Toni was playing in a band at South City High that year, and her band was going to perform at Disneyland. So the whole family came down to watch her. Mom called ahead to let Uncle O.J. know we were coming, and he said we could stay at Rockingham if we wanted to—"My house is your house," or something to that effect. But when we actually got there, it was awkward. Nicole was pleasant and cordial, and Uncle O.J. told us to make ourselves at home, but then they went about their business as though we weren't there. We put our things in the kids' rooms. Jason and Arnelle spent part of their time at Rockingham, but they were with their mother that weekend. When evening came, Uncle O.J. and Nicole sat and chatted about where they were going for dinner, and then Denise showed up a little while later with a date. The four of them went out to eat at a restaurant and left Mom and Dad with us. I was indignant, and I said so. I remember asking my parents, "Why are they going out to dinner and leaving you here? Why didn't they invite you to go along?" I couldn't imagine having someone come that far for a visit and then going to dinner without inviting them. I was angry and embarrassed for my parents.

As usual, though, they rushed to defend him. Mom said, "We don't want to go," and Dad said, "O.J. knows we don't want to go. We don't need to be involved with that." *Involved with what?* I thought. *Eating?* They were gone all evening, and we pretty much sat around and watched a movie. Eventually we found something to eat and went up to bed.

It was much later that night, well past midnight, that we heard them come in. And it was an hour or so later that we first heard the fighting. Nicole's voice was filled with rage, and she was screaming and cussing at Uncle O.J. We could hear him reply occasionally, but his voice was too low for us to tell what he was saying. She seemed to be angry about another woman, but we couldn't be sure. A short while later we heard the sound of things being thrown and of breaking glass. We could hear them storming up the stairs to the second floor, still yelling, as we stayed behind the closed doors of Jason's and Arnelle's rooms in nervous silence. After some more banging, they stormed downstairs again, and after a while a door slammed, and it grew quiet. When our hearts finally stopped pounding, we all went to sleep. We never did open the bedroom doors.

The next morning, when we made our way downstairs, there were pieces of glass all over and broken picture frames with photos of Nicole's family scattered around. Uncle O.J. was sitting in the TV room, looking very depressed. Nicole was nowhere to be seen. Nobody said anything about the mess. Uncle O.J. said Nicole had gotten really mad and pulled all the pictures off the wall to throw them at him. Then he said she'd just attacked him, so he'd had to push her out the front door until she calmed down. My parents listened to his explanation quietly, without asking questions. It wasn't until much later, when the reports of domestic abuse began surfacing during the trial, that I questioned any of the events of that night.

Besides, at that point in my life I had more interesting things to do than worry about an uncle I hardly ever saw. I graduated from high school in 1982 and entered San Francisco State as a political science major. I didn't really know what I wanted to do with my life at the point, but I'd been toying with the idea of law school, and I knew it meant the world to my parents for me to go to college. I later met my first serious boyfriend, a college student named Shaun. In the middle of my sophmore year, he was accepted to UCLA and made plans to move down to L.A. for the summer. I wanted to be with him, so I decided to spend the summer in Los Angeles working and taking classes at Santa Monica City College. I knew I could earn enough money to pay for tuition and daily expenses, but paying rent was out of the question. My solution was simple: I'd call Uncle O.J. and ask if I could stay at Rockingham for the summer. After all, he traveled so much that he'd hardly know I was there, and he had plenty of room. It couldn't hurt to ask; he could only say no. So I decided to call him. My parents weren't exactly enthusiastic about my calling him, but at nineteen I was pretty determined, so they didn't really try to stop me.

When I called Uncle O.J., he wasn't exactly enthusiastic either, but he was pleasant about it, and after a day or so he called back and said it was okay for me to come down. Mission accomplished. I packed up my belongings, and

Dad drove me down. I remember that all the way down Interstate 5 he kept warning me to be careful. He knew it was my first time away from home. My parents thought my decision to ask Uncle O.J. had been daring, and my decision to live with him risky for the whole family. They were scared to death I'd do something to offend him that would reflect on the whole family. I wasn't worried, though; I was having an adventure. At nineteen you feel immune to trouble.

The world I entered the day my father unloaded the car and left me at Rockingham was far removed from the middle-class neighborhood I'd left behind in Westborough. Uncle O.J. and Nicole lived at a level that was familiar to me only from movies and television. The house itself was large, though I wouldn't call it a mansion. It was just a roomy, two-story house. Upstairs was a big master suite, with two bathrooms and two dressings rooms for Uncle O.J. and Nicole's things. Down the hall were two other bedrooms with private baths. Later they would belong to Sydney and Justin, but when I moved in that summer, they were kept for Arnelle and Jason during their time with their father. Downstairs there was a kitchen, a dining room, a TV room with a bar, and a living room. No one ever sat in the living room, except on special occasions. Off the kitchen there was a bathroom and quarters for the maid. There was a pool out back, shaped like a football, and behind the pool there was a tennis court. In the back was a guest room.

Nicole had a real knack for interior design, and over the years she gradually transformed the house and grounds from the dark, heavy look that dominated it when I first moved in to the light, airy space it is today. The first thing she had done was to tear out the brick driveway and most of the landscaping around the house. Later, when Sydney and Justin were born, she had part of the space made into a play yard, complete with a playhouse for Sydney. Inside she had all the dark hardwood floors stripped and revarnished in a light color. The walls were also painted in light tones. She loved a light, airy feeling inside a home, and her goal was to brighten the interior of the house. After she finished the floors and walls, she remodeled the kitchen.

When I first lived there, the kitchen was done in a basic green-and-white color scene, with limited counter space. Nicole had the floor tiled in a light color, replaced the cabinets, added a central work island with its own sink, installed granite countertops, and put in new appliances. Then she expanded the space by adding a sunroom to one side. The kitchen was Nicole's pride and joy. She liked to cook with the expensive copper pans nice restaurants use. She was a good cook.

The next things she remodeled were the dining room and the TV room. She was always thrifty, so instead of getting a new dining-room set, she had the old table and chairs stripped and refinished in a light color to match the floors. In the passageway from the dining room to the TV room, she had glass cases custom made and built into the walls. The Heisman and Uncle O.J.'s other important trophies were kept in those lighted cases. She completely reconfigured the TV room. When I moved in that summer, there was a big pool table in the TV room and a long, dark mahogany bar at one end. She created a new trophy room at one end, filled the shelves with Uncle O.J.'s other trophies and sports memorabilia, and moved the pool table in there. She got rid of the big, dark bar and had French doors installed across the back part of the room. She refurnished the entire space with cream-colored furniture and big, overstuffed pillows, and she installed a huge entertainment center in place of the bar. There was a big-screen

TV in the center and two smaller TVs on top. That way you could watch three TVs at one time if you wanted to, all set to different channels. Years later, during the trial, we were all glued to those three TVs.

The last thing she remodeled was the backyard. She had an architect come in and expand the guest room into a little complex with three guest rooms, all connected, and designed to look like an extension of the house. Each unit had its own bed, sofa, and sitting area. The guest unit nearest the house, where Kato later lived, was attached directly to the house with a door that could be locked from inside the house. Out back she had the football pool torn out, removed all the brickwork around it, and had the area paved with granite-colored stone. Then she had a new rock pool designed complete with a water fountain you could slide down and a little grotto underneath. You could sit in the grotto, which she had equipped with speakers, and listen to music while water fell over the opening and flowed out into the pool. It was a magical place.

She also transformed the garden. Nicole always loved to garden, so she paid a lot of attention to the landscaping at Rockingham from the time she moved in. She completely redid all the flower beds and planted a lot of rosebushes. By the time she was done, Rockingham had been transformed from a nice house into a country villa. Uncle O.J. was very proud of her decorating ability and used to brag that she had made more than a million dollars as an interior decorator. What he usually didn't mention, though, was that he was the one who had paid her—to redecorate her own house.

It wasn't until I moved there during the summer of 1983 that I discovered how involved Uncle O.J. already was with Nicole's family. We knew Nicole had been living there for three years by then, but we had no idea that most of her family seemed to live there, too. Nicole's sister Minnie was already living in the guesthouse that summer, so I stayed in the maid's quarters. Nicole's cousin Maria was the housekeeper at the time, but she lived at home and commuted every morning. Maria's husband Rolph took care of the gardens, so between them all, virtually everyone who was there was one of Nicole's relatives.

Uncle O.J. had set Lou Brown up in business. Juditha was a travel agent, and Uncle O.J. had set it up so all his wealthy friends, many of whom traveled a great deal, did their bookings through her. I couldn't help but wonder how the Browns had made a living before Nicole moved in with Uncle O.J. Nicole's sister Denise was around a lot, too, swimming and just hanging out. I think she was still modeling for the Ford agency that year, but her career never really took off. I found the whole setup astonishing. It wasn't only Nicole who had moved in; her whole family had apparently "moved in" with her. And of course, I couldn't help comparing the situation to Uncle O.J.'s relationship with my family. Until I broke the invisible barrier and invited myself down to stay with him, he'd been disconnected from his own family for years. It was clear that part of the reason, at least since Nicole had come into his life, was that he didn't need us. The Browns had become his new family.

I had to hand it to Nicole, though. Whatever her faults may have been, laziness wasn't one of them. She might have been living off my uncle, but she earned her keep. I think that was what separated her from the blond bimbos who constantly threw themselves at Uncle O.J. Nicole was an excellent manager. For instance, she loved to have flowers in the house, but instead of ordering in plants and bouquets as most wealthy women would have, she would go to the wholesale flower mart in downtown Los Angeles early in the morning and buy flowers and plants from the produce dealers. She'd lug them all back to the house, unwrap all the newspaper, and arrange the flowers in vases herself. She was good at it; the house was always filled with beautiful, huge, fragrant bouquets that would have cost a fortune at a florist's.

She never wasted money; if we went window-shopping that first summer and she saw a dress for $200 or $300, she'd always say, "No way. I'd never spend that kind of money on one dress." She was strong and very industrious, very hands-on. She'd cook full meals, and one Christmas years later I remember seeing her up on a high ladder, stringing Christmas lights all around the roof. Every morning she'd be up early to go running or work out, and then be home in time to fix breakfast. She was ambitious to improve herself, too; she never got a college degree, but she had taken a course in interior design, and after a while she began doing design work for other people, too. I remember her redoing houses for Marcus Allen and several other friends who admired her work. That was a big part of her appeal for Uncle O.J.; she had taken his empty house and made it into a home.

Nicole seemed like she'd been born for the "good life." She fitted in as though she'd always lived that way, and at first I assumed she had. Uncle O.J. was always talking about how smart, how talented she was, how she'd been a straight-A student in school. But I gradually learned that she wasn't quite what I'd assumed her to be. For one thing, she'd never graduated from high school at all. She'd gone back later and taken the GED. And she didn't come from a wealthy family. The Browns presented themselves as wealthy, but in reality their lifestyle before Uncle O.J. wasn't far different from the families I'd grown up with in

Westborough. As time went by, I grew to see the Browns for what they were—survivors.

Nicole was only seventeen when she met Uncle O.J., much younger than he was, but from the beginning she seemed much older, much more sophisticated than her years. I always had to remind myself that she was only five years older than I was. Her sisters were the same way. It was difficult to see them as anything but wealthy, sophisticated women. They presented themselves that way.

It was also clear that they weren't going to go away. I later found out that Nicole had gone out with Uncle O.J. for over a year before she introduced him to her father, not because Uncle O.J. was married, but because he was black. She wasn't sure how her father would feel about that. But just like when we moved into a white neighborhood in Westborough, the name "O.J. Simpson" worked miracles. I don't know what her father would have said to some average black guy she'd met at school, but her father never had a problem with Uncle O.J. On the contrary. All of the Browns were glamorized by the Simpson name.

I think Nicole clearly wanted the luxury and prestige life with a wealthy celebrity provided her, and she found him even more sexually exciting because he was black. I don't know if you'd call it "jungle fever", but she definitely thought black men were more virile, and Uncle O.J. found that flattering and stimulating. She, on the other hand, was more attractive to him because she was blond and white—a living Barbie doll. Much as I dislike the theory, I do think some black men are drawn to white women because they view them as status symbols. Physically, Nicole was a trophy wife. She and her sisters all had gorgeous bodies that they liked to show off in bikinis and tight clothing, and Nicole was extremely provocative as well as affectionate with Uncle O.J. She knew good sex was essential to hanging on to him. But she wasn't only a trophy; she was also a first-class homemaker. It was a combination my uncle found irresistible.

The willingness to work hard, to be industrious, was one trait Nicole did share with my family. Different though we were from this young blond woman I'd moved in with, in that respect we were alike. All of the women in my family were strong, industrious, take-charge types. Most teenagers who wanted to spend the summer with their boyfriends would have come down to Rockingham and hung out by the pool all summer. Not me, though. I enrolled in classes at Santa Monica College, where I got straight A's, and I went to work to pay my tuition and for spending money. I got a job taking measurements for businessmen who wanted custom shirts made, nearby in Beverly Hills. They'd make an appointment to place an order, and it was my job to go to their offices with fabric swatches and a measuring tape and take their order.

Besides a commitment to hard work, though, Nicole and I had little in common besides my uncle. For one thing, I found hanging around the pool in a bikini torturous. I was the thinnest woman in my family at the time, but I couldn't compare with Nicole and her sisters. Next to them, I felt about as attractive as mud. Even when people told me I was pretty (including Nicole), I thought, *Yeah, right. Compared to what?* The women who spent time at Rockingham were often movie-star beautiful. And when I went in the pool, unlike Nicole, my hair was a disaster. Few black women do well with wet hair. So in some respects, that summer at Rockingham was hard on my self-esteem. Even when Jason and Arnelle were around, it made little difference. Unlike my other cousins, I hardly knew them. Fortunately, they seemed to get along well with Nicole.

She was too smart and too young to try mothering them, so she'd just become their friend.

When I was living at Rockingham that first summer, a typical day would start early for me because I had to get to my classes. But even when I got up early, Nicole was already up. She had a regular morning routine for herself: get up by seven take a two-mile run around the neighborhood, come back home, and make breakfast for Uncle O.J. if he was in town. By the time she got back from running, he'd be upstairs watching TV or relaxing, so she'd fix breakfast and carry it up to him on a tray. Afterward they'd often take Chubbs and Cheeba, their two chow dogs, for a quiet walk around the neighborhood, always just the two of them. Then they'd come back and spend a couple of hours relaxing together until lunchtime. Sometimes they'd go out for lunch. Afterward Uncle O.J. would go to the office, and Nicole would get on the phone and start making business calls. She was always either looking for new houses to work on, or in the middle of a project. That summer she was redecorating Marcus Allen's condo down on Montana, a couple of miles from the house. She'd stand in the kitchen for an hour or more calling clients or talking to wholesale houses, looking for materials she wanted and working out a deal. When she finished her business calls, she usually called her mother and sisters to touch base for the day.

During the middle of the day, Nicole would usually work out again. She'd sit on a stationary bicycle by the pool and sip mineral water while she rode. She was in incredibly good shape. Late in the afternoon she'd start working on dinner. She'd always cook a nice big meal. We often ate by the pool because they had a grill out back, and Nicole would often grill chicken or fish and make wonderful salads and coleslaw. The meals were always delicious and very healthful. Once everything was ready, she'd set the table nicely, and we'd all sit down together. Uncle O.J. would be home by then, and friends would drop by. If Jason and Arnelle were there, she'd check to see how they were doing, and she'd make sure Arnelle had worked with her tutor and finished all her homework. Those summer evenings by the pool were beautiful, cool, and refreshing.

Even the food Nicole prepared was chosen carefully for both price and quality. She chose only fresh, high-quality items, but she was always careful to get her dollar's worth. When Maria and Rolph, who worked at Rockingham, arrived every morning, she'd give them a list of ingredients she needed and send them to the store to make the purchases. Two or three times a week a produce truck would pull up to the house with all kinds of farm-fresh fruits and vegetables, and Nicole would go out and choose what she needed. She didn't believe in freezing meat, so she'd go down to the country mart where they had a butcher and a fresh-meat counter and pick out whatever she wanted to cook that night. The meat she grilled for us was always fresh and purchased that day. I used to wonder how someone so young (she was only twenty-three that summer) had become such a good manager. She was really quite remarkable in that sense.

Nicole was mature for her age in almost every way. I never could think of her and her sisters as being in my age group. They seemed older somehow, maybe because of the European influence in how they were raised. Nicole didn't spend money on dressing up the way most young women with that kind of money available would have. On a typical summer day she'd either wear a tennis dress (if she was playing that day) or a simple short dress and little Keds sneakers without shoelaces. Her daily clothes were basic and uncluttered, sexy but comfortable. She always wore foundation and lip gloss, even to run, but very little eye makeup unless it was evening and she was going out. Her approach to life was very European in a sense; the kind of wealthy lifestyle that is enjoyed but not flaunted, no ostentatious show of wealth. I remember going to a gym at Century City with Nicole one afternoon to work out. Afterward she wanted to go out to the San Fernando Valley to buy another cat—she loved cats, and was always giving them homes. We jumped into the Rolls Royce, put the top down, and roared off across the valley with Nicole still dressed very casually. There was a strange dichotomy about it: very rich, but always very casual.

The life she led with Uncle O.J. was idyllic, really, like something from a movie. I watched them that summer and wondered what it would be like to live that way all the time. It was so far removed from the way most people live. Uncle O.J. and Nicole seemed to be on a perpetual honeymoon. Many evenings they would stay home and cuddle in the TV room. They were a very affectionate couple, like newlyweds. At the same time they were very social; Rockingham was a Mecca for friends and family—Nicole's family anyway. Her sister Minnie was living there that summer, and Judy and Lou were around all the time. So was Denise. And there was a steady stream of friends, many of them couples that Uncle O.J. and Nicole had formed friendships with. They'd play doubles tennis and relax around the pool afterward. Nicole always seemed to have a camera handy, and she loved to take pictures of their friends. She'd frame them and put them up everywhere, all around the house. The pictures were a kind of celebration of their life together.

Besides the couples that spent time at Rockingham, there were always a lot of Uncle O.J.'s single buddies around. Some of them were celebrities. Marcus Allen was around all the time. He had a place nearby, so he was over a lot. Wherever Marcus was, there was bound to be some woman. He was the ultimate womanizer. Nicole had even told me that he had slept with Denise, but she was hardly the only one. I remember thinking, *Why would all these women want to sleep with him?*

One day I went to his house with Nicole because she'd ordered a table to be delivered for his dining room that day. He couldn't get us out of there fast enough because he was expecting some hot blond any minute. She drove up in an expensive car just as we were leaving. Like Uncle O.J., Marcus definitely preferred white women. A lot of people thought of Marcus as an O.J. wanna-be. The two of them were best buddies, but they were also intensely competitive with each other. Years later, when I heard Marcus had slept with Nicole after the divorce, I wasn't at all surprised. I always suspected Marcus wanted everything Uncle O.J. had—including Nicole.

Ahmad Rashad was around a lot that summer, too. That was before Ahmad married Felicia Allen or became as well known as he is now. In those days Ahmad was very insecure and was always phoning Uncle O.J. for advice about women. He really wanted a permanent relationship with a woman, but it never seemed to work out in the long run, and he'd be emotionally devastated when things fell apart. Uncle O.J. would always just say, "Oh, don't worry about it, man. Just move on." It was clear when Ahmad finally met Felicia that he was moving up in the world. Most of Uncle O.J.'s single friends wanted women around who would flatter them and make them feel like the stars, but Felicia was a woman with real substance. She was better known than Ahmad at the time. I remember how impressed I was when I found out they were together. Once Felicia came into the picture, Ahmad wasn't around much, which was a good thing for him. He'd never fit in completely with Uncle O.J.'s buddies, who were egomaniacs with inferiority complexes. Ahmad had too much emotional sensitivity to be happy with that way of life. He wanted something real, something that would last.

That summer Mom and Dad decided to come down and visit for the Fourth of July. They'd never been down for the holiday before, but they wanted to see me, and decided to come to L.A. that year. The holiday is also my mother's birthday, so that way we could all celebrate her birthday together. What we didn't know until that summer was that Uncle O.J. had a huge annual barbecue on the Fourth of July and invited half the planet. He and his friends would all get together for their yearly softball game between the O.J. All-Stars and their friend Jack Hansen's Daisy team. Uncle O.J.'s All-Stars really did have a lot of stars on the team: Kareem Abdul-Jabbar at first base, Lynn Swann, and Jack Gilardi (Annette Funicello's husband), A.C., Ahmad, and several others. Naturally, Uncle O.J. was the pitcher.

They'd play at Mandeville Canyon and then come back to Rockingham afterward for a big party. Nicole would barbecue piles of chicken, ribs, hot dogs, and burgers while all the kids played and the adults played tennis and swam. At the end of the afternoon, everyone got thrown in the pool, even if they had their clothes on—a real surprise to me and my sisters. There must have been a hundred people there that year, and we all had a ball partying and celebrating. But I couldn't help but think of the fact that in all the years Uncle O.J. did that, he'd never invited any of us. The omission stood out even more because all of Nicole's family was invited, and the Fourth of July was Mom's birthday. Uncle O.J.'s birthday was just five days after hers, and they'd celebrated together when they were kids. My parents never said a word about any of it, but for me, it was another uncomfortable reminder of how much we'd been separated from his life. It was hard not to take it personally. Somehow, around my uncle's friends, we suddenly looked too ordinary, too heavy—too black. Not glamorous enough for his new family and friends.

The longer I stayed at Rockingham that summer, though, the more I came to understand that there was more to the family separation than first met the eye. It wasn't just that we didn't fit the celebrity image he cultivated among his friends; it was also that there were many more serious differences between the families, too many things he didn't want us to know about the way he lived. In spite of the fact that Uncle O.J. and Nicole seemed blissfully happy together, Uncle O.J. still needed the ego boost other women could provide. One night, for example, Nicole had gone down to Laguna to spend the night with her parents, and Uncle O.J. and I were alone at Rockingham. Late that evening Uncle O.J. buzzed down to the maid's room where I was staying on the intercom to ask me for a favor. He wanted me to call some restaurant in Westwood and ask for a certain waitress. I was supposed to say, "Hi, is so-and-so there?" When she came on the phone, I'd say, "Could you please hold on a second? O.J. Simpson would like to talk to you." I buzzed Uncle O.J. to take the call, and he did. It was clear Nicole suspected it was going on, but she looked the other way as much as she could. When she was confronted with direct evidence, though, she really felt betrayed. She took it to heart, and when she did, she would confront him and there would be a horrible argument. These fights were especially bad. I would hear her on the phone calling the police. She always seemed really angry when she made the calls. At the time I thought she was trying to set Uncle O.J. up in case of a future separation.

Besides, I knew Nicole was no angel herself. She would taunt Uncle O.J. when she was angry, belittling him and comparing him to other men, and sometimes she would come on to other men herself. I never had any evidence she actually cheated on him, but she was very sexual and she liked to flirt. All the Brown women were flirts. They were proud of their bodies, too, often spending the day in bikinis or other minimal clothing. In later years Nicole got breast implants, and Uncle O.J. paid for breast implants for one of her sisters, too. Being sexually alluring was clearly a very important part of these women's lives.

I also came to realize that there were other open secrets among the fast-paced group at Rockingham. Nicole's sister Minnie was bulimic; she would eat entire cubes of butter or cups of sugar and then vomit it all up. Like the plastic surgery, it was another example of the West L.A. crowd's obsession with their bodies. Nicole chose the healthy way to deal with the problem, working out constantly and watching what she ate, but Minnie chose a more self-destructive way to keep herself thin.

I never saw either Nicole or Uncle O.J. do illegal drugs. But cocaine was everywhere in their social set in the eighties, and I had my suspicions. My brother Benny always said the differences in our families' beliefs about acceptable behavior accounted in part for Uncle O.J.'s desire to avoid contact with us. My parents strongly disapproved of the fast Hollywood lifestyle.

The summer of 1983 was a coming-of-age for me. When it was over, I decided to stay in L.A. Oddly enough, it was Uncle O.J.'s idea. I had no idea that at nineteen, I was about to fall prey to my own set of temptations.

CHAPTER 3

SINS OF THE FLESH

Things went pretty well that summer. I'd gotten straight A's at Santa Monica College and been accepted into UCLA. Uncle O.J. was pleased with my success and suggested I stay in Los Angeles instead of returning to San Francisco State that fall. I wanted to stay, too, so in late August Minnie and I decided to move into our own apartment. Uncle O.J. offered to pay my rent while I was at UCLA. He was also paying Minnie's tuition at USC. I thought it was a generous offer, and I wanted to make him proud of me. I told him what the rent was going to cost, and I assumed he'd send a check to my landlord every month to cover it, but that didn't turn out to be the case. Nicole controlled the household accounts. That meant I had to go to Rockingham and ask her to write me a check to pay my rent every month.

It was an uncomfortable arrangement. I sensed that Nicole resented paying my rent, even though it was Uncle

O.J.'s idea in the first place—and even though he was paying a fortune in tuition so her sister could go to USC. I'd welcomed the gesture in part because I thought I was finally being accepted by my uncle the way Nicole's family was. And I knew how grateful my parents had been for his offer. Yet as the months went by, it became increasingly awkward to ask Nicole for the money. Even though Uncle O.J. had suggested the arrangement, and even though I was working hard at school and my job, I still felt like a freeloader. After a while I found myself putting off the trips to Rockingham to ask for the check as long as possible. As a result, I was chronically late with my rent. This went on for months, and with each month that passed, the pressure within me built. I should have confronted the situation directly, but at that age I was too insecure to say anything. Eventually, I became paralyzed. I just couldn't go to Nicole for that check again.

I weighed my options. If I was late with my rent one more time, my landlord would kick me out. I didn't want to ask my parents, and I couldn't possibly raise the full amount on my own by the first of the month. My second cousin Carla was also going to UCLA at the time, and we used to spend time together. One day, I was at her place and I saw her bankbook lying there. I picked it up. On an impulse that I'll always regret, I decided to "borrow" some of her money from her—without asking. I rationalized that she wouldn't mind; she was family, and I could pay it back before she even missed it. It would be just like borrowing from one of my sisters until payday, I told myself.

I put Carla's savings passbook in my purse, went to the Security Pacific Bank on Wilshire Boulevard and withdrew $900 in cash to pay my rent. It was frighteningly easy. Before I had really thought through what I was doing, it was done. I stuffed the cash in my notebook, left the bank, and got on a bus to go to work in Beverly Hills. Then, in a classic Freudian slip born of guilt and denial, I forgot the notebook, leaving it on the seat with the cash still in it, and walked to work. The money was gone for good, and my self-respect was gone with it. There was no possibility of returning the money, and I hadn't even paid the rent.

I panicked and prayed for a miracle. No miracle came. Soon afterward, Carla discovered that the money had been taken out of her account. All hell broke loose. She suspected me immediately, saying, "You're the only one who could have done it! Nobody else had a chance to get my passbook!" Overwhelmed with panic, I denied taking it, but Carla knew I was lying.

Then Carla called my parents in San Francisco. My father called me, and said, "Just tell us the truth!" Increasingly frightened and humiliated, I denied everything. I was so ashamed. I just couldn't tell my parents what I'd done. I'd never done anything like that before. I was always the responsible one among my sisters. If my parents knew the truth, they'd never trust me again. When Uncle O.J. found out, he took charge of the situation. Uncle O.J. brought Carla and me to the bank to meet with the manager. The manager ran a check, and there it was on a black-and-white security video—me, withdrawing the money. A camera had captured it all. It was the worst moment of my life. There was no denying it any longer. Overcome with guilt and shame, I didn't say a word as Uncle O.J., Carla and I drove back to my apartment. I had stolen the money, and I had lied about it, too. I was a thief. Carla could have me arrested if she wanted to. I couldn't rationalize my action any longer. In my heart, of course, I d known how wrong it was from the beginning. That knowledge made me sick with guilt and shame.

Unfortunately, the nightmare was only beginning. By

the time we arrived at my apartment, Nicole and her sisters had searched my room, looking for stolen items. Apparently, when Nicole had heard what I'd done, she'd been convinced I'd been stealing from her and everyone else since I'd arrived the summer before. Nicole and her sisters went through everything in my drawers and closet as if I were a criminal. In their eyes, I guess I was. What gave them the right to go through my belongings?

I'm sure that Uncle O.J. didn't know that Nicole would be there going through my things that day. The Browns were sitting in Minnie's room and as soon as I walked in, they began to yell accusations at me and call me terrible names. I just stood there in shame, too devastated to even protest. I'd desperately needed my uncle to control the situation, but he didn't say a word. And, after a few minutes, he was gone.

I later found out that Nicole had been telling people for some time that money was being taken from her wallet, and personal items were missing and that she suspected my family. She could be very insulting to people when she was angry. She'd even complained to Uncle O.J. that whenever our family was around, things would be missing. That didn't make much sense. Except for my summer at Rockingham, we'd rarely even been there. My parents, who are the most honest people I know, didn't appreciate the implication or the arrogance that made Nicole believe she had the right to suspect us that way.

And now, in a moment of incredible stupidity, I had confirmed not only her suspicions but the ugly stereotypes that inspired them. My theft from Carla's savings account had provided the perfect excuse for her to exclude our family from their lives even more. I had been branded a thief, and it was a title I would never live down within Nicole's family. From that day on, they shunned me.

The theft of Carla's money was the end of my relationship with Nicole—and it put a severe strain on my relationship with my family for a while, too. Up until then I had occupied a special place in my close-knit family circle. I was my mother's firstborn, her good right hand, an excellent student, the cheerleader, the one who always took the lead in family volunteer work. My parents had always been so proud of me. Now I had disgraced the people I loved the most, and I had no way to undo the damage.

Worse yet, my parents were going through a difficult time. They'd given up their home and moved in with Grandma to take care of her. They were in no position to help me.

In spite of what I'd done, when I returned to San Francisco that summer, Aunt Como and Uncle Charles invited me to stay at their house, and they even paid Carla back the money on my behalf. I will always bless them for that. No one condoned what I'd done, least of all me, but they tried their best to forgive me and help me get on with my life.

When I returned to UCLA for the spring quarter, I was on my own. I had a hard time finding an apartment. Eventually I found a roommate and a new place. Her name was Bonnie; she was a young, good-looking, petite blond. Rooming with Bonnie set me up for my second big mistake.

Bonnie, I soon found out, earned money for college as a nude model. She told me how good the money was and said that, with my looks, I could make a bundle posing for photographers. It was easy, she said, and really very discreet. Lots of students did it to get through college. Besides, who would know? It was a tempting thought. My job didn't pay enough to keep me afloat, and I was desperate for cash. My extended family wasn't helping me with expenses because they thought I should move back to San Francisco (where they could help me—and keep an eye on me, too). I thought to myself, *Maybe I'll do just one shoot, just enough to get by this month.*

I contacted the photographer that Bonnie worked for, went to his studio, and posed for a one-session shoot. After I was done, I knew that this was not something I wanted to do again. The money wasn't worth the way it made me feel. I comforted myself with the thought that no one but Bonnie and I would ever know about it, and I left determined to put the experience behind me. I had enough part-time jobs to get by and went on with my classes, and soon the photo session was just an unpleasant memory.

Less than a year later I decided to move back to San Francisco nearer my family, and I reenrolled at San Francisco State to finish my degree. I took three jobs to put myself through school: delivering the *New York Times,* working as a legal assistant two afternoons a week after school, and working part-time at Macy's in downtown San Francisco. I was finally beginning to get some of my self-esteem back after the fiasco in Los Angeles. My family seemed to have forgiven, if not forgotten, what had happened. Sure enough, within months of my moving back to San Francisco, the nude photos they'd taken of me in L.A. turned up in a men's magazine. The magazine was all over.

Word spread to my family in an instant. It was a nightmare. My mother tried to visit every newsstand in town and buy up all the magazines, but by then it was too late. My dad's best friend even called him to say my picture was on the wall of a pool hall in San Diego. I was so mortified I wanted to just disappear. Worse yet, Uncle O.J. heard about it in L.A. and spoke to my mother, angry that this might affect his reputation. What if the tabloids got ahold of the photos and found out I was his niece? *Oh God,* I thought. *No one will ever forgive me after this.* It's bad enough to make a fool of yourself privately. But when your relative's a public figure like my uncle O.J., the disgrace is magnified, especially when his living depends on his public image. After all that's happened to my family since the murders, my humiliation may seem exaggerated, but fifteen years ago it was the biggest family scandal any of us could imagine.

From the day I learned my family had seen those photos, I succumbed to overwhelming shame. There was a time when I thought I'd never get over it. Sometimes I wonder if I have to this day. I went into therapy a few months later, trying to understand why I'd acted so irresponsibly, so out of character with my own beliefs. I kept asking myself, *Why?* There had to be a reason, and I needed to understand that reason if I was ever going to hold my head up again.

I tried to tell my parents that I needed help, that I'd started seeing a counselor because I was so depressed. They didn't seem to understand why I needed to do that. I remember my mother saying, "What do you need to do that for?" Going to a therapist was unheard of in our family; nobody ever had. Why would I go talk to a stranger about myself, about my family, intimate things? Only crazy people talked to therapists, as far as they were concerned.

What made it worse is that I knew my mother and Uncle O.J. had a falling-out about what I'd done, and that only increased my misery. My mom told me I'd damaged her relationship with her brother. But one thing was clear: nobody but me wanted to dig for answers to my problems. After a while, though, my family tried to put my mistakes behind them. They treated me much like they always had, and we fell back into our old patterns of family interaction. I continued to stay with Aunt Como and Uncle Charles, and on the surface, everything seemed okay. Underneath, though, I carried the shame around with me every day.

During my last year of college, I decided that political science wasn't the best major for me after all. I'd chosen the major originally with the thought of becoming an attorney, but after working as a legal assistant and seeing the attorneys trapped behind their desks all day, I decided getting a law degree wasn't for me. So as soon as I finished my senior year of college, I started my own business: Baker International Marketing and Sales. I was fascinated with the business of international trade, and San Francisco was a great base to work from.

My goal was to import fine Florentine stationery products from Italy and market them here in the U.S. These products are very popular in the U.S. now, but twelve years ago they were hard to find in the States. I spent a year and a half going back and forth to Italy, where I'd go to the trade shows and pick up merchandise. It was great fun; I'd stay a few weeks after the show and go skiing with friends I had met in the business, and then I'd fly back to the U.S. and sell the merchandise. I made enough money to cover my personal and business expenses, and I was having the time of my life.

In 1989, I went to an open vendor day for the Sharper Image store chain in San Francisco, where I met someone at the company who suggested I apply for a job as an assistant buyer. I thought it would be a good chance to learn what buyers want in America, so I took the job. Sharper Image had started as a catalog store selling upscale men's "toys" (gadgets), and in the years I worked for them they moved into retail locations with a bang, opening seventy-four stores in five years.

* * *

My family continued to have some contact with Uncle O.J. during those years, but it took a pretty big family occasion to bring us together. Grandma went down to Rockingham to visit once or twice a year for a week or two, but she nearly always ended up coming back sooner than she'd planned. I always had the feeling that even though she was proud of her son, she didn't feel very comfortable there. The lifestyle at Rockingham was so different from the one she was used to. Uncle O.J. did send her money fairly regularly, I understand, and every few years he'd buy her a car. Nicole recognized that Grandma was the one in our family that Uncle O.J. still felt a close connection to, so she was good about sending Grandma little cards and tokens. After Sydney and Justin were born, Nicole would have copies made of photos she'd taken of the kids and send them to Grandma, with notes on the back that said things like, "Hi Grandma, this is me when I was three months old. Love, Sydney." Nicole was good about those little personalized touches, and I know Grandma was happy to get them.

They saw Grandpa Simpson less often, although they did see him. He and Nicole got along surprisingly well. Grandpa was charming and an accomplished chef, which gave him and Nicole something in common. When he visited Rockingham, he would spend time with Nicole in the kitchen teaching her some of his cooking secrets. Uncle O.J. kept his distance a lot more with Grandpa than with Grandma. Their relationship had been strained ever since Grandpa had moved out of the house when Uncle O.J. was five. My sisters and I would sometimes talk about it.

Other than those visits, our family had very little contact

with Uncle O.J. during the late eighties and early nineties. It was an absence I was especially aware of because I felt somehow to blame. Because of my behavior in Los Angeles, my parents believed I might have jeopardized the family's chance to be close to him. But, there wasn't a genuine breach during those years, just the same sort of benign distance there had always been. Our lives never seemed to intersect. For all practical purposes, Nicole's family had become his family at that point.

I couldn't help noticing, when he published his book *I Want To Tell You* during the trial, that the people he constantly refers to in the book as "his family" are the Browns. All sorts of traditions in Uncle O.J.'s family, like the annual family trip to Hawaii in the winter, were traditions he shared with the Browns. The scrapbooks that were used to illustrate his book are filled with photos of the "annual Christmas trip to Aspen," the "annual Fourth of July picnic," and similar "annual family occasions." The photos invariably show Lou and Juditha Brown and at least two of Nicole's sisters smiling into the camera with Uncle O.J.

What makes our absence even more noticeable is the fact that Uncle O.J. and Nicole were so highly social, with a large group of friends who accompanied them and the Browns on these special occasions. Many of the pictures show several dozen people lined up for the camera, most of the faces white. We weren't included in these occasions.

Furthermore, even though Uncle O.J. and Nicole had a condo in San Francisco and often flew up just for dinner, I don't remember him dropping by to see my parents when he was in town. The only time he came up for Easter was in 1994 when Grandma was named Mother of the Year at church, and the church invited him up to honor her that Sunday. The only Christmas he ever spent with us was the December before Nicole died. He stopped by Grandma's house for three hours because he'd had to fly up to host the 49ers' game that day.

For me, those rare visits were agony. Uncle O.J. had never forgiven me for embarrassing him, and Nicole considered me a pariah. As far as they were concerned, I had forfeited my place as a member of his family. Grandma's seventieth birthday party was a painful reminder of that fact. Nicole was always very possessive of Uncle O.J. in public, and with her wrapped around him throughout Grandma's party, I didn't dare try to speak to him. What made it even worse is that they had Sydney and Justin with them, and that night was the first time I had seen the children. Uncle O.J. and Nicole had never brought them to San Francisco before, so no one in the family but Grandma had ever met the kids. I really wanted to meet the children, but I felt too uncomfortable. So instead I just stood aside in sadness and embarrassment.

I had tried to make amends before that night. One day, years after I moved back to San Francisco, I had worked up my courage and called Uncle O.J.'s secretary, Kathy, and asked her to give him a message. He hadn't spoken to me since the incident with Carla. To my surprise, he called me back the next day from New York. I told him that it had been a long time since we'd spoken, and I just wanted him to know how very sorry I was about everything that had happened years before. I assured him that I had never intended to damage his reputation. He replied, "Well, you know, Terri, it was a surprise to me that you stole that money, but life goes on, and we have to just keep on goin'." I thanked him for his words, but felt them hollow somehow.

In 1985, a year or so after that telephone conversation, Uncle O.J. and Nicole got married. They'd been living together for about five years by then, but Uncle O.J. had told Nicole he wouldn't marry her until she was at least twenty-five. He believed women shouldn't marry before that age if possible, so they'd establish some independence and make sure they knew their own minds before they took the big step.

I think the real reason for the marriage was that Nicole badly wanted to have children, and neither she nor Uncle O.J. was willing to take that step without marriage. No one in the family was surprised by the decision. Uncle O.J. and Nicole would only be recognizing legally a relationship that had been established seven years earlier.

The wedding was scheduled for February 2, 1985, in the backyard at Rockingham. Three or four hundred friends and family members would gather there under a big tent for a real star-studded event. On our side of the family, my grandma and grandpa, Mom and Dad, Aunt Como and Uncle Charles, and Uncle Truman and his wife were invited. The "kids"—my generation—weren't invited to the wedding. Kathy Randa handled the arrangements for out-of-town guests. She got rooms for my family at the Brentwood Motel on Sunset, a couple of miles from Rockingham. Everyone seemed excited about going. The wedding was going to be quite an event.

I've seen the wedding photo of Nicole in her white-lace wedding dress that day. She and Uncle O.J. had the traditional fairy-tale wedding. My dad came back excited about the festivities that day. It was far removed from what most people are used to. Nicole had a big tent put up over the tennis court and hired a live band to entertain. Howard Hewitt sang, and there were celebrities galore. Several places catered the event; there was a fancy veal dinner and specialty food and drink bars set up all around. Dad loved the ice-cream bar; he was as excited as a kid about eating all the ice-cream flavors and toppings. The whole event was fun, my father said, kind of like a carnival. When it was over, my parents came home happy but exhausted from all the excitement of the trip.

A year later the whole family came together again with Uncle O.J. and Nicole at Tabernacle of Faith Baptist Church. But this time the occasion was not a wedding, but a funeral. In June of 1986 my grandfather died of cancer. It had been a long, painful battle for Grandpa. During those difficult last months, all of us had tried to be there for Grandpa. I used to go over after work and spend the evenings with him so he wouldn't have to be alone. There were many crises during that time. Sometimes there would be a problem with his oxygen tank, and we'd have to get up in the middle of the night and go to the hospital with him. There were so many emergencies that we could never be sure when he might die. So when the final emergency came, we didn't know until the end. Uncle O.J. was a pallbearer at the funeral.

I didn't see Uncle O.J. or Nicole for a long time after Grandpa's funeral. In the interval, Justin had been born. I still hadn't seen Uncle O.J.'s youngest children. I kept hoping that Nicole would soften her attitude toward me since so many years had passed. One summer afternoon in the late eighties I was down in L.A. visiting, and I thought about Sydney and Justin. I was having lunch that day at Gladstone's, a popular beachfront restaurant, and thinking about how long it had been since I'd seen my uncle's family. I had just broken up with my latest boyfriend and was feeling down, so I decided to call Nicole and O.J.'s condo in Laguna and see if they'd let me come by for a visit. *Maybe I can see the kids,* I thought. I finally worked up my courage, found a pay phone, and called their house. Nicole answered.

"Hi," I said nervously, "this is Terri. I'm in town for a

few days. I wondered if I could come over and visit you and the kids this afternoon."

Nicole broke into a hysterical laugh.

"You're the nerviest bitch I've ever met. There is no way in hell I would ever let you step into my house—much less see my kids. You'd steal everything in the place."

My heart plummeted. The old familiar pain and shame washed over me. It had been so long since I'd taken the money from Carla, and I'd paid it back. And I'd never stolen a penny from Nicole or her family (or anyone besides Carla), never done anything to Nicole. Why did she hate me so much? Would she ever let me live it down? I hung up the phone. *Why do I even try?* I wondered.

In 1992, after several years with the Sharper Image in San Francisco, I was offered a job as regional sales coordinator for Polo Ralph Lauren. I was put in charge of accounts in Southern California, Arizona, and Nevada, so I moved to Los Angeles in April. My main account was Macy's, and I traveled a lot, so I still got up to San Francisco to see my family at least twice a month. Living in Los Angeles also renewed some contact with Uncle O.J. and Nicole, chiefly when my parents came down to visit me in L.A.

It soon became clear to everyone in the family that Uncle O.J.'s marriage to Nicole was in serious trouble. After a while Nicole moved out of Rockingham and took the children with her, first renting a house on Gretna Green Avenue and later moving into a condo on Bundy Drive, about five miles from Rockingham. Nicole filed for divorce. About that same time, Paula Barbieri started to become visible in Uncle O.J.'s life. From all appearances, the marriage was over. But just about the time we accepted the separation as final, Nicole seemed to be back again, spending time at Rockingham with Uncle O.J.

On a visit there with my parents in 1993, Nicole was outside, packing up things for a garage sale. Later, we saw her cuddling and kissing Uncle O.J. in the driveway. She was in such a warm mood that for the first time in ten years, she actually said "hello" to me that day. My parents and I looked at each other in astonishment at their apparent intimacy. I thought: *Nicole must really want this marriage back if she's even willing to be nice to me.* What a strange moment that was. I found the whole relationship between Nicole and Uncle O.J. deeply confusing. What did they want from each other?

I also wondered how Nicole was going to survive in the "real world" after being supported in a celebrity lifestyle since she was seventeen. Apart from the financial implications, over the years she'd developed the attitude that she was entitled to treat those beneath her on the economic scale with contempt. Michelle was the classic example. Michelle was the housekeeper at Rockingham by then; she'd been there for years, ever since Nicole's cousin Maria had left. Michelle was an excellent employee, able to meet Uncle O.J.'s exacting standards and fiercely loyal to him. Then one day Nicole took the children over to Rockingham to play in the pool, and Sydney took a cushion off one of the patio lounges and put it next to the Jacuzzi, where it was soaking up chlorinated water. The cushion was expensive; it required dry cleaning and wasn't supposed to be used near the pool. When Michelle saw it lying on the ground, she rushed over to Sydney, and said, "Get that cushion off the ground! You know you're not supposed to play with it!"

Apparently Nicole overheard this interchange and was furious that Michelle would reprimand Sydney. She went over to Michelle, and said, "This is my children's house. You don't tell them what they can and can't do here." And she slapped Michelle, hard, in the face. Michelle just stood there, so shocked she couldn't respond. Then Nicole ran to Uncle O.J. and told him what she had done. Michelle said Uncle O.J. looked uncomfortable but refused to make a decision, saying Michelle would have to handle things the way she thought best. Michelle threatened to leave if Uncle O.J. didn't say anything to Nicole about the incident, but he wouldn't do it. It was clear that he didn't like what had happened, but he wasn't willing to stand up to Nicole, even if that meant losing a loyal employee. It made me think of the day years before he'd stood uncomfortably by as Nicole and her sisters ransacked my apartment. In the end, Michelle left.

CHAPTER 4

BARBARIANS AT THE GATE

Monday, June 13, dawned hot and clear in Nevada. I had flown to Las Vegas at eight that morning, arriving at the Bullock's store shortly after it opened. Bullock's was one of our most important accounts, so I flew out to the Vegas store at least once a month. I'd been in a rush to get to the airport that day, so I hadn't even thought about turning on the morning news. As far as I knew, it was just another hectic Monday morning, and I was back to the old grind. I had absolutely no premonition that this day would change my life—all our lives—forever.

I was in the Polo department setting up a display when my sales manager came over to tell me that there was a phone call for me at the register. "Who is it?" I asked. I assumed it was one of the buyers.

"It's your mother," the manager said. The moment he said that, I knew something was wrong. In all the years I'd worked for Ralph Lauren, my mother had never called me at a store.

I went behind the counter and picked up the phone by the cash register, saying, "Mom?" The manager next to me gave me a glance of mild concern.

"Have you heard the news?" my mom said.

"What news?"

"Nicole has been murdered. She was shot in the front yard with some guy." My mother's voice was tense and dominating—her crisis voice.

For a minute I couldn't take it in. "Nicole? What do you mean, shot? When? What guy?"

"We don't know anything yet. We just heard on the news that she was shot in her front yard with some guy." My mind spun quickly. Was it a man friend? Had Nicole gotten in his face, slapped him, insulted him? I knew what she could be like at times, and if she'd lost her temper with the wrong man, maybe . . . I shoved the thought guiltily aside. What was I thinking? Then I wondered why Mom was calling me at the store. I was in Las Vegas; what could I do to help until I got home? It would have been different if I'd been in L.A. I could have gone right over to Uncle O.J.'s to see if he was all right. But then the thought came to me, that my mother was probably afraid I'd hear it on the news and be upset.

All of this went through my mind in a fraction of a second as my mother's words started to sink in. There was a silence, and I realized there was something more to come. Something else was wrong.

"Mom? What is it?"

Her voice became even more authoritarian. "They're talking crazy. They're saying on the news the police think maybe your uncle had something to do with it."

My mind went blank. Uncle O.J.? My mom's brother?

They had to be kidding. He was self-centered, distant, even irritating, but he wasn't violent, and he certainly wasn't a criminal. Criminals were gang members, lowlifes, menacing faces behind bars at San Quentin. Not members of God-fearing, caring families like mine. He might not be my favorite family member, but a murderer? Ludicrous.

My mother's voice continued, "Grandma and I will be flying into LAX later today. You need to take the next flight home so you can meet us at the airport." After an additional detail or two, she hung up.

I didn't know what to do. My parents were both in San Francisco with the rest of the family; I, on the other hand, lived only ten minutes from Rockingham. I didn't want to leave work an hour after I'd gotten there and fly back home at company expense; it didn't seem fair to my employer. On the other hand, there was no way I could say no to my mother under the circumstances. So I just looked at the manager, who still stood beside me looking concerned, and said, "My aunt's been killed. I have to go home."

Thankfully, he didn't question me. He just said, "Oh, okay. Do you need a ride to the airport?"

I told him no, I'd take a cab, and called the airport immediately. They told me the next flight left in half an hour. There was no time to wait for a cab, so I took the manager up on his offer, and we rushed down to his car and roared off to the airport. As we drove, I told him briefly what had happened. He nodded rather uncomprehendingly. I could tell he couldn't quite understand what the problem was. Either he hadn't heard the news that morning, or he didn't make the connection. I don't think he knew I was O.J. Simpson's niece. I felt confused. I knew the manager professionally, and I didn't feel comfortable talking about personal matters. I had no idea at the time that within hours an endless line of strangers would be privy to our most private family business. I suddenly felt like I'd walked into a Hitchcock movie. This couldn't be happening.

The feeling of unreality lasted throughout the short flight home to LAX. Why would the police implicate Uncle O.J.? He was a sports superstar; everybody loved him. There must have been a mistake. Maybe somebody had misidentified him, thought he looked like somebody else at the scene. *This is ridiculous,* I kept thinking over and over. *Just ridiculous.*

I'd called my dad from the airport at Las Vegas, so I knew my mother and grandmother would be arriving at LAX just an hour after I did. As soon as my plane landed, I ran over to the parking lot where my car was parked and drove back to the arrival area for their flight. Mom and Grandma were just coming off the plane, with Grandma in her wheelchair. I edged my car as close to the curb as possible, and we put Grandma in the front and wedged her wheelchair into the backseat of my old Volkswagen convertible. Mom squeezed in the back with the wheelchair, and we roared off. It was a little past noon, four hours and several lifetimes from my departure on an eight o'clock flight that morning.

We got on the freeway and headed for Rockingham in silence. I didn't have a radio in my car, so we couldn't listen to news reports. Besides, it wouldn't have occurred to us to listen to one. There might be something about the murder on the evening news, we thought. It never crossed our minds that there would be constant media coverage. As I made my way up the San Diego Freeway toward Sunset, the silence began to make me uncomfortable. Why wasn't anyone talking? We were a family of talkers; the problem was usually for anyone to get a word in edgewise. But now nobody was talking; nobody was asking the obvious questions about something so traumatic. What time was Nicole killed? Was she getting in or out of her car in front of the house? Was it a drive-by shooting? A follow-home robbery? A fight with a boyfriend? Did the police have any leads yet? Why did they think Uncle O.J. had something to do with it? Where were the kids? But nobody was saying a word. The silence felt awkward, unnatural. I could feel the tension. And then I thought, *Here we go again. Why is it that when it comes to Uncle O.J., it's always a different set of rules? Why does everyone clam up? He's not even* here, *but nobody wants to say something he might not like.* Here were Mom and Grandma, two of the most outspoken women you'll ever find, and once again they'd fallen silent in the shadow of my famous uncle.

I thought about Nicole, my uncle O.J.'s artistic, feisty, carelessly arrogant wife. I couldn't comprehend that she was dead, much less murdered. She was so young. You expect your grandparents to die, but not someone so young, and not in that way. She lived in a beautiful, safe neighborhood, not a ghetto in South Central. Things like that didn't happen just blocks from the trendiest street in West L.A. It had been on San Vincente, just five blocks from the murder scene, that I'd seen her last, just a month before. The scene ran through my mind as I drove.

I was with Michelle, the maid who'd left Uncle O.J.'s after Nicole had slapped her a few weeks before. We'd become friends and were having coffee at Starbucks on the corner of Barrington and San Vicente. I had picked up Michelle at Rockingham. Uncle O.J. had just hired a new maid named Gigi, and Michelle had gone over on her day off to help teach Gigi the procedures Uncle O.J. expected. Michelle had started a new job herself and was getting used to the transition. It was a hard time for her, so we sat at Starbucks talking about the changes in her life.

Just then Nicole walked into Starbucks. She was meeting Cora Fischman there. They bought coffee and took a table outside. I remember feeling very awkward sitting there with Michelle, with Nicole and Cora just a few yards away. When we got up to leave and walked outside, to my surprise Nicole casually greeted Michelle, saying, "Hi, Michelle," and the two of them fell into polite conversation about the kids and what they were both doing. I remember thinking how odd it was. Nicole had just slapped Michelle and insulted her, Michelle had lost her job as a result, yet the two of them stood there chatting pleasantly as though nothing had happened. I felt intensely uncomfortable, so I just stood quietly in the background, and after a minute or two Nicole said, "Hi, Terri," as though she always said hello to me.

I replied, "Hi," feeling even more awkward at the unaccustomed greeting. As Nicole resumed her conversation with Michelle, I looked her over carefully. She looked different from the person I remembered. All the time I'd known her, I'd thought of her as a lot older then I, even though there was only a few years difference in our ages. She'd always seemed more like the older, wealthy women who lived north of Sunset. She'd always worn diamonds: a diamond solitaire around her neck, two-carat diamond studs in her ears, and her big diamond engagement ring on her left hand just below her Rolex or Cartier watch. Expensive jewelry, but clean and simple. And she liked to be comfortable in shorts or jeans and a tee shirt, with unlaced tennis shoes she could slip on and kick off.

The Nicole I saw that day looked like a different woman, dressed in the trendier, more cluttered style popular with the twentysomethings in the fashionable area south of Sunset. She had on a pair of very cute, very tight jeans, and a sweater with a deep V that showed off her surgically perfect breasts. She was even wearing the cowboy-style boot-shoes so popular in L.A., which I thought especially odd since they're confining and not very comfortable. Instead of her engagement diamond, she had silver rings on several of the fingers of both hands, even her thumb. She'd had several more holes pierced in each ear, and she wore costume earrings dangling from her ears and a costume-jewelry necklace around her throat. She looked young, almost like a teenager, and for the first time in my life I thought she didn't seem old enough to be the mother of two school-age kids. She looked like a kid herself. It was like she had come full circle since I'd first met her years before when she was seventeen. She was a teenager again. I thought to myself, *She's changed. I don't even know her anymore.*

That image, of a newly young Nicole, kept floating in and out of my head as I got off the freeway at Sunset and turned west to Rockingham. Sadness was beginning to penetrate the shock. Nicole was dead. Troubled as our relationship had been, she was dead, and someone had murdered her. It was a painful thought.

There's an old cliché about "turning an important corner" in your life. That afternoon, as I turned the corner onto Rockingham Drive and approached my uncle's house, that cliché became literally as well as figuratively true for me. From the moment I made that turn, my life was never the same again.

We knew Nicole had been murdered at home, at Bundy. We knew that police would be there investigating, and we assumed the press had been at Bundy that morning. We were driving to Uncle O.J.'s to be with him, to gather together as a family and share his grief. We were driving to a place of privacy and refuge. What we found instead was another crime scene and a media storm waiting to envelop us.

I could see the crowd of reporters from blocks away. Mom and I looked at each other as if to say, "What in the world?" As I drove closer, I could also see that the entire estate was surrounded by yellow tape reading, "Do not enter. Crime scene." Police officers were patrolling the perimeter of the grounds. I was stunned. By the time I reached the entrance gate, reporters were already surging around us. They rushed the car the moment I began to slow down, shoving cameras and microphones in our faces. I got slowly out of the car to ask the officers what was going on and was immediately inundated with questions from the reporters. "Who are you? Is that his mother?" Pointing to Mom, "Who's that?" People leaned into my car, shoving cameras in Grandma's face and snapping pictures. I had no idea what was going on. It all seemed to happen at once. "Where's O.J.? Do you know where O.J. is? What was Nicole like? That is his mom, right?"

I backed away in fear and bewilderment, but I couldn't get back into my car because the reporters were surging all around me. Starting to panic, I shoved and elbowed reporters aside and forced my way back to my car. It was sheer pandemonium. I felt like I was in the middle of a carnival on a Ferris wheel while it spins full-speed backward and you close your eyes so you won't pass out. I was stunned. I kept thinking, *Why are they here? People are murdered every day, and Nicole wasn't a celebrity. What's going on? And why the crime tape? Nicole was killed at Bundy.*

Why indeed? The officer I'd tried to talk to had told me only that the grounds were closed for investigation and that no one was allowed in yet. As I backed out of the driveway and escaped back down to Sunset, the crime-scene tape and the enormity of its implications hit me like I'd run into a wall. I remembered what Mom had told me just a few hours earlier: "The police are saying your uncle's got something to do with it." I could understand the police questioning family members after a murder, but this? My God. I felt like a child had gone into a candy store and taken a dime candy bar, but instead of calling his parents, they'd sent in the SWAT team to arrest him. This was no routine interrogation. This was serious.

Where was Uncle O.J.? We didn't know what to do next, but then Mom said, "Maybe he's still at the police station. Do you know where it is?" I had a vague idea of where the West L.A. station was, so I drove to the general area, and we drove around until we found it. As soon as I got near, though, it seemed pretty obvious that he wasn't there because there wasn't a media van in sight. Still, I pulled into the parking lot and, leaving Mom and Grandma in the car, went inside and approached the officer at the front desk.

"Excuse me, can you tell me, is O.J. Simpson here?"

The officer asked me who I was. I told him I was O.J.'s niece, and then I told him, "I've got his mother waiting outside in my car. She's worried, and she's trying to find him."

The officer disappeared into a back office, and a moment later another officer came out and approached me. "He's not here. He's downtown at Parker Center."

"What's Parker Center?" I asked. "Isn't this the closest police station?"

"That's all I can tell you right now," the officer replied.

I walked back outside to the parking lot, where Mom and Grandma were still waiting in the car. The knot in my stomach had gotten a little tighter. Parker Center? Why not here where it had happened? A million things were spinning through my mind. Should we try to get to Parker Center? By now it was rush hour, and it would be a miserable, slow trip downtown. What if he wasn't even there by the time we arrived? Grandma was getting tired. If we didn't go to Parker Center, then where? We couldn't go back to my little apartment; there was no way to get Grandma's wheelchair up the stairs. And Rockingham was out of the question.

I got back in the car and explained the situation to my mom. We started driving around West L.A., trying to figure out what to do. We were getting more and more tired and frustrated. Nobody had eaten, and Grandma needed to rest. We couldn't just drive around forever. Finally my mom suggested that we check into the Brentwood Motel, which is right on Sunset less than a mile from Rockingham. Ironically, it was the same place my parents had stayed for Uncle O.J. and Nicole's wedding. It seemed like the best suggestion so far, so we drove over and checked in. As I stood there by the counter with my mother while she registered, I felt sick to my stomach. I kept remembering everybody staying there during Nicole's wedding, and I knew Mom and Grandma had to be remembering the same thing. It was the only other time they'd been there. They gave us a room key which turned out to be for the wrong room, and when we finally got inside, we saw that there were two small double beds for the three of us. The room was tiny, hot, and stuffy. I felt suffocated. Mom called San Franciso to tell everybody where we were, and then we turned to the problem at hand.

Nicole had been dead for less than twenty-four hours, but already that reality was becoming secondary. The greater problem was Uncle O.J. What on earth was going on? The signs were ominous. My mother called my dad again and said, "Get down here *right away*. We need you."

By the time we finally got through to Rockingham an hour or two later, my whole family were already on the road, roaring down I-5 for the six-hour trip to L.A. We kept in touch with them on a cell phone so we'd know where they were all the time. By then it was late evening, and the sun was beginning to set.

Meanwhile we'd gotten through to Gigi at Rockingham and found out that Uncle O.J. was on his way home and that the crime tape had been removed. We could get in. Once again we piled into the car and headed back to Rockingham. This time we braced for the worst. We found it. There weren't any police escorts set up on Rockingham yet, so when we got there, we had to fight our way through the crowd once again. The police were trying to keep people off Uncle O.J.'s property, but there weren't enough officers to really control the crowd. I inched forward, scared to death I'd run over a reporter's foot in the confusion.

It was even worse than it had been earlier. The first time we'd come, there were more reporters than vehicles, about thirty or so altogether, and an assortment of neighbors and lookie-lous. Now, though, the media was out in full force, leaving no room for the merely curious. There were trucks, vans, all kinds of equipment everywhere, and huge spotlights illuminating the house and grounds. The house had become a huge beacon in the dusk of the usually quiet suburban neighborhood. It looked like the alien invasion in *Close Encounters*. It was frightening, spooky—surreal. All those years Uncle O.J. had been in the media spotlight figuratively, but we hadn't been there. We'd never seen this kind of thing. The irony of the situation was overwhelming.

Even when we finally reached the gate and were admitted

into the grounds, we were still caught in the blinding illumination like deer frozen in headlights. We could still see the cameras on the other side of the fence bars; there were ladders all around the perimeter and reporters standing on fences and roofs in neighbors' yards. I remember seeing Maria Shriver standing on top of an NBC van with her cameraman, and I thought, *My God, what is she doing? She's a Kennedy. Doesn't she know what this feels like?* I felt absolutely vulnerable, naked before the world. I couldn't understand what was happening to us.

Still, it was first things first. We had to get Grandma in the house. We got her out of my car and helped her into the house. The living room was already crowded. Bob Kardashian was there with Ron Shipp. Kato was wandering around. There were so many people there, most of them people I didn't know. Someone told us Uncle O.J. was in the family room, so we took Grandma in there to him. He stood up when we came in and kissed her, and then he turned to my mom and kissed her, too. Everyone huddled around the couches where the TVs were going. Oddly enough, just like in the ride back from the airport that afternoon, no one was saying anything about what was happening. Nobody asked questions, and Uncle O.J. didn't tell us much at that point. The only things we learned about the visit to Parker Center were from the news reports on television.

Once again, I was puzzled. We were in the middle of the most bizarre experience of our lives, the house was surrounded by a battalion of frenzied reporters, and nobody was talking about it. I couldn't understand it. In San Francisco, the house would have been filled with family. I would have known everyone in the room. We would have sat down around the table and talked about it quietly, intimately, earnestly. Together, we would have asked a lot of questions and searched for answers. We would have tried to make sense of it all. But no one was talking about it here. In this house full of strangers, we weren't even talking to each other. What was it about Uncle O.J. that always kept us quiet?

I tried to understand it. I invented all sorts of explanations for myself. Maybe he was embarrassed about being interrogated and didn't want us to know about it. Maybe he didn't want to explain what had happened to Nicole, or when he'd seen her last. Maybe these things were too personal. He'd never shared his feelings with us before, at least that I knew of. We'd rarely even seen him over the years. In fact, we'd only been to Rockingham three or four times in the last ten years.

I looked around the room. We were all here; my parents, aunts and uncles, my sisters. We had never been all together in that house before. We'd been together so many times before—at Christmas, Thanksgiving, every holiday, virtually every Sunday of my life. But not at Rockingham, never with Uncle O.J. He was never with us.

It was the first time we'd all been at Rockingham, and it had taken something this horrible to bring it about. I felt like an intruder in his private space. Did he really want us here? Maybe he'd be more comfortable if we weren't, if he could be alone with the people he was close to. I looked at my sisters, and they looked as uncomfortable as I felt. But leaving was unthinkable, too. Our family had always come together in times of crisis. How could we leave him alone in his grief? He might need us. So we asked no questions, and when he did offer information, we accepted it graciously, without comment. There was a tacit agreement: let the important people handle it and be quiet. So, we moved from room to room, took care of the children, and watched television. Like the rest of America, we tuned in the TVs so we could find out what was going on in our lives from the people just twenty feet outside our own windows.

It was the strangest evening of my life. On one level it was like a church potluck. Everybody was eating Honey Baked ham from a buffet in the kitchen, standing around with paper plates in their hands. I remember going to fix a plate for Grandma. In other ways it was like a funeral. Nicole was dead; she'd been killed. But no one was talking about her. Justin and Sydney had lost their mother. Uncle O.J. had lost the woman who'd been the love of his life. I expected visible grief.

There'd been other divorces in the family; my sisters Kahdi and Gyne were both divorced. If either of their ex-husbands had been killed like that, we would all have felt tremendous grief, a sense of losing an important part of ourselves, a gut-wrenching agony. But none of us was crying for Nicole. We'd so seldom seen her that we didn't feel connected to her, didn't feel her absence in the family circle. None of us could have even said when her birthday was. I felt terrible that I wasn't crying for her. I wanted to; I just couldn't. We should have been talking about her. But instead we were talking about Uncle O.J. What would happen to him? How would this affect him? Even in Nicole's death, Uncle O.J. was once more the center of our attention.

Jason and Arnelle seemed to be grieving for Nicole. They were both very distraught, especially Jason. He'd been extremely close to Nicole, closer in some ways than he was to his father. Faced with her loss, and with the horror of her death, he was overwhelmed with sadness and seemed to be in a daze.

I kept looking at Uncle O.J. and thinking, *Why isn't he overcome with grief?* How could he be so calm, when the person he loved the most had just been murdered? I would have been too overwhelmed emotionally to function. I tried not to judge him; after all, I told myself, everyone showed grief differently. He'd had a long, hard day, and he'd had several hours to calm down. I shouldn't be so critical of him, especially at a time like this. Yet he just kept talking, concerned with the details of his interrogation. I wondered where he got the mental focus. I wondered why he was talking about himself instead of talking about what might have happened, who might have killed Nicole.

I don't think Kato knew how to feel, either. I was the only one in my family who even knew who Kato was, and he seemed to feel almost as out of place as I did that night.

Uncle O.J. walked into the kitchen, giving a series of dissertations to anyone who would listen, about his whereabouts and behavior for the last twenty-four hours. Uncle O.J. does that kind of thing a lot, just talks for long periods of time, while other people listen quietly. No one ever interrupts when he's giving one of his monologues.

That night he was giving one of his monologues on the police, saying, "Yeah, they're asking me all this stuff like where I got this cut and that cut." His tone of voice implied the questions were ridiculous. When Kato walked into the kitchen in the middle of all this, Uncle O.J. turned to him and said something like "Kato, you and I went and got McDonalds, and then we came back in the house together. You were with me." And he continued to go through the events of the evening with Kato, detailing what Kato "remembered." Kato never said a word. He was a basket case. He just stood there looking as if he wished he were invisible. I wasn't sure if he remembered much of anything at that moment. He seemed scared to death and very confused, so confused and overcome with anxiety that I wondered if he was on drugs. *What's wrong with this guy?* I wondered. *He seems sweet, but he doesn't seem normal. Is he high, or is he just a nervous wreck?* There was fear all over his face. He seemed like he didn't want to be there, but he couldn't leave. He lived there.

It started to get late, and my family began figuring out what to do about sleeping arrangements. I heard Mom talking to Bob Kardashian in the hall. Bob was very worried. I heard him say, "Don't leave him alone. Stay with him all night. If he goes to the bathroom, go with him."

Mom was nodding. "Of course. I'm going to sleep on the couch in his room. We won't leave him alone for a minute." It dawned on me that they worried about Uncle O.J. committing suicide. It was such a strange thought. No one in our family had ever been suicidal. We'd always been so strong. The thought frightened me.

After that the evening went quickly. We figured out the logistics of who would sleep where. Kato offered to give up his room to my sisters and their children, and I decided to camp out on the couch in the TV room. The group of visitors slowly broke up. Some of us snacked or watched TV; the more exhausted among us went to bed. I remember calling home to pick up my phone messages; there were forty-seven of them. Later, after most of the household had gone to bed, Kato asked me if I could take him over to his friend Rachel's house to pick up his car. Rachel was the one he'd been on the phone with when he'd heard the three thumps on the wall. I needed to pick up some clothes at my house anyway, so I didn't mind. Besides, I felt sorry for Kato. He looked so miserable. We made our way out through the crowd at the gate, and I drove him to the corner of Montana and Barrington and dropped him off. He said he'd walk the rest of the way to Rachel's house. I never did see exactly where he went. He just sort of disappeared into the darkness as I drove off.

Later I would be questioned about Kato's movements that night. I hadn't paid that much attention. I told them what I remembered. When I got back to Rockingham an hour or so later, my dad was worried and angry. "What were you thinking, leaving alone with that guy? We don't even know him!" By that time everything was beginning to seem suspicious. The tension was getting to us. Kato did seem kind of weird. Maybe something was wrong with him. But when he came back a couple of hours later, he just seemed sad and nervous again. *Maybe he just needed to get out of here for a while and be with a friend.* I thought. I knew how that felt. He seemed as lost as I felt. He wasn't sure he still lived at Rockingham. He didn't know if Uncle O.J. would be charged, or if that was the end of it. He didn't know if he'd have to talk to the police. That night he just wanted to get through it like the rest of us. I stretched out on the couch, and he lay down on the floor nearby. I don't think either of us wanted to be alone. We lay there in silence, watching TV until about three in the morning. At some point we both drifted off to sleep.

All around us, in the darkness and the silence, the cameras waited like enemy spies. Even in sleep, I couldn't get rid of the feeling that someone was watching me. It was like being in a glass tower built of two-way mirrors. Everyone on the outside could see in, could see us, and they longed to be inside where they thought they would find answers. But we had no answers. We were looking back out at them, waiting for them to tell us what was happening. We couldn't see anything in the glass but our own bewildered reflections.

CHAPTER 5

THE VALLEY OF THE SHADOW

I awoke late the next morning after a restless night on the couch. I looked around the living room in momentary confusion. Then I remembered; I was at Rockingham. The events of the previous day hadn't been just a bad dream. Daylight is supposed to bring relief from a nightmare, but this sunrise hadn't. The morning light shone dismally on the rich cream carpets, the light muted by the tightly closed blinds. I peered cautiously through a crack in the blind. All around us the press still lay encamped. It had been over ten years since I'd awakened at the Rockingham estate. It was a disquieting homecoming.

I wandered into the kitchen looking for the rest of the family. Tracy and Toni were there, still exhausted. Both of them were feeding their kids. I knew the events of the previous day had been especially hard on them. Uncle O.J. was nowhere around. When he still hadn't appeared an hour later, I asked my mom where he was. He'd left early that morning, she told me, as soon as he'd woken up. He'd gone out the back way to avoid the press, through the tennis court and the neighbor's gate behind the house. We later found out that Bob Kardashian had met him there, and they'd left undetected. It had never occurred to the press that he might go out the back, so no one had been watching. *Real rocket scientists, the media,* I thought, chuckling to myself. The TVs were still going in the other room. "O.J. Simpson is holed up in his Rockingham house with his family. No one has spoken to him," the reporter intoned solemnly. I laughed. With his family. Yeah, right. For the first time in our lives the whole family had come together at Rockingham, and Uncle O.J. had left. Somehow it seemed fitting.

What made it even stranger was that on one knew where he'd gone. We looked at each other, and said, "Anybody know where he went?" No one did. I knew my mother was really worried about him, and it seemed incredible that he'd just left without letting us know where he'd be. I said, "Why didn't he tell anybody where he was going?" but then my father said, "Why should he? It's none of our concern. He's taking care of business." I remember thinking, *Why isn't it any of our business? The only reason we're here is to help him.* But as usual, the thought was followed by an immediate pang of guilt. Why was I being so insensitive? Uncle O.J. must be going through hell.

My father commented that Uncle O.J. had a lot on his mind. He'd probably just forgotten to tell anybody where he was going. I remembered the constant phone calls between the rest of us the day before to keep from getting separated and thought once again how very different Uncle O.J. was from the rest of us. If I had been in the same situation, I would have nestled in the midst of my family for comfort and security. But Uncle O.J. didn't feel comfortable with us anymore. There was too much time and distance between us. He'd gone to seek comfort from the people who had become his "family" over the years, leaving us behind to wonder and worry.

It was so peculiar. Uncle O.J. was gone, his friends were gone, and there we were at his house, surrounded by hungry reporters, with no idea what to do with ourselves. There really wasn't much we could do, so we contented ourselves as best we could with watching TV and taking care of the kids and Grandma. The television had become our lifeline. It was our only means of getting information as the hours crawled by. I began to wonder what was happening to Sydney and Justin. Were they still with the Browns? Maybe Uncle O.J. had gone to get them. I could hardly stand to think about his children. What must they be going through? I hardly knew them. It made me sad.

That afternoon Kato had to go talk to Uncle O.J.'s attorneys about what happened in his interview with the police. They had questioned Kato the day before. It was becoming clear that Kato's testimony might be important. Uncle O.J. had been advising him to "just tell the truth," but I'm not sure Kato was sure what the truth was. He had left the house earlier for his daily run. When he got back hours later, Kato was pacing like a cat. The news of Kato's conversation with the attorneys had leaked out before Kato got back. It was odd, watching ourselves in the living room and on TV at the same time. It was like seeing your life in stereo, two images at once.

With every hour that passed during that long day, another rumor surfaced in the media. Nicole's companion had been identified as a young waiter from the Mezzaluna named Ron Goldman. He was referred to as an "actor and model," and he was handsome. There were rumors he'd gone to meet Nicole for a liaison. *He probably had*, I thought.

He looked like Nicole's new friends—young and hip. The rumors continued. A pair of sunglasses and a ski cap had been found at Bundy. A white Bronco had been spotted fleeing the scene on the night of the murder. Blood drops had been found in Uncle O.J.'s house. The police had found a man's leather glove at the murder scene. Most disturbingly, a detective named Mark Fuhrman had found a matching glove at Rockingham, soaked with blood.

We were beginning to understand why the grounds had been surrounded by police tape the day before, why they hadn't let us in. They'd been looking for evidence. I was confused. How could a bloody glove have gotten to Uncle O.J.'s house? It didn't make sense, and as usual, none of us was talking about it. It was so odd to sit there at the house and hear the evidence rumored on Television. Two years later Mark Fuhrman would claim that there had been blood on the light switch in the bathroom near the washer on Monday morning and a dark sweatsuit inside, still damp. I remembered our arrival that Monday night. We'd had to put the kids' clothes in the washer so they'd have clean clothes the next morning. I hadn't seen any blood. I hadn't seen any signs they'd dusted for fingerprints, either.

As each little piece of information leaked out that day, my curiosity grew. I started prowling around the estate grounds, out back, away from the press. I went around to the passageway behind Kato's room, where they were saying the glove had been found. You could see where someone had walked in, presumably to pick up the glove, but otherwise the area was undisturbed. The thick foliage covering the fence was unbroken; if someone had climbed over, there should have been obvious damage to the leaves. Overhead, between the edge of the roof and the fence, spiderwebs still hung, undisturbed. I peeked into Kato's room, where my sisters had slept the night before. It was easy to see that the outdoor air-conditioning unit was on the other side of the wall and that anyone inside would have heard thumps if someone had bumped up against it. But if someone had, why hadn't the leaves been broken? It didn't make sense. I looked at the pictures on the wall and tried to figure out which one would swing if you bumped the air conditioner.

Inside the house, everything had been cleaned up in deference to Uncle O.J.'s taste. He always insisted on a meticulously clean house. Any blood samples the police might have collected were long gone, courtesy of Gigi and Kathy. If there'd been blood in the house, though, it should have left stains on the white carpets Nicole had installed years before. I poked around the entrance area and followed the path of white carpet Uncle O.J. would have had to take to go upstairs to his bedroom. There was no blood there. Why would he have bled in the tiled hallway, but not on the white carpet? Clearly, there was a mistake. The rumors couldn't be true. Someone was bound to find that out. Everyone knew that the media weren't always reliable. Everything might still be all right. In between my little investigating forays, I returned to the TV, where the rest of my family was still keeping tabs on the latest developments.

By the time the endless afternoon had almost worn away, I was desperate to get out of the house. When someone suggested we needed a few groceries from the store, Dad and I quickly volunteered to go. It would be a relief to get out of there for a while, even if it meant facing the dragons at the gate to escape.

We got in my small car and drove out the gate as the media parted before us, craning their necks to get a good look at my father. At that point rumors of Uncle O.J. were almost as prevalent as Elvis sightings, and every black man in the vicinity was rumored to be my uncle. It was amusing in ways. My dad had always said that white people seem to think all black people look alike. He meant it as a joke, but maybe he had a point. People had been identifying me as Arnelle from the minute I'd arrived.

As I drove down Sunset toward Bundy and the nearest Ralph's supermarket, I realized that we were only a couple of blocks from Nicole's condo. I looked at Dad. I don't remember either of us saying anything, but somehow I just knew what we were both thinking. I turned down toward Montana and the alley that ran behind Nicole's house. They hadn't shown much footage of the murder scene yet, and we wanted to see for ourselves. We needed to make it real, to see with our own eyes what had happened. We had only an electronic image of Nicole's still form wrapped in a sheet. It wasn't enough.

We pulled up behind the condo, half-expecting to see police guards and media all over the grounds. No one was there. We parked in the alley behind Nicole's jeep, still sitting by the garage, and got out. She always parked in the driveway when she was in a hurry or thought she might go out again. It seemed strange that the jeep was still sitting there, right where she'd left it, as though she might be back any minute. It was covered with dust from the fingerprint analysis, and it had been searched. I looked through the jeep window. Her lip gloss was lying on the console, and her hairbrush was next to it with a few strands of blond hair still in the bristles. Nicole usually kept her lip gloss handy. For the first time since I'd gotten the news, it began to sink in that this was *Nicole*. Something about that lip gloss and the strands of her hair made me shiver. *My God*, I thought, *she was just* here. *How can she be gone?*

Scattered on the ground near the jeep were coins, mostly pennies. I remember looking at them and wondering why they were there. It looked like someone had been rummaging in his pockets for keys and spilled the coins accidentally. It made sense. I wondered if they belonged to Nicole's friend, the man who had been killed with her. As we came closer to the back gate, we could see the familiar police tape strung around the premises. It was then that I noticed the blood. One day later, but they still hadn't cleaned up the blood. I went numb. We stood by the back gate, staring at the splashes of blood. There was blood smeared all over the bottom crossbar on the inside of the back gate and what looked like a partial footprint, as if someone had shoved the gate open with their foot in their hurry to leave. We looked at it in silence. That image would come back to me months later, when the prosecutors showed photos of the same gate taken three weeks later. *It wasn't at all like that,* I remembered thinking during the trial.

We went on around the corner and started toward the front, we could see bloody pawprints where Nicole's Akita, Kato, had walked the night of the murder. We followed the trail of bloody prints to the front of the condo. It was then that the full impact of the scene hit us. Nothing had prepared us for the amount of carnage in that yard. There was blood everywhere, pools of it, so much that I couldn't even comprehend it. I stared at the place Nicole had died, and over and over, like a broken record, I kept thinking, *How could she have that much blood in her body? It isn't possible. It wouldn't fit.* Images of her tan, firm, healthy body flashed in front of me as I stared at the life fluid spilled out before me. I couldn't take in what I was seeing. We followed the walk down to the gate by the grass, where the police had been. It was even worse. The gate was covered with blood, clotted blood, and what appeared to be lumps of flesh. The depressions in the ground made it clear that there had been a struggle. My father said, "If she died over there, how come there's all this blood here?"

Later I would find out that was the place Ron Goldman had fallen, and that's where he'd died. Much later, when I saw the photos from the crime scene, I would find a photo of Ron Goldman leaning in that same spot, his eyes wide-open and staring in death. The images would haunt me forever. I thought, *My God, this is real.* As I stood there looking down at the carnage in that space, I felt suddenly overpowered by a sense of imminent danger. It was as though the murderer were still there somewhere, and somewhere in the back of my mind, a voice was shouting, "Run! Run for your life!" But I couldn't run. I could only back away.

My body had gone completely numb by then. The world was a blank, and I couldn't hear or smell anything around me. The only thing that went through my mind was Uncle O.J.'s face. *No,* I thought, *no. Impossible. Incomprehensible. Uncle O.J. do this?* This was the act of a maniac, a deranged psychotic, someone like Charles Manson. How could anyone think, even for a moment, that my charming, affable uncle could be capable of such a thing?

Dad and I walked back to the car in silence. I didn't understand the nature of dissociation back then, so I didn't realize I was in shock. We got back in the car as if nothing had happened. I think one of us said something about going to Ralph's. I didn't feel a thing. If you'd asked me, I'd have said I was fine. But my hands were inexplicably clumsy. I had trouble getting the key in the ignition, and for the first few blocks I couldn't seem to remember how to change gears. My hands felt stiff and awkward on the steering wheel. I could hear my own voice talking to my father, but it didn't feel like my voice. It was like listening to someone else. Somewhere deep in my being I could feel my heart and spirit filling with a reservoir of tears, but I couldn't cry. Even my tears seemed far away, beyond my reach. In the coming year that well of sorrow would become deeper and deeper until I was drowning in it, but the tears would never come. Somehow, they were a luxury I couldn't afford. My family needed me. There was no safe place for me to grieve for Nicole, to grieve for her children, to grieve for myself.

It was like being in a nightmare. Everything was distorted, grotesque, surreal. It wasn't until we got back to Rockingham that I began to come back to myself. Walking into the house again with a bag full of milk and diapers, and my family waiting for us, brought me back to a sense of reality. It was like waking up again. I shoved the images of the Bundy condo firmly out of sight and stepped back into the moment. Dad and I didn't say a word about where we'd been. Not even to each other.

That night when bedtime approached, for the first time in my life, I reached for a bottle of wine to help me go to sleep. I needed it, to shut out the images, to bottle up the tears.

The next day was the wake. By that time the rumors about Uncle O.J.'s involvement were swirling around us like the helicopters hovering overhead. We had become prisoners in a home that wasn't even our own, trapped behind the tightly closed drapes of the mansion or the darkened windows of the limos. We were like fugitives, eyed curiously by the press and suspiciously by the Browns. The enormity of the situation was slowly, relentlessly, dawning on us. We'd done nothing wrong, yet in the eyes of the world, we were undergoing a gradual metamorphosis into criminals, accomplices after the fact. We closed ranks against those ever-watching eyes. In the chaos swirling around us, we clung tighter than ever to each other.

We returned to Rockingham after the wake and once more turned on the TVs. Again all the stations announced that Uncle O.J. had taken refuge at the house after the wake. He hadn't. We didn't know where he was. We'd met him at the wake, of course, but afterward he'd slipped out again without telling us where he was going—or where he'd been—and we did not feel free to ask him. Besides, he'd been in such bad shape at the wake that it had shocked me. I had never seen him like that. He looked like a broken man.

As the evening drew to a close, I went back to my house to get a few things to wear. My neighbor was home, and we sat across the street and talked together for hours, until it was time for me to go back to Rockingham and my family. I remember thinking how odd it was that he and everyone else in the world seemed to know what was going on in my life. It was Wednesday night. That Monday morning no one in America but our friends and coworkers had even known who we were. Two days later everyone in the world was watching us go through the greatest tragedy of our family's lives. And it was only the beginning.

The funeral was the next day. I wondered if it was going to be open-casket again. Surely not. The children would be there this time. My heart ached for them. Once again we struggled with the logistics of the sleeping arrangements. As more news had leaked out about police statements that the murderer might have gone to Rockingham that night, my sisters became more and more frightened about sleeping in the guest rooms outside the house. When it came time to go to bed the third night, Toni and Tracy said, "I'm not sleeping out in that guest room again tonight. I don't feel safe out there. What if whoever killed Nicole comes back?"

For some reason, I never had that fear that the murderer

would come to Rockingham. Besides, even if he did, he'd have had to fight his way past a hundred reporters and trucks full of floodlights to get in. Kato offered me his bed, and I accepted it gratefully. After two nights on the couch and all the stress, I ached from head to toe. Kato didn't want to be alone any more than my sisters did, though, so he asked if he could sleep on the floor in his room. I told him it was fine with me (I didn't mention it to my father).

Kato had sort of latched on to me by then as a familiar face; I think he sensed the family's suspicion of him. As far as I was concerned, he was just a harmless guy. My previous suspicions of him had faded with the light of day. That night we were awake for hours talking, not about the case, but about life and relationships. He talked a lot about his little daughter, who was Sydney's age, and his relationship with her mother, his ex-wife. He still seemed sad and very, very nervous; he paced a lot, and it was a long time before he could relax enough to fall asleep. We finally drifted off in the wee hours of the morning. Four hours later it was time to get up for the funeral.

The funeral was held at St. Martin de Tours Catholic Church on Sunset, not far from the house, at eleven that Thursday morning. Directly across the street from the preschool Nicole enrolled Justin and Sydney in, St. Martin's is not too large, and relatively plain by Catholic standards. There was no ornate architecture, just a simple modern building that blended pleasantly with the surrounding homes. As we came down the aisle to take our seats, I noticed that the coffin wasn't there. But there were lots of flowers, and more photos of Nicole, just like at the wake. And what huge photos they were, poster-size, blown up as big as possible and arranged all around the altar area. I remember thinking, *How in the world did they get those posters made so fast?* The picture of Nicole and the kids in a shiny white Ferrari stood out from all the rest. It seemed an odd comment on her life—a sports car, fast, slick, beautiful, expensive. I sat and stared at the photos as we waited for the ceremony to begin. Just as I had a month before at Starbucks, I thought how little I knew about Nicole's life, especially the last few years. I recognized so few of the images before me.

I didn't recognize many of the people there, either. I'd expected the church to be mobbed, but it wasn't. There were about a hundred people there, no more. I sat in the third row with my sisters and some friends; in front of me sat my parents, Aunt Como and Uncle Charles, and Nicole's sisters; and in the first row, right in front of the altar, sat Lou and Juditha Brown. Many of Uncle O.J. and Nicole's old friends were there, too, Bob Kardashian and his fiancée Denice, Bobby Bender and his wife—familiar faces. I wondered where Marcus Allen was. I didn't see him. I didn't recognize anybody else. I searched the crowd for other familiar faces, but there weren't any. We were so estranged from their lives, I thought once again. I didn't even know these people. And they didn't know us. People glanced at us without recognition. I remember thinking, *They must wonder who all these black people are, and why we're all sitting in the front rows.* We were nearly the only African-Americans there.

Sydney and Justin had been waiting for Uncle O.J. at the entrance to the church when we'd arrived. They wanted to walk down the aisle with him. As I saw Uncle O.J. and the children sit down in the front row next to the Browns, I wondered if the children even understood what was going on.

They'd been sleeping upstairs when their mother was killed; the police had found them sound asleep in their beds, wrapped them up in blankets, and carried them out the back way in the middle of the night so they wouldn't see what had happened. They'd taken them back to the police station and called Arnelle to come for them as soon as they discovered who the children were. The little ones had been both sleepy and confused, and the police didn't want to tell the kids what had happened until they'd contacted Uncle O.J. and he could come for them. A female police officer had said Sidney had called her mother all night afterward, saying "Mommy, Mommy, where are you? Pick up the phone. How come we're here?" Tears filled my eyes as I looked at them both, solemnly perched next to their father in the front row. I knew they'd been told their mother was in heaven with God, but I didn't know what that meant to them. I wondered if they'd overheard anything else. It was heartbreaking.

The service started, and the pallbearers carried the coffin in. Ron Shipp was one of the pallbearers. I remembered him doing crowd control at the wake the evening before. He looked so sad. Nicole's parents seemed overcome with grief. Sydney looked sad, solemn, as the coffin went by, but I don't think Justin really understood. He was squirming, restless. He seemed confused. I felt sad, sad and guilty because I couldn't grieve for Nicole. I knew that if one of my sisters, or my brother's wife, were lying in that coffin, I would have felt terrible grief. For Nicole I felt sadness, great sadness, but no grief.

The service was unremarkable. Denise Brown spoke, and Cora Fischman. Juditha Brown was supposed to speak, but she was too overcome to do so. Everyone talked about what a good mother, sister, and daughter Nicole was. Then they played music, and the service was over. Everyone filed by the coffin which, thankfully, was closed. Most people placed a flower on Nicole's casket and then stopped to kiss her family. It seemed to take a long, long time. Each of us gave Uncle O.J. a hug and kiss. I remember putting my arms around him and saying, "You have to stay strong. You have to get through this and be there for the kids. It'll be all right. We love you." He thanked me. I'm not sure he even registered what I'd said. When it was finally over, we went back into the bright noon sun to face the battery of cameras once again as we filed to the limos for the ride to the cemetery.

The ride to Orange County seemed even longer than it had the evening before on the way to the wake. We were all exhausted. Jason, Arnelle, Tracy, Toni, and I all rode together in one limo. We didn't say much. The noise of the media helicopters overhead drowned out everything, making it difficult to talk, even to think. When we finally pulled into the cemetery and wound our way back to the burial site, we could see a large crowd waiting, many more people than had attended the funeral service in Brentwood. I guess a lot of people thought it was too far to make the drive to both services, especially with all the media and traffic.

Once again, Ron Shipp was handling the security. Nicole was to be buried in her mother's plot, chosen years before. It was a long walk from the limo to the burial plot, and it seemed even longer as we were tracked by telephoto lenses. Again I was astonished by the media's behavior. No press were allowed on the property for the burial service, so they'd bought their way into the houses with backyards along the fence closest to Nicole's grave. Some of them were climbing over the fence; others were hiding in the bushes in the neighbors' lawns.

When we got close, we could see Uncle O.J. sitting by Nicole's casket, just staring blankly off into space. Someone had brought the posters from the church and set them up around the casket again. It seemed so bizarre, so Hollywood—like publicity photos. I didn't think that was the intention, but to me the giant posters seemed out of place, somehow inappropriate. Nearly everyone was standing, for there were very few chairs available. Most of the faces in the crowd were new to me. There was an Asian girl with Denise. I later found out that her name was Eve Chin. She was Nicole's best friend from high school. The one face that stood out to me was Faye Resnick's. She was wearing a big hat, looking very Hollywood, with costume jewelry on both arms and hands. And I looked at her, and thought, who the hell is she? I thought she must have been close to Nicole, because she seemed to be in a great deal of emotional pain. There was a very brief ceremony, Lou Brown said good-bye to Nicole, and once again people began coming forward to put flowers on the casket. Sydney and Justin put flowers on their mother's casket. Almost everyone was crying.

Afterward, while the adults talked and tried to comfort each other, the children ran around on the soft spring grass and played. Uncle O.J. was sitting with my parents by the casket, talking to Lou, so my sisters and I kept an eye on the kids. As I watched Sydney and Justin laughing and playing chase, it hit me all over again that they were just children. They still didn't seem to understand what had happened. They were playing like two kids in the park on a Sunday afternoon.

After it was all over, we piled back into the limos all over again and joined the caravan to the Browns' house. Uncle O.J. and A.C. were in the front limo with Sydney and Justin, and the rest of us split into the other two cars. The kids were hungry and wanted to get something to eat on the way to their grandparents' house. None of the rest of us had been hungry all day, but we decided to pick up something for the kids' sake. The only place we passed was Jack in the Box, and the kids wanted hamburgers and french fries, so we decided to go through the drive-through. What an absurd picture we made: three limos pulling up at the drive-through window at Jack in the Box with the media trailing behind. The kids gave their order, someone else decided to order something, too, and once a burger was passed through the window, we all realized how hungry we really were. The next thing we knew everybody was saying, "Get me a burger. I'd like some fries," and so fourth. It was the first normal moment we'd had all day. We pulled back out on the highway in our limos, munching burgers and fries the rest of the way.

They admitted us into the gated community where the Browns live. Once at the Browns' house, we repeated our procession out of the limos and into the house. I'd spent most of the last twenty-four hours in a limo—my first taste of the "celebrity lifestyle." Lucky me.

As we walked into the Browns' living room and I looked around, I was very surprised to see how comparatively humble their home was, a simple A-frame house with three bedrooms. I'd always seen them in glamorous settings: at Rockingham, or in photos taken at Aspen, Hawaii, or some celebrity function. It surprised me that their home was so middle-class and ordinary. Except for the fact that it was in a gated community, it looked like every other Orange County house built in the late seventies. I wondered how so many of them lived in such a small space (both Denise and Minnie with their children had moved back in sometime before). The inevitable posters of Nicole were there, transported from the cemetery. It made their small house look like a shrine.

After the years of estrangement from Nicole, I felt almost guilty about being there, as if I had invaded their private space. Being there was like reading someone's private letters without permission. I felt torn between my desire to support my uncle and show the Browns respect as part of our family, and a desperate desire to get out of there and give them back their privacy. Nobody said a word about the circumstances around Nicole's death. Uncle O.J. went in another room with Lou and Juditha, and the rest of us sat around awkwardly, wishing to pay our respects but not having the faintest idea what to do. Every now and then someone got up and got a drink or a snack from the food piled in the kitchen or offered to help the Browns carry plates in and out. Earlier that day Sydney and Justin had met my sister's children, their second cousins, for the first time. Later, in the backyard, I could hear them jumping up and down on the trampoline, with Denise and Minnie's children, with whom they were very familiar. We were all very uncomfortable being in that small space together. What must the Browns be thinking? There was nothing overt; everyone was polite, pleasantly cordial, but there was little eye contact and little attempt at conversation.

There was already tension between our family and the Browns. Denise had spoken out publicly that week, accusing Uncle O.J. of abusing Nicole, voicing her belief that he was the murderer. I could see the grief and pain in her face, but I couldn't understand how she could think Uncle O.J. had done such a horrible thing. Then my mind drifted back to the day two months before when I'd talked to my father about Uncle O.J.'s relationship with Nicole. They were trying one more time to work out a reconciliation, but both of them were ambivalent about it. This time they were arguing about Kato and whether he should live at Bundy or Rockingham. Uncle O.J. didn't think Kato should be living under the same roof with Nicole and the kids, but he didn't especially want him at Rockingham, either, and as usual tensions were running high between them. For the umpteenth time I thought how strange and entangling their divorce had been; they still couldn't live either with or without each other.

It had been such a poignant statement at the time, but sitting there the day of the funeral, my father's words had a different, chilling meaning. Had they been a premonition? But no—it was unthinkable. People hurt each other all the time, but not like this. The murder scene at Bundy forced itself briefly into my consciousness. I looked at my uncle's sad face, listened to the voices of his children outside. No. It was impossible.

After an hour or so it was time to start leaving. The helicopters were hovering close overhead, so A.C. decided to provide a diversion—an end run, if you will. He and Uncle O.J. traded suits, and then A.C. partially covered his face and ran to the limo Uncle O.J. had taken earlier. The press bought it. As the limo zoomed away, the helicopters followed in hot pursuit. Meanwhile, once again Uncle O.J. went quietly around the side and got into a car with Bob Kardashian, who drove him away undisturbed. Mom and Dad left to take Grandma home. It was past six by then, and Grandma was exhausted. The rest of us "kids" piled in another limo and headed back separately. Thankfully, nobody was interested enough in us to follow us with cameras. We got back to Rockingham a little after eight and turned on the TVs. We wanted to know where Uncle O.J. had gone. Miserable as the press made us, they were still our primary source of information. We watched the coverage on different stations until they finally went off the air about 1:00 A.M. Afterward I went back out to Kato's room alone. Kato hadn't come back with us after the funeral, so I had the room all to myself. Too tired to think about anything, I fell into a deep sleep. If I dreamed that night, I don't remember it.

CHAPTER 6

THE KILLING FIELDS

A few months ago some friends and I rented a movie called *The Killing Fields*. It's a brilliant, gut-wrenching film about the war in Cambodia in the seventies. There's a moment in the film when a huge army evacuation helicopter hovers just above ground as people stream toward it in a desperate attempt to climb on. Some hold their children up, begging those on board to pull their little ones to safety. The noise of the engine and the whirling blades is deafening as dust and wind swirl around the desperate faces underneath.

As I watched those electronic images of human suffering with my friends, I felt suddenly overwhelmed with pain, the pain of recognition. I started to cry. *That's it,* I thought. *That's the feeling. That's what I felt that day three years ago when we all huddled together at Rockingham watching our family plunging toward destruction.*

The day started out calmly enough. With the wake and the funeral behind us, we hoped the worst was over for a day or two. We sensed something was imminent legally, but we hoped that since it was Friday, nothing would happen over the weekend at least. We desperately needed a respite from the continual chaos and the media onslaught. There were so many things to do, simple things. Buy milk for the kids. Wash clothes. Take a nap. Deal with work. And most of all, figure out what to do next.

Grandma wanted to go home. She announced that fact in no uncertain terms that morning. She said she was having heart palpitations, and she wanted to go see her doctor in San Francisco. I wasn't really surprised that she wanted to go. The week had been grueling for her, certainly, but it wasn't just the physical strain that was bothering her. In our family, Grandma has always been the center of attention. No matter what the situation, her comfort has always come first. She was used to having my mother's full attention. Mom cooked for her, waited on her, and, most important, doted on her. My mother had always been Grandma's girl. Nobody, not even my father, ever came between them. Grandma was used to being the center of every family circle.

But this week, Grandma hadn't been the center of attention: Uncle O.J. had. Mom had slept in the room with him that first night instead of spending time with Grandma. Everyone talked about Uncle O.J. all day long—worried about him, sympathized with him, hung on every word the media said about him. We had all been glued to the televisions at Rockingham, and when we'd left for the wake and the funeral, my mother had attached herself to Uncle O.J. most of the time, not to Grandma. I figured Grandma felt neglected, left out. This had never happened to her before.

It was an interesting family dynamic. Both Grandma and Uncle O.J. took being the center of attention in the family circle for granted. Yet we'd spent so little time with Uncle O.J. over the years that there had never been a conflict of interests. On the rare occasions my family came down to Los Angeles to visit him, Grandma was usually at home in San Francisco. On the even rarer occasions that Uncle O.J. visited the family in San Francisco, it was usually for one of Grandma's special occasions and they could share being the center of attention for the hour or two he was there. When Grandma came down to visit in L.A., she came alone, and Nicole had catered to her. But now, with the family all together for four days in a row (the first time that had ever happened), it was impossible to give both Grandma and Uncle O.J. the exclusive attention they were accustomed to. I'm sure Uncle O.J. didn't notice, but Grandma did. She wanted to go home to her own doctor for a little comfort and reassurance, and she knew my mother would go with her. It was a test of allegiance, and we all knew it: Mom had to choose between them. She chose Grandma. I knew she would.

I was angry. We all knew an arrest was imminent, and that we should be there to support him until the worst was over. I couldn't understand how Grandma could leave, knowing her son was about to be arrested for murder. She had a comfortable room, plenty of people taking care of her, and Uncle O.J.'s family doctor more than willing to come over and make sure she was all right. When it became clear that there was no way to keep Grandma in L.A., I tried to talk my mother out of going with her. We could take Grandma to the airport, put her on the plane ourselves, and have another family member waiting in San Francisco to take her off the plane. My sister Gyne would be glad to meet her there. They could go straight to Grandma's doctor, and then Gyne and an array of family and friends would take care of her around the clock. I thought my mother should stay in Los Angeles, with the rest of us. If they did arrest Uncle O.J., we would all need her help. Mom was the family organizer, our tower of strength. We were accustomed to her functioning as the family representative.

It was no use. My mother would not be talked out of it. She and Grandma took the next plane to San Francisco, where Grandma insisted on checking directly into the hospital. Once there she was examined and pronounced to be suffering from "nervous exhaustion." With all the publicity the murder case was attracting, Grandma was immediately surrounded by sympathetic and nurturing nurses and staff members, and as usual, my sisters and mother did round-the-clock hospital shifts so my grandmother wouldn't have to be alone. Grandma was in her element. Her heart palpitations disappeared.

Meanwhile, I was struggling with my own scheduling conflicts. My best friend Jerri Churchill (Jerri Lucas at the time) was getting married the next day, and the wedding was in Virginia. The rehearsal dinner was that night, the ceremony was the next afternoon. I was in the wedding party. I badly wanted to be there. Jerri had already told me not to worry about coming under the circumstances, but she was my oldest friend and I really wanted to be there. My flight to Virginia was scheduled out of LAX at a little after 10:00 A.M., so I had to make a decision in a hurry. I talked it over with my dad, who urged me to go ahead with my plans. I could come back the next day, right after the wedding. Dad knew how important Jerri's wedding was to me.

Relieved but still a little torn, I packed quickly, and my dad took us all to the airport. When I got there, I picked up my boarding pass and hurried down to the departure gate. After all that rushing, I was a few minutes early. But the plane was delayed for an hour, so I decided to go into the little cafeteria by the departure gate and get something to eat while I waited. I hadn't had time for breakfast. There was a TV on in the corner of the cafeteria, and I'd no sooner sat down than the news report came on the screen: "O.J. Simpson has fled arrest. He is now officially a fugitive." I was stunned.

I rushed to the nearest phone and called my dad at Rockingham. I knew my grandmother's flight had already taken off, and I was hoping Dad had time to get home. I was panic-stricken. Dad had just gotten back to Rockingham, but he turned right around and came back to get me. I jumped in the car and we drove back to the estate as fast as we could get there. The media, which had started to thin out there over the last twenty-four hours, was back in full force. We shoved the car through them and rushed into the house. Our family was gathered together in the family room, with all three televisions going on different channels. Everyone was standing, rigid with anxiety, drawing closer and closer to the TV sets as if we could force the broadcasters to tell us something.

Then Bob Kardashian came out in front of the cameras at his house and read aloud what he described as Uncle O.J.'s suicide note. My heart stopped. I was sick with fear and anger. How could this be happening? As Bob Kardashian's voice went on and on, reading my uncle's words, I heard name after name mentioned. Uncle O.J. was thanking all the people who had loved and supported him through the hard times: Bob Kardashian, his and Nicole's friends, Paula Barbieri, even his golfing buddies. But nowhere in that damned letter, not even once, did I hear him mention anyone in his own family. I listened in vain for my mother's name, *his* mother's name. I began to tremble with rage. How dare he? How dare he take his own life just five days after his children had lost their mother? Over and over again I kept thinking, *How can you do this? How can you leave your own children alone at a time like this? They need you. How can you be so selfish?* He was about to kill his children's only other parent, and he was thanking Paula Barbieri, the woman whose main attraction was that she provided him with "incredible sex."

Everyone was panicking, desperate. Jason and Arnelle got on the phones and started calling around, trying to find out where he'd gone. We just needed to talk to him to see if it could possibly be true. We felt so helpless. Then a news report said that he'd called the Browns at the Bundy condo, where they'd gone to pack up Nicole's things, and that he was on the way there to kill himself in the same place Nicole had died. My anger was swallowed up in fear. *Oh God, no,* I thought over and over.

Ron Fischman was at Rockingham with us, and Ron immediately ran outside to his car. He was going to drive to Bundy to try and see Uncle O.J. I ran out right behind and jumped in the car with him. I couldn't just sit there and let this happen. I had to see him, to stop him, to beg him not to do it. All of the years of estrangement dissolved for me in that moment. O.J. Simpson was no longer the distant celebrity relative; he was my *uncle*, and I didn't want to lose him. All I wanted to do was to get to him and say, "We love you, we love you, we love you. Please, don't do this. It's not the way."

Ron roared past the media and over toward Bundy at top speed. We pulled into the alley to avoid the media, jumped out of the car, and went running around the side to the front entrance, which the police had put under heavy guard. The police tape was still up, but Nicole's cousin Rolph had just washed down the sidewalk to remove the blood. The grass and cement were still wet. We told the officers who we were, and after sending someone inside for permission from the Browns, they let us through.

We entered through the front door and into the living room. It was eerie. I'd never been inside before. Everything about the place reminded me of Nicole—cream carpets and overstuffed cream furniture, big fluffy pillows, candles and bunches of fresh flowers she must have arranged in the vases a few days before, family photos everywhere. The place even smelled like Nicole's favorite perfume, Caylix. It was overwhelming.

Lou and Juditha, Denise and Minnie and Tanya were already packing up Nicole's things. Apparently the officer had just sent in Ron's name, because the minute they saw me, Minnie got really angry and upset. She pointed right at me: "What is *she* doing here?"

They called the police officers back inside and took them into the kitchen. A moment later Denise and Minnie came back out with the officers and stood there next to them. One officer approached me, and said, "The family is uncomfortable with your presence. They don't want you here. You're going to have to leave immediately." I looked at Minnie's and Denise's faces. They were masks of hatred and contempt. Suddenly I flashed back to the day they had ransacked my apartment with Nicole, the day Nicole had called me a filthy little thief. I had seen the same expressions on their faces that day. Over ten years had gone by, but they hadn't forgotten. They still saw me through Nicole's eyes. I was humiliated to my soul. One of the officers escorted me out through the garage and into the alley, where I waited alone. After a while Ron came out, and we drove back to Rockingham. If Uncle O.J. had been coming to Bundy, we thought, he would have been there by then.

Everyone was on the lookout for Uncle O.J. at that

moment, so the minute we approached the gate at Rockingham the press descended on us to demand if we knew anything. People began shoving microphones at me from all directions. We had already been told not to comment to the press, so we said nothing and went back in the house. Once inside, I discovered that my family had watched me live on television as I stood shaking trying to get into Nicole's condo just a short time before.

Less than five minutes after Ron and I got back, the announcement broke that the Bronco had been spotted on the freeway. And the long chase ordeal began. People were screaming and cheering all along the freeway, hanging on the walls of the overpasses. It was pandemonium. After all the shocks of the week, I thought nothing could surprise me, but this was the most bizarre thing I'd seen yet. Why were they all cheering? This wasn't a football game; this was his life.

We knew that A.C. was with him, but with Uncle O.J. in the back with a gun, there was little that A.C. could do except talk to him. We kept saying to ourselves over and over, "Please don't let him kill himself. Please God, don't let him kill himself." We were terrified we were going to watch him blow his brains out on national TV. Then they began to announce that he was trying to talk to Grandma, and we all panicked even more. He thought Grandma was back at Rockingham. He'd been out of touch with us all since Monday night, except for brief moments at the wake and funeral. He had no idea Grandma was in San Francisco. The irony of it seemed cruel at that moment. His habitual indifference to our comings and goings could cost him his life.

We immediately started trying to get in touch with Grandma at home, but she had gone straight to the hospital from the airport. By the time we tracked her down through the doctor, the press was already reporting that she'd been hospitalized with heart problems. My brother Benny and his wife had gone to the hospital to stay with Grandma while my mother ran home to pick up some things Grandma needed. It wasn't until my mom got home and turned the TV on that she had any idea what had happened. She panicked. Meanwhile, Benny had found out what happened and rushed to Grandma's house to be with Mom. My sister Gyne had heard on the news that Uncle O.J. was trying to get in touch with Grandma, so she rushed in a minute after Benny did, looking for Grandma. It was absolute chaos. Benny told me later that during the confusion someone in the family had said, "Oh my God. He must have caught them in bed."

My mother started dialing over and over, trying to get through to the cell phone in the Bronco. She even called the police trying to get them to break in and tell Uncle O.J. that his mother was in San Francisco, to try to get the call put through to the hospital there. My sister said that Mom got more and more frantic with every minute that passed. She was pleading with anyone who would listen to please put her through to her brother. His secretary and old friend, Kathy Randa, had the cell phone number but couldn't get through on the line. All the while back at Rockingham, I kept thinking, "Oh God, why did Grandma leave? Why did she leave? He's going to come here and she'll be gone, and then he will kill himself." It was an escalating nightmare.

A few minutes later A.C. turned onto 405 and it became clear that they really were heading toward Rockingham. We desperately wanted him to come home, yet we were afraid of what would happen when he got there. If he had a gun, the police might kill him before we could even get to him. This was right after the Rodney King beatings and the movie *Panther,* and our minds were filled with images of unprovoked police assaults. We were paranoid. I remember thinking, *What if LAPD shoots him down right in front of us before he can surrender?*

We were watching the television screens as the Bronco neared the Sunset exit off the 405 freeway when all of a sudden all hell broke loose. The door burst open and at least twenty members of the SWAT team rushed into the house and surrounded us, shouting, "Get out of here! *Now!*" They were all wearing bulletproof vests, and they had fanned out through the house almost before we knew they were there. We were frightened and bewildered. I remember saying, "Why do we have to leave? This is our home, our family. He's not going to shoot us." But they paid no attention; apparently, they thought he might shoot anybody in his frame of mind. And once bullets started flying, no one would be safe. Our worst nightmare was coming true. They told us to leave by the front gate immediately. My sister Toni ran up to a detective we later found out was Tom Lange and pleaded with him not to allow anyone to shoot Uncle O.J.

The last thing I remember before we walked out the front door is looking back at the family room, piled with our jackets and purses, and thinking, *Uncle O.J. is going to kill us when he gets here and sees what a mess we've left.* And with that absurdly irrelevant thought, I walked outside. The whole thing couldn't have taken more than one minute, but we'd lost all track of time.

It was even more terrifying outside. The grounds were filled with SWAT team members; I remember looking at Sydney's dollhouse and seeing an officer hiding inside, gun at the ready. Helicopters converged overhead with a deafening roar, scattering dust and litter in every direction. We were in a war zone.

Sobbing and clinging to each other for support, we made our way to the front gate and out onto the sidewalk. It was sheer mayhem. People had descended on us from everywhere, hundreds of them, many of them running. The media were screaming into their microphones over the din. People all around us were cheering hysterically, chanting, "Go, Juice," like they thought he was running for a touchdown and the gates of Rockingham were the goalposts. We couldn't see the Bronco yet, but we could tell by the noise of the crowd that it was coming. They were giving a running commentary, like at a sports event. The police were trying to hold back the crowd, shoving them back to the end of the block to clear a path for the Bronco.

We huddled on the corner of Bristol and Ashford, a few feet from the crowd, on the edge of the lawn by the tennis court. All around us there was turmoil, an ocean of people surging and screaming. There in that little circle we clung to each other, joining hands, crying and praying together. Something about joining our hands in prayer at that moment changed everything for me. I'd never felt very close to Arnelle; she always seemed distant like her father, not close like family. But in that moment of desperate communion, I was overwhelmed with love for those standing around me and for the man in the back of the Bronco spinning invisibly toward us. Uncle O.J. was my flesh and blood, connected to me by body and spirit. I loved him. Losing him would tear a hole in the fabric of my family that could never be repaired.

Suddenly the crowd began to fall back, scattering as the outline of a large white vehicle roared into our line of vision. It was so odd; on television for the last two hours, it had been a small white dot on a gray background moving at what seemed to be a slow, smooth pace—what the police call a low-speed pursuit. But the reality of the Bronco's size and speed were frightening. A.C. swung around the corner toward the gate a few yards away at a dangerous speed to pedestrians. The police were pushing people back, desperately trying to clear the way for A.C. But we held our ground. We kept saying, "No, no, we're not going. We're not in the way. We're staying here." As soon as the Bronco had swung into sight, Arnelle had started jumping up and down, waving and screaming at her father: "We're *here*. Over here, Dad!" The police grabbed us and pulled us back out of the Bronco's path, but Jason was too quick for them. Before they realized what he was doing, he had dashed toward the Bronco's back bumper and followed it through the gates as they swung shut behind him. With the gates shut we knew it was no use trying to get in, and we backed out of the way.

Steve, Uncle O.J.'s neighbor and Jason's childhood friend, had joined us, and he shouted, "We'll go to my house!" There would be a television there to show us what was happening behind the closed gates. It was less than a block to Steve's house, but with the crowd now surging back toward the gates, it was almost impossible to move. We split into smaller groups; Arnelle, my father, and I locked our arms tightly together and forced our way against the tide of onlookers until we reached Steve's front porch. He was waiting for us there to let us in. Aunt Marguerite, Uncle O.J.'s first wife, and her husband Anthony—they'd been with us at Rockingham before the SWAT team had arrived—were already there, and we rushed to the television to watch what was going on just fifty yards away. The camera showed Jason behind the van, looking uncertain about what to do next. He seemed lost as he moved around the side of the Bronco and called out, "Dad? Dad?" The police were afraid to come out in the open and grab Jason for fear Uncle O.J. would shoot, but after a moment's hesitation we saw the SWAT team grab Jason and throw him in the house out of range.

Then A.C. got out of the car, very slowly, with his hands in the air and I thought, *No!* I didn't understand why he was leaving, why he had his hands up. Somebody had to stay with Uncle O.J. or they'd kill him. It didn't make sense, but in my mind Uncle O.J. would somehow be safer in that car if A.C. stayed with him. For some reason I didn't think they'd shoot A.C. Someone shouted, "No, get back in the car! Don't leave him alone!"

An officer came out to get A.C., and I thought, *Oh God, I wonder if Uncle O.J.'s seen the guys in the bushes and the sharpshooters in the trees. They're going to shoot him now that A.C.'s out of the way; I know they will.* One way or another, whether they shot him or he shot himself, at that moment we were certain he was going to die. He seemed absolutely desperate at that moment, and I thought, I know what it feels like to be desperate. I've felt that, too. We were all focused on him so intensely that it seemed as if we could feel what he was feeling at that moment, feel his pain. We were holding our breaths and clinging to each other. And then finally he put the gun down and climbed out, and nobody shot him; they just stepped carefully forward and put handcuffs around his wrists. Relief flowed over that room like a cool wind; we started crying, saying, "Thank you, God, thank you, thank you." When other people look at the tape of that moment they always say, "How terrible for you. They're taking him to jail." But we were sobbing with joy and crying out, "He's going to jail! He's going to jail! Isn't that wonderful? He's going to jail! He's going to be safe!" And I remember thinking at that moment, *Even if he has to spend the rest of his life in jail, he's alive. He's safe. We haven't lost him.*

The police took him in the house for a little while. We tried to go back to Rockingham and see him, but they wouldn't let us in, so we went back to Steve's house and the television set. While he was inside, Mom finally got through to the police officers and hooked him up with Grandma at the hospital. Apparently they also gave him some juice and let him rest for a while. Then they took him back outside, and we watched as they put him in the police car and drove away. The helicopters overhead followed in a convoy behind him. No one was paying attention to us anymore. We made our way back to the house once again. Then, at last, they let us go back to Rockingham.

Inside, we turned the televisions back on and then just sat there, trying to absorb what had just happened. It didn't seem real. We watched reruns of the Bronco chase, and we watched ourselves huddle outside the estate. We watched the SWAT team enter the house we were now sitting in. We watched as they took Uncle O.J. out of the police van downtown and went inside to book him. They ran the television footage over and over, and we just sat there watching it, hypnotized with shock and exhaustion. We were beyond functioning. We couldn't process what had just happened to us all. It was too much. Everything, the whole week, it was too much.

Later that evening my friend Jerri called from Virginia. She'd watched the chase with the rest of America and called to see if I was all right. She told me that she and her fiancé, Frank, were flying back to California right after their wedding the next day to be with me and try to help, even if that just meant being there for moral support. I was deeply touched.

A little later my brother Benny called from San Franciso to tell me my mother was all right. He and my sister Gyne had been there with her through the whole thing. He said she'd been incredibly focused through the whole ordeal, but that the minute Uncle O.J. stepped out of the Bronco and it was clear he was going to be all right, she'd dropped the phone and collapsed full length on the floor sobbing. He'd never seen my mother cry like that. It was shocking, painful to watch. She was all right now, though; they all were. Gyne had gone to the hospital to spend the night with Grandma, and my mother's cousin Gwen was coming to spend the night with her. "Get some sleep," Benny told me. "Get some sleep."

I went back out to the guest room and crawled into bed like a wounded animal. Sleep. I wanted to sleep forever and not have to wake up. As I lay there in the darkness, it flitted through my mind that I had poured my soul out for Uncle O.J. but that I still couldn't grieve for Nicole. I felt the familiar twinge of guilt, but I was too exhausted to worry about it. Sleep. We all just needed to sleep. Maybe when we woke up, things would be better.

CHAPTER 7

THE GLASS TOWER

There's nothing like the light of day and two crying babies to bring you back to reality. My sisters' babies, Joshua and Madison, had been sleeping in a strange place and eating off schedule for five days by the time we woke up at Rockingham that Saturday. They needed to go home to San Francisco, where they could have a normal schedule and some peace and quiet. Dad wanted to go home, too, to make sure Grandma was all right and to help my mother. Next week was Father's Day, and we'd all planned to be together in San Francisco. I needed to get back to my place and regroup. So the next day Dad and my sisters packed up the babies and headed north. I climbed into my little Volkswagen and made the short trip home.

I looked forward to the respite. Uncle O.J. was under suicide watch in the jail infirmary for a few days and couldn't have visitors, so we didn't have to worry about organizing visits yet. We'd been told that he was heavily medicated and was being cared for around the clock by psychiatrists and by his regular doctor, Dr. Maltz. It was a period of emotional breakdown for him, and the best thing was to let him go through it, to let his feelings out. We knew that he had a strong support system and that he would be safe. After the trauma of the day before, we were relieved to know that he was being taken care of. And I was relieved to be going home.

I live in a three-unit building that was built on a hillside in the twenties as a bed and breakfast. Even though my part of the canyon is very close to Los Angeles, it has a secluded, intimate feeling to it, and a sense of community. The manager lived upstairs from me, and a very close friend lived just above me. My neighbors across the street were also good friends. We used to get together and barbecue every week. I didn't feel alone even though I lived alone.

I also went home to another long series of phone messages, more than fifty in all. People I hadn't heard from in years had called. All the messages were loving and supportive, expressing concern for me and my family. That Sunday I went to First AME Church, where my sister Cynthia is a minister.

In the middle of the week my parents drove back down, and we started trying to sort out the situation. We really wanted to see Uncle O.J. by then. We knew he was very uncomfortable, in a tiny cell with a sink, a urinal, and a bed with no pillow (they don't allow one under suicide watch). We'd heard it was pretty bad. Just thinking about him trapped in that tiny space with very little to distract him really bothered me. He was able to make phone calls, and he spent a lot of time on the phone those first few days, to his friends and to Paula Barbieri. I don't know whether or not he talked to my parents. But talking on the phone isn't the same as having someone in the same room with you.

Ordinarily you can only visit on weekends, but his attorneys had already come up with a way around this. They'd devised a plan by which anyone on the list of potential witnesses could see him during the day as long as an attorney was present; The judge approved it. They'd retained Nicole Pulvers, a young legal assistant who'd just graduated from law school, to be with him all day, so that he could see visitors but still keep his attorneys free to work on the case. Her being an attorney was a technicality, of course, as Nicole's only job was to sit with Uncle O.J.

Our first chance to visit him came in the middle of the week. I went with my parents. It was a remarkable experience. To begin with, the press were there seven days a week, camped out all day in beach chairs, trying to talk to anyone who came to see him. Unlike Rockingham, where we'd usually been in a car when we passed them, we now had to walk right through the middle of them to get to the jail entrance. They could get right up in our faces with their cameras and microphones. That took considerable getting used to.

Once we ran the gauntlet of the press, we began the check-in routine, which quickly became a ritual. First we had to turn over our drivers' licenses, fill out a visitation card, and walk through a metal detector. There was a guard station up above with two or three deputies behind bulletproof glass, and they would have to push a button to open the door—a thick, heavy, door painted an ugly green. Once we walked through, we had to wait for that door to close behind us before proceeding through the next locked door. The sound of that heavy door closing behind us with a thud gave me the shivers. Once it shut the deputies would press another button to open the second door. When you go through that door, you're actually in the jail. Something about hearing the hollow, heavy metal latch slide and lock behind us brought home to me that this was a real *jail*. It's one thing to see one on TV but something else entirely to be in it. I'd been in a minimum-security jail once during college to interview inmates for a class project, but nothing like this. Standing trapped inside that door was poignant, painful.

We were taken to the area where inmates see attorneys for our visit. Only four people could be in the cubicle with him at a time (an attorney and three visitors), so we had to wait. Some of Uncle O.J.'s buddies had gone in to see him. In those early weeks we all thought he'd be out on bail, so everyone was trying to cheer up Uncle O.J., telling him he'd be home in no time. None of us had any idea at that point what an endless process it would turn out to be, how familiar that visitors' cubicle would become. My mother was on pins and needles waiting to get in. It was traumatic for her to be visiting her brother in such a place, and she didn't know what shape he was in. All the reports we'd had were secondhand.

Nicole Pulvers came out to greet us. I'd never met her before. She was young and pretty. It gave me a start that her name was Nicole. I'd wondered if Uncle O.J. would fall in love with her. That happens to people in traumatic situations, and I knew they'd be spending a lot of time together. *But no,* I thought. *She's not Uncle O.J.'s type. Not glamorous enough.*

We also met his psychiatrist and his doctor. They said that he was still heavily medicated, but that he was stabilizing and they were optimistic. He was also going through the process of adjusting to his surroundings, a difficult adjustment under any circumstances, much less after losing his wife. In some respects it was like going to the hospital to see someone who's really ill. We were whispering, "How's he doing?" and conferring in hushed tones in the corridor outside. I could see my mother struggling to be cordial and patient, but it was clear she was fighting to keep her emotions in check.

When our turn finally came, I waited outside so my parents could go in first. I knew my parents wanted some time alone with him so that he could express whatever he was feeling in ways he wouldn't do with me there. I was still a kid to Uncle O.J., and he always tried to maintain some sense of dignity around us "kids." As it turned out, I wasn't able to see him that first day. By the time my parents finished their visit, it was time for him to meet with his attorneys again.

When we were ready to leave, the marshal at the front desk said, "By the way, he's got an awful lot of mail here. What should we do with it?" Inmates are allowed up to twenty-five pieces of mail at a time, so usually the mail is just passed on through to them, but they had more mail than they could handle with Uncle O.J. inside. Having no idea what we were getting into, we said, "Oh, okay, we'll just take it with us." We were picturing a bag or two that we could easily carry to the car. Instead they brought out three big satchels. It was only the beginning. Within a week or two he was getting hundreds of thousands of pieces of mail each week, and it became part of our routine to lug it out to the car, past the horde of reporters, every time we visited.

That Friday I finally got to see him. On weekends we could only see him if he was in the infirmary, but during the week we visited him in the attorney-consulting rooms. My parents were already inside when I was told I could go in. There was a row of six glass cubicles on the left side set aside for consultations; Uncle O.J. was always in the last cubicle on the left, right in front of the guard's desk. There was a glass wall about six or seven feet high separating the visitors from the inmates. You could look down the row and see other inmates talking to their attorneys. Since all the walls were glass, there was really no such thing as privacy. That first time, Uncle O.J. wasn't there when I first walked in and squeezed myself into a chair with my parents. He'd gone to the rest room and would be back in a moment.

I wasn't prepared for his return. I knew he was an inmate, of course, but nothing had prepared me for the shock and horror of seeing him in that place. Here was my glamorous uncle, the sports hero, whom I'd always seen well dressed and impeccably groomed. Now he came toward me dressed in jailhouse greens, wearing tennis shoes with no shoelaces, his feet bound together in chains so he could only take small, shuffling steps. His hands were cuffed in front of him and then chained to his waist, and two deputies walked behind him. My eyes flooded with tears. As he sat down awkwardly, with all the heavy metal hanging on him, I tried not to look at him. I didn't want him to see the horror in my face. My first impulse was to stand up and try to reach over the partition to hug him, but the deputies immediately said, "You can't touch the inmate." I sat back down, overcome with emotion.

He had been on top of the world, socially and financially, and now here he was, reduced to the position of a common criminal, the lowest position on earth. I couldn't take it in. I don't remember much of what we talked about that day. I do remember talking about the children. He was distraught about the children and kept asking how Sydney and Justin and Jason and Arnelle were. We tried to reassure him, to think of something comforting to say when there really were no words for the enormity of the situation. The hardest part was pushing back the tears. But even though we couldn't touch him, even though we hadn't been as close as we'd wanted for many years, at least we were there. We comforted ourselves with the hope that we were some support for him. When it came time to say good-bye, we didn't want to leave him, but it was time for him to talk to his attorneys. As we turned to go, I glanced back. He was already engrossed in discussion of legal matters with Bob Kardashian. *Good,* I thought. *It will keep his mind off other things.*

That was the first of many visits for me. I had no idea that day just how many there would be. When he was incarcerated in June, he was hopeful that he'd be home in time to go trick-or-treating with Sydney and Justin that fall. But Halloween would come and go, followed by Thanksgiving, Christmas, and another Father's Day before he would come home again. And as the days turned into months and we waited for the trial to begin, the visitation routine would become commonplace to me, and the glass-and-metal maze that felt so foreign that first day would become as familiar as the hallways at work. Somehow, when you're black, a lot of people assume you're familiar with the penal system, that it's just part of your life. But it was as foreign to me and my family as to any white family on the hill in Westborough, in suburban San Franciso where I grew up. I never quite got over the feeling that I was walking into TV-Land, the modern equivalent of Alice through the looking glass. There was a part of me that never got used to it, a little voice in my head that continued to whisper disbelief that any of us were there.

After that first day a routine developed. Kathy Randa, Uncle O.J.'s faithful secretary and friend, put together a schedule of visitors so Uncle O.J. would never have to be alone during the day. Kathy became information central the whole time he was in jail. She kept track of Uncle O.J.'s appointments and commitments while he was on the inside just as she had when he was on the outside. When he gave up his office lease a short while later, Kathy just moved quarters to Nicole's old office at Rockingham and continued from there. From the beginning we kept in touch with her about when we should go to see him.

I usually went in the early evening, after work, with my parents. I never felt comfortable going alone; it was hard for me to know quite what to say. I'd like to say it got easier after the first time, but it didn't. I dreaded going down the shark-infested media path, through the clanging metal doors, and through the glass cubicles like a rat in a maze. I dreaded the struggle to find something cheerful and comforting to say to a man I'd never been comfortable talking to, in a place that made any words of encouragement sound empty. But I went, because not going was even worse. I couldn't stand to think of him alone there, and if I could give him even a crumb of comfort, like the widow's mite in the Bible, I wanted to give it. I wanted him to know I loved him, for whatever it was worth.

The hardest part was not being able to touch him, especially when we left. Hugging and kissing are as natural as breathing in my family, but we could only look at him through the protective glass barrier. The best we could do was to hold our hands up against the glass. Each time when we left, we'd put our hands up against the glass between us, and he'd put his hands against ours on the other side. We'd swallow our tears, and then we'd go. That was the closest I'd felt to him—even when I could touch him.

It didn't matter anymore that Uncle O.J. and I had never been close. That was history. Old resentments evaporated in the face of the terrifying new reality. He was family, and

That's me with Uncle O.J. and Nicole at his Fourth of July party in 1983.

Nicole in 1983, when she still had long hair.

Dad, me, Uncle O.J., Jerri, and Toni at the Fourth of July party, 1983.

Uncle O.J. at our house in Westborough in the 1970s.

Uncle O.J. and Arnelle at their first home in Los Angeles in the early '70s.

Uncle O.J. and Aunt Marguerite attending church shortly after their wedding.

Grandpa Jimmy.

Arnelle, Grandpa, and Jason when Uncle O.J. was playing for Buffalo.

That's me on the right, with my sisters Tracy and Khadi, at one of my high school track meets.

My mom, Grandpa, and me at my South City High School graduation in 1981.

That's Grandpa with me just before my senior prom.

All dressed up for graduation exercises at San Francisco State in 1987.

Hanging out in the guest room at Rockingham where Kato would later live, 1983.

Feeding Uncle O.J.'s dog, Chubbs, in the foyer at Rockingham in 1983.

Posing with Minnie before a Halloween party in 1983.

Dad, Michelle, and me hanging out in the TV room at Rockingham in early 1994.

Ron Fishman and me outside Nicole's condo the day of the Bronco chase.
(Reuters/Sam Mircovich/Archive Photos, Inc.)

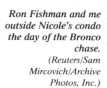

Kato and me leaving Rockingham for Nicole's wake.
(Andrew Taylor/IPOL International Press Online Inc.)

During the trial, Uncle O.J.'s fans left goodwill posters and letters of support at the front gate at Rockingham.

My mom and me at Johnnie's Christmas party.

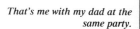
That's me with my dad at the same party.

Grandma Simpson in 1993.

At Johnnie's homecoming party for Uncle O.J. Uncle O.J. did not attend.
Back row (left to right): Benny, Panzy, Cindy, Gyne, Tracy
Front row (left to right): Toni, me, Johnnie and Dale
(African American Press Photo © 1996)

Aunt Como, Jason, me, my mom, and Arnelle at a birthday party for
Jason.

Toni, Tracy, and me with A.C. at a surprise birthday party for Arnelle in 1994.

Aunt Como, my dad, Grandma Simpson, Arnelle, my mom, and Jason in front of the Criminal Courts Building. Mom is responding to comments made by Fred Goldman.

(African American Press Photo © 1996)

My family and the entire defense team, minus Bob Shapiro, the night after Johnnie finished his closing arguments.
(African American Press Photo © 1996)

Mom, Dad, and me with one of the jurors from the criminal trial at Johnnie's Christmas party for the jury.

Toni, me, Tracy, Cindy, and Gyne standing in the kitchen at Rockingham the night before the verdict. We were all pretty worn out.

Uncle O.J. the day he came home after his acquittal with me, Toni, Tracy, and my nephew Josh.

My mom, Johnnie, Uncle O.J., Denise Halicky, and me listening to a gospel performance by Tim Story.

Uncle O.J. and me after hearing Tim Story sing a moving song.

My friend Jerri and I at high tea at the Beverly Wilshire Hotel about a month before the trial ended. I was drinking heavily then.

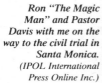

Ron "The Magic Man" and Pastor Davis with me on the way to the civil trial in Santa Monica. (IPOL International Press Online Inc.)

Grandma Simpson and Uncle O.J. at Rockingham in 1997. Uncle O.J. was taking Grandma to the hospital for knee surgery.

Taking a lunch break with Grandma Simpson on the first day of the civil trial. It was Grandma's 75th birthday.

Leaving the court after the verdict in the civil trial. We were determined to keep our heads high, the press was determined to tell a different story.
(John McCoy, LA Daily News)

he needed us. We would be there. That was all there was to it.

A few days later it became apparent just how much he was going to need us all. A grand jury had been convened and then disbanded because of media leaks and charges of bribery; then there was a hearing. I had never paid much attention to the actual workings of the criminal-court system, so like the rest of America, I was just learning how it worked as we went along, often from TV. Eventually they charged him with two counts of first-degree murder with special circumstances. We were shocked. In spite of the media leaks, I was unprepared for reality. *This is serious,* I thought. *They must have an awful lot of evidence.* It was troubling—confusing.

Then on Wednesday, June 22, one of Nicole's 911 calls was released to the media. I wasn't shocked that Nicole had called 911; I wasn't even shocked by what she said. I knew Nicole had called the police before; she was always calling the police, but I had never understood why. It had seemed to me at the time that she was just being melodramatic; after all, I had never seen any evidence that Uncle O.J. had ever hurt her. On the contrary, I had seen her lose her temper and fly in his face (and other people's faces) more than once. Uncle O.J.'s explanation of years ago that he'd "just tried to calm her down" had always seemed perfectly plausible to me.

But listening to that tape for the first time shook me up. I had never heard my uncle so much as raise his voice to anybody; if anything, I thought he backed down too often with Nicole. The voice on the tape, though, was not the voice of the man I knew. Oh, I recognized it, all right; I never thought the tape was a fake. But the rage, the yelling, the cusswords thundering in the background— this wasn't the uncle I was used to seeing. It frightened me; *he* frightened me. I kept thinking that if someone were yelling at me like that, I'd be terrified. A vision flashed into my head of a man on a football field, a man big and heavy-handed enough to inflict real damage on the other players. A man that seemed to be out of control. I shivered.

The family, though, had a different perspective, one I gladly embraced. From their point of view, the situation wasn't what it appeared to be. First of all, if she was so scared of him, they reasoned, why was she staying there in the house with him? Why did she just go upstairs and pick up a phone instead of going out the front and getting away? Secondly, why was everybody making such a big issue out of this when he didn't even hit her? All he did was yell at her. Finally, and most important, they reasoned, this was when Nicole was threatening to leave him. What better way to get a good settlement than to set him up in the eyes of the law as a wife-beater? It was no secret that Nicole liked the celebrity lifestyle she enjoyed as his wife. She was setting a record, we reasoned, a record that would look good for her in a divorce court.

When we talked to Uncle O.J. about the tape, he echoed all our theories and added a few details of his own. He hadn't broken down the door that night, he told us. The lock on the back door was already broken, and the door was ajar when he got there. He'd just walked in. I stilled the little voice in my mind and accepted his explanation. I was anxious to believe him. Not believing him would have been too disturbing.

This was the beginning of an ongoing process that took over our lives and eventually became a matter of public record—the process of explaining, rationalizing, and defending every aspect of Uncle O.J.'s behavior. As I was gradually to learn, there would never come a time when he would accept responsibility for even the smallest mistake on his part. Many men would have listened to that tape of themselves, and said, "Oh, man, I shouldn't have done that. I really almost lost it that time." Instead he rejected responsibility automatically, without pausing long enough to reflect, to consider—to feel the pain. That's what it was really about, I think, feeling the pain. Thinking through his past behavior and accepting responsibility for where he'd done wrong would have been too painful for him. He'd never had to do it, and he wasn't going to start now. He had to defend his fragile self-image at all costs, even from himself. Especially from himself. And, for better or worse, we helped him do it.

It would be fair to say that we became almost as quick to defend him during that period as he was to defend himself against the constant media leaks about "evidence"—evidence we had yet to see, always from "unnamed sources." Nothing is less convincing than an unnamed source when the information they're reporting contradicts everything you already believe. The media leaks were so constant, in fact, that I actually brought a car radio with a TV scanner on it so that I wouldn't miss anything while I was driving to and from work. I also began scanning the tabloids, not to mention the more legitimate papers, looking for every detail of the investigation as it unfolded, right down to the tiniest rumor. I made a point to read every little piece of information that was published about Uncle O.J. so I would have something to say to him during my visits.

In those early weeks of his incarceration I also began meeting the whole "cast of characters" that would become the Dream Team—not only the attorneys, but the people behind the scenes as well. I already knew Bob Kardashian as a friend of Uncle O.J.'s. The first of the new attorneys I met was Robert Shapiro. He was there the first day we went to visit Uncle O.J. in jail. He came into the glass cubicle as we were getting ready to leave, and Uncle O.J. introduced us all. I stood up to shake his hand, and he took my hand, and said, "Hi, Terri," looking directly into my eyes with such warmth, such a sense of connection, that I was immediately taken with him. He was so welcoming; he made me feel I was important, that we were part of the same team. I remember thinking, *What a star, this attorney! He's so warm, so personable, so magnetic!* I was impressed. Initially, I was less impressed with the man who became Bob Shapiro's adversary, F. Lee Bailey. He came into the waiting area one weekend with my parents while I was sitting there, waiting to see Uncle O.J. He came through the door with an air about him that said, "I'm very important." The media followed him in and waited to follow him out again when he came back later. My parents introduced me to him, and he shook my hand. He was nice, and very formal. I remember thinking, *Oh, F. Lee Bailey, he's the famous one.* But when I stood up to shake his hand, I realized that at 5'4'', I was eye to eye with him. And when I sat back down, I noticed he was wearing high-heeled boots—not regular bootheels, *high* heels. I'd never seen a man in high heels before. They were like the kind Prince wears in the videos to make himself look taller. Something about the contrast between his height and the size of his self-importance struck me funny. As he strutted toward the elevator in those heels, I thought with considerable amusement, *Another illusion shattered. Why does everyone look so much more impressive on TV?*

Then, of course, there was Johnnie Cochran. Johnnie didn't disappoint me. Meeting Johnnie was like meeting someone from home because he was black, like us. I felt comfortable with him. He quickly began to seem like family; my mother, Aunt Como, and Johnnie's wife Dale struck up a friendship almost immediately.

But of all the people I encountered behind bars during those endless visits, the capper had to be Paula Barbieri. I'd met her once before, about six months before Nicole died. My parents had come down one weekend to visit. My sister Cynthia was being ordained at First AME Church in L.A. that Sunday, so I went with Mom and Dad to visit Uncle O.J. that Saturday, the day before. We had just walked into the living room and said hello to Uncle O.J. before going into the kitchen with him. Paula was sitting there reading at the kitchen table. Uncle O.J. introduced my parents to Paula but didn't introduce me (he rarely introduces us "kids"). Paula was friendly to my parents, but not at all friendly to me.

Later, after I walked into the other room, Paula asked Michelle on the side who I was. Michelle told me later that Paula was angry and suspicious at seeing an anonymous young woman on intimate terms with Uncle O.J. As soon as Michelle told her I was O.J.'s niece, Paula apparently said, "Oh, thank God." Suddenly she got very friendly with me, exuding Southern charm and asking me about myself. I thought the whole incident was pretty funny when Michelle told me about it because I'd always felt so unglamorous around Uncle O.J.'s gorgeous female friends. Evidently Paula was insecure about Uncle O.J. and other women. The two things that Uncle O.J. always said about Paula was that she had a horrible temper and that she was insatiable sexually. Two things she had in common with Nicole.

We didn't see Paula during our early visits to the jail, but we heard about her. Uncle O.J. talked to her every day. To us she was kind of the invisible girlfriend, but eventually she did materialize. And what a picture she was.

On one hand, she was the epitome of the good little girl, the traditional woman who only wants a husband and children. She nearly always had her Bible with her when she visited Uncle O.J. She would read it aloud to him in jail; she even sat and read it in the waiting room while other people were visiting him.

One day many months later, she said to me, "All I want to do when this is over is get married and have kids and only have to worry about dropping them off and picking them up from school every day."

I said, "How are you going live?"

Paula drawled, "Oh, O.J. and I will get married and move to Florida. Of course, we'll have to get rid of our matching white Broncos, because it would draw too much attention in a little Southern town."

I thought, *Who is this little twit, and where did Uncle O.J. find her? His wife had been murdered, and he's interested in her?*

"Twit" is actually one of the kinder words that went through my mind when I watched Paula in action. When she wasn't spouting scripture, she was talking about sex. She was obsessed with it. She'd talk to anyone who would listen about how much she missed sex with Uncle O.J. At times like that she acted like a naughty teenager.

The first time she started going on about it to my parents, I couldn't believe it. They were so embarrassed they couldn't say a word. She seemed to have had no sense of how inappropriate her conversation was. Not only that, but I heard her joke with Uncle O.J. about giving him "sneak peeks" during her visits. I remembered seeing Nicole play the same sort of sex games—usually while they'd walked the dog together. She'd wear a skimpy little tennis skirt with a very slight G-string underneath and occasionally "flash" Uncle O.J. from behind. Paula's version was somewhat more discreet, involving her very short miniskirts.

There were other visitors. Rosie Greer was there from the beginning, offering counsel and support. A.C. didn't come for the first couple of weeks, which I thought was odd, but my dad pointed out that A.C. was still working on his own legal problems with the Bronco chase and probably didn't want to add fuel to the fire. Also, A.C. was still in contact with the Browns, still visiting with the kids there. I hadn't really realized it until Nicole died, but A.C. was very close to Nicole, and he grieved for her. He and Uncle O.J. had been like brothers since they were kids and he took Nicole's death hard. You could tell he felt split down the middle between his loyalty to Uncle O.J. and his feelings for Nicole's family. It was really hard for him. So he visited at the jail a few times, but not that often. I don't remember hearing about Marcus Allen's visiting him, which brothered me. I thought about that later when he avoided testifying. We all knew he'd had an affair with Nicole after the divorce, so we thought he might feel a little awkward even though he was married by then. I also wondered where Ahmad Rashad was. All those golfing buddies mentioned in the suicide note. Where were they? Not at County Jail, that's for sure, at least not that I knew of.

As far as family was concerned, Grandma came once or twice in the beginning, but it was hard on her, and she stayed at home in San Francisco most of the time with the rest of the family. Mom kind of took it on herself as the oldest sister—and the family matriarch after Grandma—to watch out for her little brother. Uncle Truman never did make it to lock-up, but he did make it to a tabloid TV show. Sydney and Justin were too little to come, and Uncle O.J. didn't want them to see him there, anyway. He thought it would be traumatic for them. I agreed. The one part I didn't understand, though, was Jason and Arnelle. Where were they?

When Uncle O.J. was first incarcerated, Jason and Arnelle visited once, maybe twice. And that was it. Arnelle went shopping with me to Logos, the Christian bookstore in Westwood, to buy inspirational items for Uncle O.J.'s cell. I remember we bought him a plaque that told the story "Footprints in the Sand," about how God carries us through the hardest times of our lives. But apart from sending in the occasional message or gift, Arnelle and Jason had almost no firsthand contact with their dad. My visits were sometimes attributed to Arnelle publicly because the press continued to confuse us, but Arnelle's own visits were extremely rare. Most people's perception was that they couldn't cope with the media frenzy and with seeing their dad in jail. To me, though, it was incomprehensible. How could they stand not seeing him? *If it were my dad in jail,* I thought, *I'd be camped out all the time.* One day I asked my father, "Why don't they visit him? If it were you, I'd be there every day!"

He just said, "Everybody copes in their own way. Besides, he's busy with his attorneys. It probably doesn't bother him that they're not coming."

Doesn't bother him? I thought. *How can it not bother him? How can we all be part of the same family and think so differently?* Once again, it hit home with me how differently we'd been raised. Their father/child relationship was light-years away from my father's relationship with me and my siblings. Even my adopted sister would have been there to see Dad if he'd been in that position. Stranger yet was my parents' reaction to Jason and Arnelle's absence. If any one of us had acted that way in a similar position, my parents would have been horrified. They would have felt we had let the family down. I knew they hoped I would be there several times a week since I lived in West Los Angeles. It's not that I minded; I wanted to help. *Besides,* I thought guiltily, *how could I worry about family politics at a time like this?* It made me feel petty. The important thing was for us all to stick together until this nightmare was over. We would just have to take it one day at a time.

CHAPTER 8

OUR DAILY BREAD

Uncle O.J.'s world wasn't the only one that collapsed the day Nicole died. In a sense, the world collapsed for all of us. Nobody teaches you how to cope with the kind of family emergency we faced. Victims' groups offer some sort of support, psychological and financial, for families who are hurt by violent crime. But nobody wants to support the family of the accused. In a strange form of guilt by association, the families of the accused are despised by many as thoroughly as the one on trial, even before there's been a conviction. During all those years we'd been left out of Uncle O.J.'s life, we'd never shared the celebrity spotlight, the glamorous lifestyle he'd led with Nicole, her family and his dozens of friends. But now, in a bitter twist of fate, we would share the public stigma and financial calamity that were about to overtake him. And we had to find a way to cope with it all. Coping presented an ongoing series of practical and logistical problems that often seemed overwhelming. There was nothing to do but pray for help and take it one day at a time.

The first problem for me was my job. That first week following Nicole's death I took personal/sick days off from work to be with my family and attend the wake and funeral. The second week I took vacation time. Fortunately, I had a lot of unused vacation time saved up. My parents also took time off from work during those first weeks, but naturally, that couldn't go on forever. The third week after Nicole's death I went back to work, and the routine of working and visiting started. I would go to work in the morning, work all day, and try to get to the jail after work to visit two or three times a week. We could visit until 8:00 P.M. I'd also try to visit once on the weekends. With my parents back in San Francisco much of the time, taking care of Grandma and trying to hold on to their jobs, they couldn't visit Uncle O.J. as often as they wanted to, so I took on that responsibility to make sure he had regular family contact. I would keep my parents informed about how he was doing when they couldn't be there. It was exhausting for me, but a great comfort to my mother, so I was happy to do it.

The next problem, and bigger practical difficulty even than work, was coping with the mail. Uncle O.J. received a truly phenomenal amount of mail daily, and it was our responsibility as his friends and family to pick it up and process it. The jail wasn't set up to deal with a mail problem of that magnitude, and legally they couldn't just throw it out. So their problem became our problem. Whoever came to visit on a given day would pick up as many bags or boxes as she could carry, lug it out to the car, and either take it home or over to Uncle O.J.'s for sorting. I'd take the letters home, open as many as I could, sort them, rubber band them, and then take them over to Rockingham for storage.

The best ones I'd keep out, to take to Uncle O.J. and read to him during our visits.

It quickly became clear that virtually all of the letters fell into one of four categories. We learned to sort them accordingly. The first pile was the really good ones, the special ones. These letters were usually passionate about his being innocent. Some of them were very touching, especially the ones from children. The second pile was the pleasant, relatively neutral letters from people who just wanted to offer their support. This was the biggest group. These people rarely commented on his guilt or innocence; they would say things like, "I'm praying for you and your family no matter what happened." The third pile was smaller, the ones from people who thought he was guilty. I nicknamed this group the Bible Belter pile. Some urged him to repent, saying things like, "If people like you repent of your sins, God will forgive you." Others strongly implied that they thought he was guilty, followed by statements like, "But we love you anyway." We never showed him those. The last pile would be the letters with donations. It was especially important to keep track of those so we could send an acknowledgment.

My aunt Laura, in San Francisco, and Kathy Randa took on the task of chronicling all the donations. They listed them all on a computer so we'd have a permanent record and could send a thank-you to everyone. Kathy and my mother worked hard to come up with a nice thank-you letter to send all those people. They wanted to make sure that no one was forgotten. Many of the donations were very small, often just a dollar bill in an envelope. Little children sent their allowances. It was incredibly touching. I knew that for many of these people, that dollar bill was a genuine sacrifice. Kathy Randa would take all the donations, large and small, and deposit them into Uncle O.J.'s account.

I had mixed feelings about that. Part of me was happy; everybody kept telling me that he really needed money. It was clearly important that Kathy get the ones with money and make the deposits as soon as possible. I thought, *He must really need the money. Everybody says it's important.*

On the other hand, it bothered me to accept money from people who were so needy themselves, people who would never live the lifestyle he had for even one day. The money was a real sacrifice for them, yet I knew it wouldn't make a dent in the expenses he was facing. It would be miraculous if all of it together paid a single one of his bills. It made me sad. I thought, *He can't need the money that much.* I didn't know in the beginning how high his legal fees were; Bob Shapiro alone was being paid $100,000 a month from the beginning, and the process dragged on for such a long time. Still, I didn't feel comfortable accepting some of the money.

Eventually the volume of mail simply became overwhelming. I would open letters for hours at night, until I fell asleep on the couch surrounded by them. My tiny apartment gradually filled with boxes and bags of mail, stacks of them, until I could hardly walk around. I couldn't keep up with it. Every time I finished a batch I'd take it to Rockingham, and soon the garage was filling up there, too We didn't throw a single letter away. We piled them all into large, long boxes, and stacked them in the garage. By the time the criminal trial was over, there were at least fifty of these big boxes stacked up at Rockingham. They're still there, piled with all the scrapbooks and other material chronicling the trial. Just reading them all was a monumental task. Answering most of them was out of the question.

As weeks wore on and turned into months and the trial

still hadn't started, those piles of letters began to take on a symbolic meaning for me. I was, quite simply, over-whelmed. The adrenaline and emotional energy that had carried me through the early weeks inevitably wore off as the "temporary emergency" became a way of life. My life became an endless cycle of work, mail, and visits to County Jail, constantly punctuated by calls to my family in San Francisco with the daily O.J. report. Like the obsessed media, my own life had been taken over by my famous uncle's. It was gradually turning into a scheduling night-mare.

As Uncle O.J. recovered from the first shock of Nicole's murder and his arrest, he slowly began to slip back into his old habits. Even in jail he was back on top of everyone again, maybe more so than ever because how could you resent someone who's incarcerated? I remember thinking, *He's back up on the throne again. He's in control behind bars.* He had an entourage at his beck and call seven days a week—not only his attorneys but his business associates, his secretary, a virtual production company of his own. He'd already made the deal to write his book and raise a little cash behind bars, and he was strategizing to come up with new financial ventures. Kathy was soon keeping an appointment book for his activities in jail. We had to call her for an appointment if we wanted to see him. She'd say, "Such and such a time is open. Maybe we could squeeze you in then."

If my parents weren't coming with me, it was hard to get in at all because there was always someone more important he needed to see. It was bizarre. It went from needing to be on the witness list to get in to see him, to needing to be on the A-list if you wanted to see him. There was all kinds of maneuvering within the family to make "the list" and then stay on it once people started getting dropped. My sisters badly wanted to come down and see him, but they never got a chance because they never made the list. Their feelings were hurt. Just as before he was incarcerated, it became intensely important to each family member to get in to see him, not only because they were concerned, but because being on the list spelled acceptance. It meant you were important to the most important member of the family. It was the Fourth of July barbeque all over again. Even when you made the cut, so to speak, you nearly always had to wait a long time to get in, and you usually had to leave early because some VIP (as I thought of them) would show up. After a while I was surprised that I was even on the list anymore.

Nicole, the resident attorney, wasn't blind to all of this. Her attitude toward us went through a progressive but clear change as time when on. In the beginning, she was very friendly and congenial. She would ask how we were all doing, and she and I would talk about getting together and going rollerblading. Her assumption seemed to be that because we were his family, we must be important in the scheme of things. But as time went on and she saw how he prioritized his visitors, the friendliness wore off. She seemingly placed me well down the scale. I came to believe that she had picked up on Uncle O.J.'s value system and categorized us accordingly.

It came to a head for me one day when I ended up visiting Uncle O.J. alone with Nicole. It was the first time I'd been in the cubicle without other people, and I was overwhelmed with anxiety at the thought of visiting him alone. What on earth would we talk about? I ended up talking about a problem I was having at work, and Uncle O.J. told me I should get a lawyer to write a letter for me. That small amount of interest on his part warmed me, and I found myself suddenly opening up to him about the struggles I was going through in my own life. I started sharing my worries with him like I might with other family members. After a few minutes of this, I remember turning to Nicole, and saying, "Do you think maybe you could help me write a letter that would be okay?" She said she could look into it for me, and then I looked at Uncle O.J. for his tacit approval. His face had gone completely blank. His mind had wandered, and I realized he hadn't heard a word I'd said.

A second later, without even realizing what he was doing, he said something completely unrelated, something about an article about himself he'd seen in the newspaper. If it had been anybody else in the family, I would have said, "Hey, I was talking about something important!" But I couldn't say that to him; instead I was concerned I'd bothered him, as if I'd done something wrong. Nicole turned her attention to Uncle O.J.'s remark as if I hadn't said anything, and I felt even more mortified at his obvious indifference to me in front of this girl. And as usual, the embarrassment was accompanied by the familiar pang of guilt: why was I bothering him with my stupid little problems when he was in jail, on trial for his life? No wonder he wasn't interested

The obvious question at this point is, Why did I keep seeing him if he didn't care about seeing me? My friends asked me that question with increasing frequency. There's no simple answer. One reason was the family loyalty that had been pounded into me from birth. I had inherited an extra measure of it because I was the first Simpson grandchild of the oldest daughter. Just as my mother, Shirley, was the keeper of the family among her younger siblings. Another reason, paradoxically enough, was because I wasn't as close to Uncle O.J. as I was to the rest of my family, and I wanted to be. I thought this might be my only chance to really get to know him. *After all,* I thought *he's a captive audience for the time being. He has to talk to me.*

Most important, though, I visited him because it meant so much to my partents. It hurt them deeply that they couldn't be with him as often as they wanted, and it was a source of tremendous comfort to know I was there. Each time they left for San Francisco, my mother would remind me to go see your uncle while they were gone, to make sure he was all right. They worried that if I didn't go, my name might be dropped from the list and there'd be no one to go while they were out of town. I would call them in San Franciso on the weekends to let them know I'd seen him, and that he was all right. It meant so much to them; I couldn't let them down. And truthfully, I think it was healing for me, too; after all those years of being the one who'd let them down, who'd shamed them with Uncle O.J., I was now the good daughter, living up to my responsibilities. I needed them to be proud of me.

As time wore on, our persistent loyalty did seem to bring rewards. Uncle O.J. had always spent a lot of time on the phone, even before he was incarcerated, and as the weeks and months passed he began calling my parents more and more frequently. For the first time in our lives, he called us on every holiday.

The first—and one of the hardest—was Father's Day. He'd only been incarcerated for nine days at the time. My sisters wanted my father to come home to San Francisco to celebrate with them, but I decided to stay behind so Uncle O.J. wouldn't have to be alone. I was still powerfully moved by my first visit with him the day before, and the thought of his being alone on Father's Day was too painful for me. He'd received a lot of wonderful Father's Day cards from people he didn't know, so I took some of them over on Saturday afternoon to visit with him in the infirmary.

Then I found out that I wouldn't be able to see him the next day anyway because he'd be meeting with attorneys all day, so I decided to catch a late flight to San Francisco to celebrate with my father.

That Sunday morning we went to an early service at church and then came home for a special Father's Day meal. We were all sitting around the table when the phone rang. It was Uncle O.J. We couldn't call him, so everyone was glad that he called us. We all tooks turns talking to him, passing the phone from person to person, saying, "We love you. This will all be over soon." He was strong with my sisters and brother and me, but then my parents went into the back room and talked to him privately. When Dad came back out, he looked depressed, and said, "He's having a hard time. A real hard time." Apparently he'd pretty much fallen apart talking to my parents. It was sad. He'd talked to Justin and Sydney on the phone that day, and to Jason and Arnelle. I don't know if they went to see him. It was the first time we had ever spoken to him on Father's Day.

Thanksgiving was equally tough. I think Jason and Arnelle went to see him that day. The rest of us were in San Francisco. It was a tug-of-war for my mother because she was torn between being with Grandma in San Francisco for the traditional Thanksgiving dinner and being in L.A. for Uncle O.J. The whole situation was complicated by the fact that even if she stayed in L.A., there was no guarantee she'd get in to see him because of his scheduling conflicts.

As we stood around the table in Grandma's dining room on Thanksgiving day and said grace, we prayed for him. Grandma asked God to send him strength and to give us all the strength to continue being there for him. It was a difficult day. We felt almost guilty. How could we enjoy our delicious dinner and the people we loved with him locked away? Christmas was another struggle. We were even more depressed at the prospect of his spending Christmas behind bars. At first I told Mom, "I won't come home for Christmas. I'll stay here. I can't stand the thought of Uncle O.J. spending Christmas alone." Those sentiments were quickly followed by another reality check, though. His schedule was already overbooked. I felt a little rebuffed, but relieved as well. The period between Thanksgiving and Christmas is the busiest time of the year in retail, and I'd been working six days a week all month.

By the beginning of the trial in January, I was already wearing down. Things had gotten increasingly difficult at work. Two months before the murder I'd gotten a rave review for my job performance; the average increase at that time was 4.2 percent, and I got a 10 percent increase. Everyone seemed enthusiastic about my job performance. Over the months following the murder, however, I started getting written up as being "not really there." I was there literally by then; after the first two weeks of vacation time, I returned to my regular schedule until the trial began. But I wasn't there psychologically. I tried to be, but I was in over my head by then. My boss told me that if I couldn't give 110 percent to my job, I shouldn't be working there. I thought he was right. I was already starting to break down under the long strain, although I didn't know it yet. I finally decided it would be better to leave voluntarily than to be fired. I talked to a doctor, who examined me and said I was suffering from post-traumatic stress and recommended a disability leave for a couple of months. The company agreed, and I gratefully accepted it.

The endless pretrial grind had become overwhelming. I was still buried in mail, and I was frustrated and angry about the thankless task of opening and sorting thousands of letters every week. Uncle O.J. had begun losing interest in them; he was too tied up with legal issues to have time or energy for anything else. When his book, *I Want To Tell You,* was published that December, I had no desire to read it. *More letters,* I thought, knowing that many of them had been published in his book. *Just what I need.*

Besides, I saw the book as just another money-making scheme to raise funds for his defense. At that point I gave up on the letters. I hauled home boxes when I had to, but I no longer read them. I'd begun to resent reading letters for a man in jail who had trouble squeezing me into his schedule. I was beginning to lose all sense of myself. People in and out of the family had begun saying, "Terri, you have your own life. Don't worry about this stuff so much." But it was easier said than done.

As the only family member on the witness list who lived in driving distance of the jail, my family continued to depend on me to give them reports. When they flew down to L.A. themselves, they needed me to be their driver. They didn't have a car down here, and they couldn't afford a cab, so that meant I became their driver. They needed me to pick them up and drop them off at the airport, give them rides to wherever they needed to go. It never seemed to stop.

The visits to the jail got harder and harder. Not only were they difficult to schedule, but they were taking a toll on my self-esteem. Each visit was another reminder of my own unimportance in my uncle's eyes. It was depressing, almost degrading. He paid lip service to my visits, thanking me for coming, but he was so clearly uninterested in me as a person. It became harder and harder to go.

By that time jury selection had begun, and since I was the only family member available to do it, I attended when I could. Whenever I had a day off or could rearrange my schedule I would go because the attorneys were telling us any kind of visible family support would look good for his case. Just my being there would send a message to prospective jurors, they believed. My parents were always very happy when I called to say I'd attended a session. They'd always say, "Really? That's great. Did you see your uncle? How did he look?" They were hungry for any first-hand information they could get.

One day especially I'll never forget. It was near the end of jury selection, right around New Year's, and Rosie Greer had come that day, too. During the break, Uncle O.J.'s attorneys invited me and Rosie to have lunch with them. We went back into their conference room, next to Judge Ito's chambers, and sat down around a big table. They were having a strategy meeting to get themselves pumped up and ready to go now that the trial was actually beginning. They went around the table, and each person introduced himself and told me what aspect of the trial he or she was working on. The whole team was there, not just the lead attorneys. When they finished, I stood up and thanked them on behalf of my whole family for believing in my uncle and being there to support him. After all I'd been through those last months, it felt wonderful to stand there as a representative of my family and show them that it wasn't just Uncle O.J. they were helping; it was all of us. I felt honored, and I felt humbled, too. I felt so vulnerable at that moment. *Our lives are in these people's hands,* I thought. It was up to them now.

Then Rosie Greer had us all stand up and hold hands around the table, and Rosie prayed. It was deeply comforting. For the first time in a long while, all the struggle and humiliation seemed worthwhile. Everything might still be all right. We might still come out of this whole. Maybe even better than ever. I was anxious for the trial to start.

But before that all-important opening day, we had some problems to solve.

My parents never considered moving down to Rockingham full-time for the trial. My mother was responsible for taking care of Grandma, and Grandma wasn't planning to be in court until she testified for Uncle O.J. Simply getting my parents to court in Los Angeles every week was a gigantic problem. It had been hard enough managing the jail visits. Commuting to L.A. by car twice a week was out of the question, and airfare was expensive. Fortunately, Southwest Airlines had their "Friends Fly Free" promotion at the time, so my parents bought advance tickets to take advantage of the savings.

The attorneys suggested a minimum of three family members in court every day, and we knew it was unrealistic to count on Jason and Arnelle to be there so often. So my parents and Aunt Como worked out a schedule. Aunt Como would commute down and be in court on Tuesday, Wednesday, Thursday, and Friday. On Friday night she would fly home, work on Saturday, Sunday, and Monday, and return to L.A. on Monday night. My parents would come down for court on Monday, Tuesday, Wednesday, and Thursday. They'd fly home on Thursday night and come back on Sunday night. I'd be there every day if possible, definitely on Mondays and Fridays, when either Aunt Como or my parents would be in San Francisco. That way the family bench in court would always be filled. It would also be my responsibility to make the runs to the airport to pick up and deliver my folks. *Why,* I wondered, *wasn't Uncle O.J. offering to help with airfare?* He expected the family to be there for him, but he wasn't offering to help pay any of their expenses. My parents just said he had money problems of his own, so it was up to us to manage however we could.

The one thing he did help with was allowing the family to stay at Rockingham. They couldn't begin to afford a hotel. Yet as luxurious as Rockingham seemed to outsiders, it wasn't very comfortable for my parents. Uncle O.J.'s large bedroom and bath were kept locked at all times. Only Paula Barbieri was ever allowed to sleep there. Various other friends and associates were installed in the guest rooms, so my parents had to sleep in the children's room. The beds were too small for them, so they were never comfortable at night, and it was the only bedroom in the house without a TV or telephone. My parents are devoted television watchers who never sleep without the TV on if they can help it, so not having one available to help them relax was hard on them. And without a phone in the room, they had to go all the way down the stairs to answer the phone if it rang after they'd gone to bed. It wasn't what you'd call an ideal arrangement. I knew my mother looked forward to being home in San Francisco on weekends, to sleep in her own bed, and take care of her own house.

Since my parents and Aunt Como would be flying down for court, their cars would be in San Franciso. My VW was too small to fit everyone in unless we tied someone in the trunk. Uncle O.J.'s Bentley was sitting gathering dust in the garage at Rockingham, but my parents still treated all of Uncle O.J.'s possessions like holy objects. They refused to ask him if they could drive it, and he didn't offer. When I got mad and told them to ask for the key, they were horrified. "Hell, no! We can't be driving his Bentley!"

It's just a car, I thought, *just a damn car. This is ridiculous!* We didn't have the money to rent a car. Fortunately, my Aunt Como had a brother-in-law in L.A. who said we could borrow an old car that he wasn't using. It wasn't exactly a Bentley; it was, in fact, a Geo Storm. It held one more passenger than my little convertible. He said we could use it to get back and forth to the courthouse every day. The plan was for everyone to leave from Rockingham in the morning and carpool.

The biggest problem was our jobs. I was still on temporary disability leave. My mother had to take a temporary leave from her employer, an unpaid leave. This meant that for the first time in her adult life, she would be counting every quarter. It hurt me to see the woman who'd always had money to share walking around with two dollars in her purse. Aunt Como worked out an agreement with her employer to rearrange her hours so she could work an extended shift on Friday, Saturday, and Sunday, and attend court during the week. This meant that even though she'd be working seven days a work week and exceptionally long shifts, she'd still have to take a big pay cut. We were putting our financial lives on the line for Uncle O.J. It was frightening. But what else could we do? My uncle's life hung in the balance, not figuratively, but literally. If he lost the case, he'd spend the rest of his life in prison. Or worse.

As I laid out my clothes on the night before court, that thought haunted me. A lot of things were haunting me by then, but I couldn't seem to put my finger on any of them. I kept telling my friends, "I don't know what it is. I feel like I want to cry all of the time, but I can't. I need to cry so badly, but I just can't. I don't know why." I had been feeling that way for months by then. It was getting harder and harder to sleep at night. When the long days were over and I was alone at home, I'd be so stressed it felt unbearable. On the really bad evenings, when I couldn't relax, I'd been having a few beers or a couple of glasses of wine. Since I wasn't used to drinking, the alcohol had a powerful sedative effect on me. It relaxed me and made me sleepy. After a couple of drinks I could veg out or even fall sound asleep on the couch. I didn't realize it was becoming a habit. I was too busy surviving the days to think about much of anything.

After months of waiting, the day of days was almost upon us. Marcia Clark would be giving her opening statement tomorrow in what would soon be called the "trial of the century." And my whole family would be there.

CHAPTER 9

AND JUSTICE
FOR ALL

On Wednesday morning, January 25, at 8:30 sharp, my heart still pounding from fighting my way through the media, I took my seat in the packed courtroom of Department 103, on the ninth floor of the county courthouse. The big day had finally arrived. Johnnie would be making his opening statement that day. Just getting a place on that bench had been a major accomplishment. It was the A-list all over again. It made my head hurt just to think of it.

First of all, there had been the usual family politics to deal with. Nobody but my parents and I had been around during the seven months Uncle O.J. was incarcerated waiting for the trial to start, but when it came time for the "television premiere," people started coming out of the woodwork demanding a front-row seat. Jason and Arnelle wanted to be there, naturally, and space was limited. The bench would accommodate seven skinny people, or six full-size ones. My family was full-size, and we couldn't fit everybody on that bench. Counting my parents and Aunt Como, we were already crowded when another problem arrived in the form of a hanger-on named Larry Schiller.

I'd met Larry for the first time on one of my jail visits. Larry was supposedly a writer and a photojournalist, but as far as I was concerned, he was just another deal maker trying to cash in on Uncle O.J. And of course, Uncle O.J. was glad to let him do it if he could make some money for himself along the way. Uncle O.J. always had an eye for a good deal. Larry had put together the publishing deal for Uncle O.J.'s book *I Want To Tell You*, making a tidy profit from his percentage of the million-dollar advance. The plan was for Larry to tape Uncle O.J. in jail, collect some of the letters, and then hire a ghostwriter to patch it all together into a book. As a result, Larry was on the A-list for visitation, and for several weeks I'd seen him coming and going in the jail while he taped the interviews with Uncle O.J. The book was timed to go on sale that weekend, to coincide with Johnnie's opening statement. Uncle O.J.'s attorneys decided Larry deserved a reserved seat on the family bench.

Mom was in charge of seating arrangements for the trial, and the responsibility was very important to her. The constant scheduling problems with the jail visits had made her even more sensitive to the question of who had the right to sit on the family bench. She had so little real power in what was going on all around us, and this tiny bit of jurisdiction gave her some sense of control. Uncle O.J.'s attorneys had stressed the importance of having family members in the front row every day, and we'd gone to great lengths to make that possible. Then the night before the trial was to start, Larry Schiller had suddenly announced that he'd been guaranteed a seat on the family bench by Bob Kardashian and Skip Taft. This was news to my mother.

She was furious. What right did this stranger have to sit with our family? She told Larry, "I don't think there's room."

"O.J.'s attorneys have already agreed to it," he replied.

Fuming, Mom said, "It's not their decision to make. It's mine and my brother's." When my mother gets really angry, she's a force to be reckoned with, and she was mad now. "We'll just see about that," she told him. Then she told me privately, "It's time to zip up my nigger suit and take care of this," which meant "I'm tired of being nice—listen up, this is the way things are going to be." When Mom zips up that suit, watch out.

That night, when my mother and I went to visit Uncle O.J. in jail, Skip Taft was waiting outside the attorneys' room. Mom was in his face about Larry Schiller in record time. At first he didn't want to give in, but she said, "You know what, Skip? I'm telling you, and I'll tell my brother, that if I'm not in charge of these seats—the only thing his family has any control over in this mess—then I'll take my black ass home and *none* of us will be there! How's *that* going to look in court?" Skip dried up. He mumbled something about Larry's importance without really answering Mom one way or another. Since nothing was getting settled in the hallway, we took the fight into the conference room.

As we walked into the little glass cubicle, I said to my mother, "You need to settle this with Uncle O.J." She didn't need any encouragement. We'd hardly said hello to Uncle O.J. when she launched into the subject with him. She wanted a decision made right then, in front of Skip. As usual, Uncle O.J. was reluctant to get involved. Just like with Michelle and Nicole a year before, he preferred the coward's way out. He hated confrontation. But there was no putting off my mother. Finally he told Skip, "Shirley's in charge of seating. Whoever wants seats has to go through her."

In the end, Mom provided a seat for Larry in court part of that day. But needless to say, things were a little strained between the five of us. *Lucky me,* I thought as I sat there that morning. *I get to sit next to him.* He sat on the end of the bench to my left. To my right were Grandma in her wheelchair, Mom, Dad and Aunt Como. My mother sat proud and straight, ready to face down the world if she had to. Nobody was going to hurt her brother if she had anything to say about it.

It had been quite a morning. We'd met at Rockingham to carpool as planned. Gigi had put out some coffee and rolls for us in the kitchen, but nobody could eat. Arnelle had told us the night before that she'd be there, but when she wasn't ready in time, we decided we'd better go ahead without her. Mom and I crammed ourselves into the backseat of that borrowed Geo Storm, high heels and all, and we were off. I thought, *Great! Mommy's hunched under that hatchback like a turtle with arthritis. I hope the press doesn't see us drive up. O.J. Simpson's family, traveling in style.* I knew I shouldn't complain; Aunt Como's brother-in-law was kind to lend us his car, and we were lucky to have it. But I couldn't help thinking about the Bentley sitting unused in the garage as we drove away. We'd fought through traffic, parked our car in the overpriced lot, struggled through mobs of reporters, and made our way into the courtroom onto the family bench.

We sat on the left side of the chamber, directly behind the defense table. In front of me and Larry sat the "Dream Team," as the press was already calling them. Sitting there I took a look at what they were wearing. Apparently the fashion rules they'd given to us didn't apply to attorneys.

Bob Shapiro, whose dark tan hinted at too much time under a sunlamp, was making his usual flashy fashion statement, wearing an expensive suit that was a little too Hollywood for me. Bob's charm had worn off on me long ago. He'd turned out to be about as sincere as a Hollywood casting director—"We'll have lunch." Yeah, right. Uncle O.J.'s paying $100,000 a month for this, I thought. Next to him sat F. Lee Bailey, dressed in an ordinary-looking suit and wearing his usual high-heeled boots. By that time, he and Bob Shapiro weren't speaking. Barry Scheck, looking cute in a rumpled suit, was sitting with us. They'd run out of room at the defense table.

Johnnie, on the other hand, looked great as usual. He was dapper in a dark blue suit, striped shirt, and maroon tie. His distinctive glasses, a gold bracelet, and the small gold cross on his lapel rounded out a look that was perfect for the occasion—not too flashy but not too sedate. His appearance commanded attention. The jury'll be impressed, I thought, especially the women.

I was getting nervous waiting for court to start. After all, we'd waited seven months already. As I sat there trying not to fidget, my eyes wandered around the courtroom, over the judge's bench, and then up the wall to the large, bronze-colored California State Seal. In a way, I thought, being there was like being in church. The raised bench was like a pulpit, and the judges who sat there wore robes like preachers and had a God-like authority. The bailiffs were the deacons, reminding us that we were supposed to be quiet and reverent. And, of course, we were dressed in our Sunday best. Church, though, was familiar. I'd spent most of the Sundays of my life in church. When I went to church, I felt at home. Here in court, I felt a sense of uneasiness and dread. We were completely vulnerable in that place.

The judge's robe, the seal, the gavel—symbols of justice (at least to most white Americans) were, for me, painful reminders of the inequalities of life for African-Americans. I didn't know a single black man who hadn't had a bad experience with the police or the criminal justice system. Even my own father, as good and upstanding a man as you could find, had been unjustly harassed by the police; so had my brother, Benny. If you're black, the court can be a frightening place, even if you're innocent. Especially if you're innocent. My dad had a theory about that. He thought there was a conspiracy in white America to take down all the black status symbols. I was naive, my dad had told me. Black men were being set up to take a fall. My uncle O.J. was one of them.

Could Uncle O.J. find justice here? I didn't know. I felt the anxiety gnawing at my insides. A big part of me didn't want to be there. But since I had to be, I was glad we were finally going to meet my uncle's accusers head-on. I was sick of the waiting.

Whatever the outcome, I knew this courtroom was going to be the place where a spiritual crisis for my whole family would be acted out. My mind went back to the day of the Bronco chase, when all of America had watched our personal agony. Prayer had gotten us through that day. Prayer would get us through this day, too. We had all grown up good Baptists, and we knew that this trial was a test of faith as well as of justice. This was going to be an ordeal by fire, one of biblical proportions. I prayed for the truth and the strength to survive it. At Rockingham that morning, before we left, we'd held hands and prayed. Sometimes it felt like we'd never stopped praying since that day last June when Uncle O.J.'s life had hung in the balance. Today his life was hanging in the balance again. We needed all the help we could get for the ordeal ahead. We knew the world was looking over our shoulders, questioning our motives, probing the deep and secret places of our family's lives. Under the eyes of the cameras, it seemed we'd lost the privacy even of our own souls.

After a small eternity, a door opened and through it, single file, the jurors came out, found their seats, picked up their notebooks, and waited. They looked as nervous and self-conscious as I felt. I recognized several black faces from the jury selection. Uncle O.J.'s lawyers were happy with the jury. So was I. *They'll be fair,* I thought. *They'll listen to Johnnie. They won't believe everything the media has been saying.* The media had been tearing our family apart for months now, and we hadn't been able to defend ourselves. We'd get that chance today.

A moment later Bob Kardashian entered through a side door, and then Uncle O.J. came in, escorted by a bailiff. He smiled and nodded at Mom before turning to face the judge's bench. She kept her dignity, but I knew she must be fighting back tears. Dressed nicely in one of his expensively tailored suits, he looked more like the uncle I remembered than the convict I'd been visiting for so many months. He looked handsome as ever; well groomed, like the commercial superstar he'd always been. Until he was arrested, Uncle O.J. had been considered one of the most "watchable men in the world," the top black American celebrity spokesperson. No other black sports star before him had managed it: not Willie Mays, or Hank Aaron, or Muhammad Ali—no one. Well, the whole world was watching him now. An American hero was on trial for murder. It felt good to see him looking like himself again. He had his game face on, looking solemn and dignified. Then he sat down at the defense table between Johnnie and Bob Shapiro. I sighed. *This is ridiculous,* I thought for the thousandth time. *This is my Uncle O.J. He's no murderer. Why are we even here?*

"All rise!" the bailiff said in a loud voice. We got to our feet as Judge Ito walked briskly to the bench, up the two steps, and sat down. I stood uncomfortably for a moment, and then sat down, too, on cue. I felt like I was back in kindergarten class. You do what you're told, keep quiet, and if you're good, you get to stay. We had already been instructed that if we left the courtroom, we couldn't get back in, or if we were even a minute late, we would not be admitted. We'd also been told we couldn't chew gum, and that if we dozed off, we'd be ejected from the courtroom. Who made these rules? I looked at Judge Ito, trying to read his face. I'd seen him before, at the jury selection. My family was glad he was Asian; neither white nor black. He'll be fair, we thought.

After a few preliminaries, Judge Ito gave the signal, and Johnnie walked up to the jury box to begin his opening statement. A hundred pairs of eyes, and one remote-control camera, followed his movement in that courtroom. Outside the courtroom, we knew, the world was watching. The big moment had come. My spirits rose in excitement. I trusted Johnnie. He wouldn't let us down. Finally, we would get to defend Uncle O.J. from the months of accusations.

As soon as Johnnie started to speak, I felt a great sense of relief. Unlike Chris Darden or Marcia Clark, who had buried their opening statements in melodrama and technicalities, Johnnie spoke with the friendly ease of a good preacher. He didn't resort to complicated arguments; he simply told the jury a story. Uncle O.J. could not have committed the crime, he argued. It was simply impossible, and he was going to prove it. Then he put the case in a larger context, using one of his favorite quotes from Martin

Luther King, Jr.: "Injustice anywhere is a threat to justice everywhere." He reminded the jurors that they were the conscience of the community, participants in a search for justice and truth. He told them they would be making the most important decision of their lives. He reminded them to keep an open mind. It was a powerful moment.

Next, Johnnie moved on to the particulars of the defense, working down a checklist of witnesses he intended to produce, and providing hints of what they would say. He promised to bring forward people who would contradict the prosecution's claims. He challenged the prosecution's time line, saying that it was full of mistakes. Johnnie had made some impressive promises. If he could deliver on them, I thought, he could prove Uncle O.J.'s innocence. I felt my heart lifting further.

Then Johnnie argued that Uncle O.J. had accepted the fact that Nicole was out of his life, and that he had a new girlfriend, Paula Barbieri. I had my doubts that Uncle O.J. was really over Nicole, but I understood why Johnnie said it. Johnnie wanted to get at the issue of motive. How could Uncle O.J. be angry enough at Nicole to kill her if he'd already moved on? Of course, I knew that Paula was important to Uncle O.J. because she was beautiful and good in bed, not because she was a replacement for Nicole. Paula might be talking marriage, but Uncle O.J. wasn't.

Johnnie also suggested to the jury that he could account for Uncle O.J.'s time while the murders were taking place. Nicole and Ron Goldman had been killed after 10:15, he said, and a defense witness named Rosa Lopez would testify later that she saw Uncle O.J.'s Bronco parked on Rockingham, near the gate, at 10:15 that night. Alan Park, the limo driver mentioned by the prosecution in its opening statement, couldn't raise O.J. on the intercom because Uncle O.J. was chipping golf balls on the lawn, then taking a nap, showering, and packing. I knew that Uncle O.J. frequently chipped balls in the front yard. *But,* I thought, *not at night.*

Johnnie continued. There was a witness, he said, by the name of Mary Ann Gerchas, who was going to testify that she saw four Hispanic and Caucasian men, all wearing knit caps, run away from the crime scene that night, get in a car, and speed away. A detective that the prosecution had failed to mention, Johnnie said, had interviewed her. The detective's name was Mark Fuhrman. I didn't know anything about this witness, and very little about Mark Fuhrman, but if Johnnie could deliver this testimony, it would be very powerful. It would mean that other suspects had been seen in the area, and they were still at large. I thought this bit of information would be devastating to the prosecution, but when Johnnie mentioned Mary Ann Gerchas, I could hear snickering. Bob Kardashian leaned back and looked over at the prosecution's table. Marcia Clark was whispering something in Chris Darden's ear. She was smiling, which didn't make sense to me. Did she know something Johnnie didn't?

Whatever Marcia Clark thought was so funny, she was in no position to criticize. Her opening had been terrible; she'd lost the jury out of pure boredom. And Chris Darden had been ridiculous; according to him, yelling at your wife made you a potential murderer. Johnnie, on the other hand, understood that the jury needed to like him and understand what he was saying if he had any hope of convincing them. The prosecution didn't seem to realize that obvious point.

By noon, we were all relieved. It was going well. When Judge Ito banged down the gavel and announced that court was recessing for lunch, I felt much less worried than

I had in the morning. We headed for the elevator that would take us to the cafeteria. As we stood in the crowd of people waiting for the elevator, I could hear a woman's voice speaking loudly behind me. It was Marcia Clark, talking to Bill Hodgman. When I glanced back, she spotted us and stiffened up, motioning to Bill Hodgman to stop talking. There was an uncomfortable silence as we stood there awkwardly, wondering if we should say hello.

To my relief, Bill Hodgman made eye contact and pleasantly said hello. We all nodded and said hello to him, too. He seemed like a nice man. He knew we weren't the enemy. But Marcia kept silent. Her face hardened with anger and hostility. She looked away. *Can't she even be polite,* I thought. *We haven't done anything wrong.* Didn't she realize how painful this was for us? But she didn't even want to acknowledge our presence. I know that attorneys need to keep distance from all parties during a trial. It protects them from any accusations of impropriety. But, it seemed, the trial was more personal to her, and her anger at Uncle O.J. had spilled over onto us. It made me angry. Would she treat a white family the same way? It was a long ride down on that elevator. I was glad to get off.

Lunch turned out to be anything but relaxing. The courthouse cafeteria was surrounded by glass walls, and when we arrived, the media hordes were already outside, looking in. Another glass house. It was like dining in a fishbowl. We got our food and looked for a place to sit. The only available table was right by the window wall, at the end of the room. We sat down and tried to eat, the video cameras outside recording every mouthful. Across the room sat the Browns at a table with their friends. I tried not to look at them. We hadn't seen each other since the week of Nicole's murder. It was miserably awkward—our former relatives, now our enemies. The cafeteria was also open to the public, of course, so reporters didn't hesitate to come over and chat while we choked down our food. We couldn't say much, but that didn't stop them. I could hardly wait for lunch to be over. I hope they don't follow us to the bathroom, I thought. That may be the only place we can get minute of privacy.

After lunch, we resumed our place on the family bench. The afternoon session would be short, we'd heard, because there was a legal wrangle over some of the witnesses Johnnie had mentioned in the morning. Sitting right behind them, I could feel the tension among Uncle O.J.'s attorneys. There was some confusion about who had been responsible to notify the prosecution of the defense's witness list—a major procedural screwup. Carl Doulgas was responsible for the list now, but he taken the job over from Bob Shapiro, and Johnnie apparently felt that Bob had screwed up big-time and forgotten to make some very important disclosures. There were already problems between Bob and Bailey and now Bob and Johnnie were barely speaking. From three feet away, I could feel the tension. Why had Uncle O.J. even hired Bob Shapiro, I wondered. Bob's specialty was plea bargaining, and that had never been a possibility. Why would Uncle O.J. plea-bargain when he was innocent? I wish we'd just hired Johnnie in the first place, I thought. He was the one with the courtroom experience.

I felt better when Johnnie stood up and resumed his opening statement. His pleasant voice revealed none of the behind-the-scenes tension. Immediately, he worked to introduce a new doubt in the jurors' minds. Uncle O.J., he argued, was not physically capable of committing a violent murder. After discussing Uncle O.J.'s football injuries, he asked Uncle O.J. to stand and walk over to the jury box. Uncle O.J. stood up with apparent difficulty and walked slowly by the jurors, making eye contact with as many as he could. As Johnnie described his injuries, Uncle O.J. stood so close to the jurors that they could touch him, and held up his pants leg to show his arthritis-damaged knee. I knew perfectly well that Uncle O.J. was still a powerful man, but it was a good move on Johnnie's part. It gave Uncle O.J. a chance to make close contact with the jury, so they could see him as a human being, not as a criminal. The jury seemed very interested, even touched, as they leaned forward to look at Uncle O.J.'s hands. As Uncle O.J. sat down again, Johnnie concluded for the day. And with that, Judge Ito banged down the gavel and excused the jury for the day.

On the way home to Rockingham that evening, jammed in under the hatchback of that little car again, I wondered how many days this grueling routine would go on. I was already exhausted, and it was just the first day. Meanwhile, the prison visits would need to continue, too. I tried not to think about it. *If I think too far ahead*, I thought, *I'll never make it.*

Meanwhile, where were Jason and Arnelle? They had been there for the prosecution's opening. Why not today? It was the jail visits all over again. Where were they when their dad needed them? Johnnie wanted us all there as often as possible. My parents were coming all the way from San Francisco to be there. Arnelle was still living at Rockingham. She was a Hollywood stylist who worked periodically, so I figured she could find some time to get to court. Jason was working at a restaurant in West Hollywood. Arnelle had said she was coming last night, and this morning she'd told my mother, "I'll meet you guys down there." But she'd didn't make it. Lucky for her the press thinks I'm Arnelle, I thought sarcastically.

By the time we got back to Rockingham, I just wanted to go home and collapse among the bags of mail with a glass of wine. My little apartment, cluttered but private, was my refuge. But I knew I couldn't stay there long. My life had been taken over.

CHAPTER 10

NO RECUERDO

I didn't get back to court until the following Tuesday. Bill Hodgman, the only prosecutor who had been pleasant to us, had been admitted to the hospital with chest pains, and Judge Ito had called for a recess. He was still in the hospital, but the trial went on without him.

My parents had gone home for the weekend, and I'd picked them up at the airport Sunday night. That morning we had all piled into the car again and made our way through the rush hour downtown. I hoped we could get into the parking lot unnoticed. Fortunately, we managed to slip out of the car without attracting attention and made it halfway to the courthouse steps before the media barrage began. At least this time I knew what to expect. I was becoming an unwilling media expert.

We skidded onto our bench seconds before the courtroom doors closed. The attorneys were already in their seats, talking quietly. In a moment Uncle O.J. entered, followed by the jury, and finally Judge Ito. There was a lot of tension on the Dream Team as we waited to begin. I could feel it in the air. Johnnie and Bob Shapiro had been fighting over the weekend about who would be in charge. Bob had wanted to cross-examine more of the witnesses, but Johnnie had refused. They had tried hard to keep the infighting to themselves, but it was an open secret now. The press knew about it. It wasn't news to us. I just hoped the problem wouldn't compromise Uncle O.J.'s defense.

Johnnie was in charge this morning, and Bob obviously wasn't happy about it. He hadn't let go of any power willingly. I noticed that Uncle O.J.'s position at the defense table now reflected the rift. His broad shoulders separated the two factions. Bob sat on his left, at the very end, and Johnnie on his right.

I knew that the prosecution would begin their case by trying to prove that Uncle O.J. was a wife beater.

The prosecution's first witness was Sharon Gilbert, the 911 operator who had taken Nicole's call in 1989. Since I'd heard the tape already, I didn't expect to learn anything new. I didn't. Next up was John Edwards, an LAPD detective. He had answered Nicole's call and driven to Rockingham that night. His testimony was a little unsettling. According to him, Nicole had run out of the bushes when he arrived, saying "He's going to kill me!" The words didn't really bother me, since I assumed Nicole was being melodramatic. But Edwards had taken photos of Nicole's face, which were displayed on TV monitors in the courtroom. They made me uncomfortable. I hadn't seen her bruised like that. She'd obviously been hit. I assumed, however, that she'd been beating on Uncle O.J., too. Maybe he'd bruised her inadvertently while defending himself.

Why, I wondered, would she forgive him but then put the pictures in a safe-deposit box? I rationalized it again. It's got to be a setup, I thought.

The last witness of the day was another cop, Mike Farrell. He had been the second officer to investigate the 1989 incident. He backed up what I had been thinking. When he had questioned Uncle O.J. that night, another story had emerged. Uncle O.J. had told him that the fight was a "mutual wrestling match"; he'd hurt Nicole in the act of defending himself. Farrell said that Uncle O.J. had apologized for his behavior and promised to get help from a professional counselor. When Johnnie cross-examined Officer Farrell, he wanted to know if any other cops from the West L.A. station had been out to Rockingham in 1989. "Were there any other incidents?" he asked. Farrell said he could only think of one. "And who went out on that call?" Johnnie asked. "Mark Fuhrman," Farrell replied.

That was all. It had taken all day, and only three witnesses had been called. I knew there were dozens more to come. This was going to be a long trial.

Every morning and afternoon, there would be a short recess. It was my only chance to go to the bathroom, but it was risky if I did. If there was a line, as there had been today, or if I got stuck in the crowd that always mobbed the hallway and didn't get back exactly on time, I couldn't get into the courtroom until the next break. But if I decided not to go to the bathroom and just hung out in the courtroom or the hall, it was clear I'd have to deal with the media, or the Browns, or the Goldmans.

It was especially difficult to be around the Goldmans. My dad had approached Fred Goldman that morning during the break, and extended his hand. He said to him, "I'm really sorry for your loss." He meant it from the bottom of his heart. Dad's a very caring and ethical man.

But Fred responded very coolly. Every time I looked at Kim Goldman, I thought of my brother Benny, who's always been so special to me, and imagined the agony of losing him the way Kim had lost Ron. I wanted to say something to her, but never felt she'd be open to it.

Even sitting on the bench was stressful. We knew that we were on camera frequently, being watched by people all over the world. It made me extremely uncomfortable and self-conscious. There wasn't a single moment when I could let down. When the camera wasn't turned on. I had to look dignified all the time. I was acutely aware that I represented more than myself. I represented Uncle O.J. and the whole family. I felt the pressure of it every minute of the day.

Two days later I was back in court. Today Ron Shipp was going to testify. I had thought in the past that he was a friend. He had been with us through much of the crisis, arranging security at the wake and the funeral. He had been at the house a lot in the weeks following the murders, and Uncle O.J. had known him for years. But now he was being called by the prosecution. After the usual preliminaries, Judge Ito motioned to Chris Darden, and Darden called Ron to the stand. Ron looked extremely uncomfortable, and as he walked forward, he avoided looking at Uncle O.J. Darden started by asking Ron if he and Uncle O.J. were still friends. Ron said, "I still love the guy." Then Darden asked him about Uncle O.J.'s relationship with Nicole. What he was really asking about, of course, was abuse. Nicole had confided to him, Ron said, that Uncle O.J. had beaten her. The more he talked, the more painful it seemed for him.

After a few minutes of pursuing the abuse theme, the

questions turned to the night Uncle O.J. had returned from Chicago. Ron claimed that he had been with Uncle O.J. that night, in the master suite at Rockingham, and that Uncle O.J. had told him that he'd dreamed of killing Nicole. Because of the dream, Ron said, Uncle O.J. had told him he was afraid to take a lie-detector test. If this testimony was true, of course, it was devastating. But it didn't make sense to me. I was there that night. Uncle O.J. was depressed, and the whole family had been worried that he might commit suicide. Someone was with him all night in his room, mostly Mom and Dad—but never Ron Shipp. No one could even remember Ron having been upstairs. It didn't make sense.

I also knew that a few months earlier Ron had told this same story to a writer, Sheila Weller. She had used a pseudonym for him, "Leo." My whole family believed that "Leo" was really Ron. Until then I'd always thought that Ron, an ex-cop, was a straight-ahead guy. I was disappointed in him.

When Darden got through, Carl Douglas cross-examined him. He was tough on him, and I couldn't help but feel sorry for Ron. Finally Ron looked at Uncle O.J., and said, "This is sad." A moment later Douglas turned to Judge Ito. "We can stop now, Your Honor," he said. As Ron left the stand and walked by Uncle O.J, he looked right at him and mouthed, "Tell the truth, man. Just tell the truth." It was such a strange thing to say. Uncle O.J. was telling the truth—wasn't he? Judge Ito brought down his gavel and walked out the door. Another day in court was over.

By the end of the week thirteen witnesses had been called to testify about Uncle O.J.'s domestic abuse. Marcia

Clark and Chris Darden had tried their best to make my uncle into a monster, a man who stalked Nicole. It had all been so long ago, and most of it came from witnesses who were either prejudiced or really didn't know much. At that point in the trial I was looking at every witness with a suspicious eye, and I thought the prosecution was exaggerating things. It seemed to me that some of the witnesses just wanted to be in the spotlight, and others who testified had taken things out of context.

The worst one, from my point of view, was Denise Brown. What a hypocrite, I thought. I'd always thought Denise was jealous of Nicole and Uncle O.J. When Nicole and Denise were younger, Denise had been the glamorous one, the Ford model. But when her modeling career ended and her marriage fell apart, she was stuck living in her parents' three-bedroom house with a young son. Meanwhile, Nicole had moved into Brentwood with a celebrity. It had always seemed to gall Denise. I had no doubt that she and Nicole had been close, but I also knew how important it was for Denise to get what Nicole had. If any of Uncle O.J.'s friends had offered to marry her and give her Nicole's lifestyle, I believe Denise would have jumped at it in a New York minute.

And when had Denise become such an expert on abuse? A week after Nicole's murder, Denise was speaking out on TV on behalf of women's groups on the importance of getting out of abusive marriages. If Denise was so concerned and knowledgeable, I thought, why hadn't she ever tried to get Nicole away from my uncle? On the contrary, whenever Nicole and Uncle O.J. were together, Denise was usually there to join the party. What this meant to me was that Denise hadn't really seen what she was now claiming. She was just seizing the moment to get into the limelight, the way she'd been in her modeling days.

I was still of the opinion that in all of the arguments I'd ever overheard between Uncle O.J. and Nicole, Nicole had been the aggressor anyway. I'd heard her screaming obscenities at him. Besides, Denise hadn't done anything to endear herself to me. She'd been not only insensitive but cruel to me. Sometimes I'd think bitterly, Nicole's murder was the best thing that could have happened to Denise. Now she's in the spotlight again instead of her little sister. Even her testimony seemed like a performance to me. I couldn't help feeling the difference between her and Kim Goldman, sitting to my right. I couldn't see any of the agony on Denise's face that I saw on Kim's.

The next two days were consumed with the boring testimony of witnesses the prosecution had lined up to establish the time of Nicole's death. There were ten of them, and the testimony was endless. The prosecution was trying to set the time of the murder based on Kato—Nicole's Akita dog. Several witnesses said they heard Kato barking at around 10:15 P.M. Amazingly, I could see that the jury was paying attention. The prosecution was making it all seem so melodramatic. A dark night, a broken-hearted, howling dog. I remembered what Johnnie had said in his opening statement—it was absurd to build a murder case around a barking dog. Then I remembered the bloody pawprints my father and I had followed one day after Nicole's death, and it sobered me for a minute. Still, I thought the prosecution's "dog tale" was largely a waste of everyone's time.

The following weekend, however, promised to be anything but boring. On Sunday the jury would be touring Nicole's condo, and then the house at Rockingham. Uncle

O.J.'s attorneys were anxious for the jury to see both places. Taking the jurors inside Uncle O.J.'s house would allow them to see him as a human being, a man with a home and a family and a lot to lose. Why would anyone risk all that? Bob Kardashian telephoned Kathy Randa a few days before to let her know the jury would be visiting.

Kathy got off the phone, and said, "Oh my God, O.J.'s coming home!" She wasn't as concerned about the jurors, lawyers, cops, and Judge Ito as she was Uncle O.J. By Uncle O.J.'s standards, the house was a mess. Gigi hadn't been keeping the place up to its usual spotless standard because she was in the kitchen most of the time, cooking for the steady stream of guests. When she wasn't cooking, she was taking care of her son, who was now living with her at Rockingham.

We considered the jury visit a homecoming for Uncle O.J. It was important for us to make the house warm and inviting for him. And we didn't want him to get upset because the house didn't look the way it usually did. Kathy thought we should hire a few people to help clean, but we decided to take care of it ourselves. The whole house was dusty, the corners were full of spiderwebs, and the windows were dirty. Kathy, Gigi, and I did the grunt work, with help from one other cleaning person. We worked for almost two days, scouring the whole place. I even went onto the patio outside Uncle O.J.'s bedroom and scrubbed it on my hands and knees with bleach. It was looking pretty good by late Saturday. Kathy's sister came over to help that afternoon. Her sister is an interior decorator, so we relied on her to arrange everything in the house. Everything was to be in its place. Then Robert Kardashian and (his fiancée) Denice came over with flowers. They had been to the wholesale flower mart and bought several large arrangements. We had flowers in practically every room.

We did change a few pictures around, although not many. Kathy had gotten hold of a few old pictures of Grandma and Grandpa when they were young and had them enlarged. We put one on the side table in Uncle O.J.'s bedroom and a few on the bar. A couple of photos of Paula Barbieri were put away. They weren't nude photos, as some people thought. (The only nude photo we put away was one over the bar of Uncle O.J. and his buddies at the beach mooning the camera, which seemed inappropriate under the circumstances.) This was part of Uncle O.J.'s usual routine, anyway. Before Nicole died, he would have Michelle switch photos, depending on who was coming over. If Paula was staying over, her photos would be sitting out. If Nicole was visiting, the photos of Paula would magically disappear, and their wedding photo would be sitting on a table downstairs. I'd always thought it was funny, a typical "man" thing to do. The photo gallery going up the stairs was pretty much left intact. We put up a few more of Grandma and Grandpa, but for the most part, it was the same. We certainly didn't change everything over from white folks to black folks. The changes were minor.

We worked until five minutes before the jury arrived. We were still running around, fine-tuning things, until they got there. I suggested we light fires in the fireplaces. I wanted the place to look warm and inviting for Uncle O.J., like a Hallmark card. However, when Marcia Clark arrived, she objected to the lit fireplaces. Judge Ito ordered them extinguished. No one was allowed in the house while the jury looked around.

Outside it was a circus. The big black-and-white bus with tinted windows and bars was parked outside the gate, along with several vans, police cars, and motorcycles. The cops had nearly shut down the whole neighborhood. Uncle

O.J. was standing over near Sydney and Justin's play area, uncuffed, talking to the deputies that were assigned to guard him. Gigi was making the rounds, passing out sandwiches, chips, and soft drinks. Uncle O.J. was smiling and kidding around with the bailiffs. After the jurors had finished their tour, Uncle O.J. was allowed into his house and went in with Johnnie, Carl Douglas, and Bob Kardashian. He seemed pleased with the way it looked. The only thing he mentioned was the flag. We hadn't raised the American flag on the pole out front. It was the one thing we'd forgotten. The jurors toured the grounds as Uncle O.J. walked around the house, talking quietly with his lawyers. After the jurors had filed around the yard, they got back on the bus, and the whole entourage headed back downtown. Rockingham was silent again.

On March 9 I got my first look at Mark Fuhrman. The talk on the defense team was that he was a racist and a rogue cop; that he might even have planted the bloody glove at Rockingham. But I was surprised when I'd seen him on the news. At the crime scene he was unremarkable. He didn't stand out or seem like some evil kind of guy. I thought to myself that he looked kind of upstanding. But when he began to testify in court, I started to change my mind. His story about coming over the wall at Rockingham to "make sure everyone was all right" didn't ring true. *He's lying to cover his back,* I thought. *Just a typical cop.* But I also thought, *He's good at what he does.* He seemed so cool and professional. So my feelings fluctuated. I'd expected him to be a racist cop, but when I saw him on the stand, he didn't look like he was lying.

After Marcia Clark finished with Fuhrman, F. Lee Bailey rose to conduct the cross-examination. I was anticipating a lot from him. *Okay, let's see you go to work,* I thought. I was rooting him on. But I was disappointed. There were no fireworks, no Perry Mason stuff. Fuhrman stayed focused. When Bailey finally got around to asking him if he had used the "N" word in the last ten years, I thought to myself, *This is irrelevant.* Ten years? What did it matter? Bailey was grasping at straws. I thought he was trying too hard. I didn't realize, and I don't think anyone else outside the defense did either, that he was skillfully setting Fuhrman up for later.

When Bailey was done, the prosecution called Patti Goldman. Her testimony was really hard to listen to. She talked about the moment she had learned that Ron was murdered. I could feel her pain. Her words made me feel awkward and uncomfortable. I remember my father's attempt to talk to Fred Goldman. I didn't like the gulf that separated us. I didn't want people to think it was our family against theirs. *Why,* I wondered, *did they have to send four cops to Rockingham and scale the fence, but not tell the Goldmans until the next day—and on the phone? My God, the news reports were already out. Those poor people.* It was so insensitive.

A week later, Phil Vannatter was called to the stand. He wasn't an impressive man. *This guy's a joke,* I thought. He answered questions about the search warrant that he'd signed, made several lame excuses for his behavior the morning after the murder, and claimed unconvincingly that he'd asked Mark Fuhrman to scale the wall because they were worried about Uncle O.J.'s safety. No one was convinced. Bob Shapiro conducted the cross-examination. He asked Vannatter about the procedures he had used to collect the blood samples. Vannatter had been there at Parker Center when a blood sample was taken from Uncle

O.J. Instead of sending it to the lab, he'd put the vial of blood in his pocket and driven it to Rockingham. In the twenty years he had been a cop, he admitted, he had never carried blood around in his pocket. But instead of owning his mistake, he tried to justify it, pretend it was normal procedure. *Why didn't he book it downtown?* I wondered. If you take blood down to a crime scene, and you've never done that before in the twenty years you've been a police officer, it seemed to me there had to be some reason. But Vannatter wasn't forthcoming. I had to wonder why. If he'd made a mistake, I thought, he should just say so. He was just one more cop trying to justify his actions. But because he denied that anything was wrong or unusual, it just made the inconsistency stand out all the more to me.

Vannatter was on the stand for two miserable days. Next up was Kato Kaelin. I hadn't seen him since the weekend after Nicole's funeral. Marcia Clark wanted to ask him some questions about the bumps he had heard outside his guest room the night of the murders. His testimony seemed out of sequence. Clark pushed him hard, but she didn't get the answers she was looking for. It was Friday now, and when Judge Ito adjourned for the weekend, Clark wasn't through with Kato. When next Tuesday came around, she resumed. But the more she pushed, the more confused and sad-looking Kato became. I felt sorry for him. He was in a bad spot. Everyone thought his behavior on the stand was calculated, a performance, but I didn't. He'd acted pretty much the same way in the days just after the murders.

In the first few days after the murder he'd looked disheveled and disoriented, like a lost puppy-dog. It was awkward for him to be around the family. The day he left Rockingham he'd left a message on the answering machine at my apartment. He said, "Terri, it's Kato. I'm going to be staying somewhere else for now, but I just wanted to tell you that I really love all you guys and hope that everything works out well." I respected him for that. I thought the tape was so supportive, I gave it to one of the defense investigators.

But now I thought his testimony was confusing. I saw him walking a very fine line. I could understand the position he was in. He wanted to tell the truth, but he didn't want to get Uncle O.J. in trouble, either. Kato had been under pressure from the beginning. That night last June when Uncle O.J. had spoken about what he and Kato had done that night, Kato was completely confused. He couldn't remember. He really hadn't been paying that much attention. Kato didn't have a memory for detail. We had talked about the thumps on his wall the week it happened. He'd said, "I heard thumps, and I went outside because I didn't know what they were." He had said it with a sense of confusion at the time. So the Kato I saw on the witness stand was the same Kato I knew from experience. He wasn't faking confusion, as the prosecution wanted everyone to believe. He really was confused.

Kato finished up on Tuesday, March 28. That same afternoon Alan Park, the limo driver, was called to the stand. Park was an honest-looking man, and I believed what he said. He was one of the few people associated with the trial who hadn't sold a story to the tabloids. He had no vested interest in the outcome. He seemed totally sincere. The prosecution wanted to make the point, among others, that Uncle O.J.'s Bronco wasn't in front of the house when Park arrived to pick him up. The defense, of course, wanted to establish that the Bronco was there, parked by the gate on Rockingham Drive, when Park arrived, but that he just didn't notice it. Uncle O.J.'s alibi was on the line.

A couple of things bothered me when Alan Park was testifying. Everyone agreed that the Bronco was parked on Rockingham later that night. It was still parked there when Mark Fuhrman jumped over the wall. But why Rockingham? And why outside the gate? Every time I'd seen the Bronco parked there, it was inside the gate. When I'd lived at Rockingham, and all the times I'd visited there, no one had ever parked their car outside the gate, unless it was over on Ashford. Uncle O.J.'s house was on a corner and had two gates. The one nearest to the front door was the one on Ashford. Alan Park had come up Rockingham and turned the corner onto Ashford. How could he miss a big white jeep like the Bronco? It seemed highly unlikely. I thought Uncle O.J.'s attorneys were being a little disingenuous when they implied that cars were parked there all the time. The Rockingham gate led to the garage, and you had to have a remote control to get through. You'd only go through that gate if you were going to park inside. We always let people in and out on Ashford. That's where the intercom was. The inconsistencies in our defense bothered me.

The other testimony, about seeing someone who looked like Uncle O.J. crossing the yard, never concerned me. So what? Uncle O.J. had always said, "Yeah, it was me. I was outside in my robe." The prosecution was trying to imply that something odd or sinister was going on, that the dark, shadowy figure Alan Park saw was actually Uncle O.J. It was. But it raised a question in my mind. Uncle O.J. had said he was awakened by Alan Park's phone call. So why was he walking around in his robe before that? Why would he say he was asleep?

* * *

The only comic relief of all the days in court through February and March was the testimony of the confused maid, Rosa Lopez. Johnnie had mentioned Rosa prominently in his opening statement. But no sooner did he mention her than she disappeared. She was a housekeeper for one of Uncle O.J.'s neighbors, and she spoke only Spanish. When the press found out who she was, she'd resigned her job and fled to her daughter's home. Uncle O.J.'s lawyers had hired a detective to keep track of her, but she had managed to give him the slip. A Spanish-language radio reporter had found her there several days after she disappeared. Rosa had claimed that she was out walking her employer's dog and had seen the Bronco parked at Rockingham at 10:00 or 10:15 P.M. on the night of the murders. If this was true, Alan Park was wrong, and Uncle O.J.'s alibi would get a much-needed boost.

The press began chasing Rosa Lopez relentlessly. She decided to go home to El Salvador to escape the pressure, and when word of her decision got to Johnnie, he decided that he'd better get her on the stand right away, before she disappeared for good. The problem was, the prosecution was right in the middle of its case. It wasn't our turn yet. Johnnie petitioned to have her heard out of sequence, and Judge Ito agreed to hear from her without the jury present, and decide what to do. When she got on the stand, Chris Darden asked her if she was planning to leave right away and go to El Salvador. She said she'd made a reservation already. While she was on the stand, Cherri Lewis, another prosecution lawyer, called the airline. There was no reservation. Darden confronted her. "They don't show a reservation for you," he said.

"I am going to reserve, sir," she replied. "As soon as I

leave here, I will buy a ticket." Judge Ito decided she would probably flee the country and agreed to let her testify—but with an unusual twist. She would testify in court and be videotaped without the jury present. They would make a decision later about whether the jury would see it.

The next few days were a comedy of errors. First of all, the defense had forgotten to disclose a taped interview with Rosa that one of its investigators, Bill Pavelic, had made. He'd forgotten to tell anyone on the team that he'd made it. Then Chris Darden asked her some embarrassing questions. She had on new clothes. Had Johnnie paid her? Had she received a five-thousand-dollar payment from the tabloids. Had she told a friend that if she would say that she saw the Bronco, she would also get paid $5,000? To all these questions she replied, "*No recuerdo* [I don't remember]." A simple "no" might have settled the matter. In the end, I couldn't tell whether she was telling the truth or not. If she couldn't even convince me, she was worthless as a defense witness. Her line, "I don't remember," became a joke among the reporters. She became a recurring character in Jay Leno's *Tonight Show* monologues. Her fifteen minutes of fame over, she fled to El Salvador for good. I'm told she accepted a marriage proposal shortly after she arrived. So at least it wasn't a complete waste of her time.

C H A P T E R 11

TRAIL OF BLOOD

From the beginning of the investigation into Ron's and Nicole's murders, the detectives had claimed that when they went over the wall at Uncle O.J.'s, they were just following a trail of blood that led straight from Bundy to Rockingham Drive. At first they'd claimed the blood might have led to a victim, that they'd gone to Rockingham to rescue my uncle, not to arrest him. I didn't believe it for a minute. That was just a story they'd made up later to cover their backsides. They'd gone to Rockingham that night because they thought Uncle O.J. was a murderer—what Johnnie called their "rush to judgment." But the fact remained that there *was* a trail of blood, and it bothered me. Where had it come from, and where would it lead?

I remembered the blood trail Daddy and I had followed the evening we went to Nicole's condo. That trail had been made by Kato, Nicole's Akita dog. I'd seen those prints for myself. But the detectives claimed there was another trail. They said they'd found the murderer's bloody footprints at the scene as well. The crime photos showed prints from size 12 Bruno Mali shoes—Uncle O.J.'s size. They also claimed there was blood from the murder scene on the floor of the Bronco, blood they claimed came from the murderer's shoes. They said they'd also found drops of blood at the scene paralleling the killer's footprints, blood that had apparently dripped from the murderer's left hand as he left the scene. Uncle O.J. had cuts on his left hand the next day. They claimed there was blood on the door handle of the Bronco, on the console, and on the street next to the Bronco where it was parked at Rockingham. Supposedly there was blood in the foyer at Rockingham that night, blood in the drains in Uncle O.J.'s bathroom, and blood on a pair of his socks, left sitting at the foot of his bed. And, of course, there was blood on the glove Mark Fuhrman claimed he'd found in the walkway behind Kato's room. I'd heard that the prosecution had run DNA tests and identified the blood at the murder scene as Uncle O.J.'s. It disturbed me. I remembered standing at Nicole's condo that terrible day, with her blood all around me, and thinking, *No way Uncle O.J. could have done such a horrible thing. No way.* I still believed that. But how to explain all the blood evidence away? I hoped Johnnie could do it. I needed for him to do it, not just for the jury, but for me.

The trial had gone on for two months now. It had worn me down. To date, I hadn't heard any testimony I found convincing. I had an explanation for everything the prosecution presented. Witnesses weren't credible. People contradicted themselves, or each other. There were a hundred reasons to doubt the prosecution case, it seemed to me.

And no reason to doubt my uncle. The picture of him presented by the prosecution bore no resemblance to the man I knew. But the blood evidence. There was so much of it. My family kept saying, "It's all a conspiracy." But I thought to myself, *Wait a minute. How many things can you write off to a police conspiracy? This would have to be a really elaborate plot.* I kept my doubts private, of course. This was something I couldn't talk with my family about. I found myself going back and forth in my mind. As the blood evidence portion of the trial wore on, the prosecution would present evidence that looked pretty convincing, but then the defense would cross-examine a witness and raise serious questions about it. I was constantly confused.

The most important witness was Dennis Fung. Johnnie and the rest of Uncle O.J.'s lawyers thought the whole case hinged on Barry Scheck's cross-examination of Fung. If he could raise doubts about Fung's handling of the blood evidence, there was a good chance Uncle O.J. would be acquitted. If he couldn't, the defense would be in big trouble. As the prosecution presented it, the blood evidence was devastating, and so far Fung had been composed and seemed very professional. But the question was, could Barry punch holes in Fung's testimony?

One thing was clear. Barry Scheck was much better prepared than anyone else on the prosecution team. He had mastered all the confusing, contradictory material. He'd dissected every detail of every report, every photograph, and every inch of videotape. As March faded into April and we entered the third month of the trial, Barry confronted Fung and began to hammer away.

Right away, Barry put Fung on the defensive. He accused him of being reckless and irresponsible in the way he had collected the crime-scene evidence. The evidence was hopelessly contaminated, Barry implied. No one had used proper procedure, or even ordinary common sense, he argued. He got Fung to admit there was a possibility the samples had been cross-contaminated. He raised the point that Fung's assistant, Andrea Mazzola, was a trainee who had only been on one previous murder case. He got him to say that Mazzola had worked unsupervised. By the end of the day, Fung's testimony had been shredded. "Barry's really smart," I thought. His intelligence was appealing. I congratulated him as we got up to leave that Wednesday. I was already starting to feel better.

The following Tuesday, after a five-day recess, Barry resumed his torture of Dennis Fung. He was very good at it. I almost felt sorry for Fung. Barry argued that Fung had handled evidence without gloves on, that he had failed to make a record of all the blood samples he had collected, that he had been sloppy. Then he produced a photo of the back gate at Nicole's Bundy condo. It was a shot taken the day after the murder. Fung hadn't collected the blood sample from the back gate until three weeks later. But the blood spot couldn't be seen in the photo. Barry asked him about it. "Where is it, Mr. Fung?" he said, his voice rising. "I can't see it," Fung answered. The clear implication was that the blood had been planted there, later, by someone else. I thought back to the day when Dad and I had gone by the murder scene, one day after the photo was supposedly taken. We had seen blood on the back gate that day. But it had looked different. Was this the blood Barry was asking about? I couldn't reconcile that photo with what I had seen for myself. Barry's right, I thought; somebody must have planted it. The implications filled my mind with doubts. What's going on? Maybe my parents were right. Maybe they were framing my uncle.

The poor, hapless Dennis Fung was grilled by Barry for a total of eight days. I couldn't help but identify with Fung's misery. Anyone could. Barry challenged everything about Fung. He questioned his competency, his memory, his knowledge of LAPD procedures, his common sense. He was utterly destroying Fung. This was going to acquit Uncle O.J., I thought. But I was bothered with a nagging little doubt. Was it incompetence or conspiracy? Could anyone, even the most conscientious technician, withstand an examination as grueling as this one? Did sloppy lab work invalidate the evidence? I didn't know. When it was finally over, Fung looked tremendously relieved. Hank Goldberg, one of the prosecuting attorneys, asked him, "Have you ever testified in a case where you were on the stand so long?"

Fung answered, "Never." With that, he rose from the stand, walked over to the defense table, and shook hands with all of Uncle O.J.'s lawyers, and then Uncle O.J. "Good luck to you," he said. I thought it was a strange thing to do. If Fung's information was correct, my uncle was probably a murderer. If it wasn't, he was part of the plan to frame Uncle O.J. His career could be ruined. Why on earth, then, would he be wishing Uncle O.J. luck? Then I thought about Marcia Clark; one minute she was implying that the defense team was unethical, and the next she was cuddling up to Johnnie between camera "takes," flirting with him in the most outrageous manner. No wonder she was getting a divorce. And Bob Kardashian, engaged himself, was flirting with a woman on the defense team. I didn't understand any of them.

Dennis Fung was supposed to be the star witness for the prosecution, but he ended up making the defense's case instead. Our defense team was clearly delighted. They'd demolished a powerful enemy. Fung's assistant, Andrea Mazzola, was up next. She looked like a rookie trying to act strong. It was Peter Neufeld's turn to cross-examine.

The prosecution questioned her for one morning, and then concluded. She'd done pretty well, but since she had virtually no experience with investigations anyway, I didn't take her opinion seriously.

In the meantime, a revolt was being staged by the jurors. I didn't know the whole story, but it seemed that they were unhappy with each other, and upset that their guards had been reassigned. Judge Ito adjourned court until the situation could be resolved. The Dream Team was a little nervous about the adjournment, but they calmed down as court was reconvened and Peter got his chance to unravel Mazzola. He quickly challenged her testimony, resuming the attack that had started with Barry. In his Brooklyn accent, he asked pointed questions and soon had Mazzola on the retreat. She tried too hard to justify things that she should have just left alone. By the time he was done, she had admitted to several errors, and had even said that the prosecution's charts and visual aids were incorrect. The defense was on a roll.

The next several days were filled with more blood testimony. Greg Matheson, the LAPD's chief chemist, was questioned, and then Robin Cotton of Cellmark Laboratories was called. Much of this testimony was really boring, and highly technical. Even Uncle O.J. was having a hard time keeping awake. *I wonder what the jury thinks about all this*, I wondered to myself. Only a scientist could love this kind of stuff. The prosecution was attempting to give everybody a short course on DNA identification. The only problem was, it wasn't short enough. I fought drowsiness. I knew that if I nodded off, Judge Ito would be on my case immediately. He would tolerate all kinds of media nonsense, but God forbid you nod off.

Even with the boredom and the technicalities, though, the DNA evidence didn't look good to me. Uncle O.J.'s

DNA appeared in blood samples taken both at Bundy and at Rockingham. Dr. Cotton, the prosecution's expert, testified that Uncle O.J.'s DNA markers only appeared once in every 170 million whites and African-Americans. If you factored in Hispanics, too, the odds that someone else would have the same markers were one in 1.2 billion. *Pretty steep odds,* I thought. The details of the science may have been a mystery, but this part was easy to understand. The jury was paying attention—and taking notes.

I knew that Uncle O.J.'s attorneys were planning a vigorous defense. Barry Scheck and Peter Neufeld were working like dogs, late into the night, analyzing every last detail of the prosecution's case. But as the DNA evidence kept piling up, doubt began to gnaw at my mind. Up until now I had been thinking, *All of this can be explained.* But now I wasn't so sure. How could you explain away all of this DNA evidence? I'd heard of DNA evidence before Uncle O.J. was arrested, and I knew that it was considered extremely accurate—conclusive, in fact. DNA didn't lie. It was considered so conclusive, in fact, that it had been used to free several people who'd already been convicted. So as I listened to the DNA findings for Uncle O.J., it seemed to me that all of the other stuff didn't matter much, but the DNA was crucial.

My family was working hard to deny everything. They didn't even bother to deny it out loud; they just rejected it out of hand without even thinking about it. They didn't allow themselves to think about it, because the implications were too terrifying. And it wasn't only them; I'd been doing exactly the same thing until then. *We're all in denial,* I thought. At that point it occured to me that we weren't just there supporting Uncle O.J. in any objective way. We weren't saying, like many of the letters to him said, "We love you and we're there for you, whether you did it or not. We love you either way." On the contrary, there were certain questions we had never allowed ourselves to ask. I had been so swept up in my support for Uncle O.J. that I had just gone along. When I did have questions, I'd just choked them back. But now the questions in my mind were coming faster and faster, and it frightened me. The tiny doubts that had nagged at me off and on in the beginning now loomed larger. *My God,* I thought, *even if they had a picture of him commiting the crime, my family would be saying, it's not him; the picture's doctored.* If Uncle O.J.'s lawyers had made the claim that his head had been superimposed on an incriminating photo, they would believe it! I could imagine them saying "That's an impostor!" In fact, they probably wouldn't look at the photo at all. They wouldn't want to know what it might show.

From the day more than a year earlier when my mother had called to tell me Nicole had been murdered, I'd been waiting for answers to questions I wasn't even allowed to ask. There were so many things I wondered about, so many things I needed to know. Yet even asking a question had been a kind of a violation, breaking the code of silence my family had imposed from the beginning. As the trial went on, the questions and the doubts had multiplied, and the silence that surrounded us in our most private moments had begun to suffocate me. One day in the car with my parents, my frustration had overflowed.

We were driving back to Rockingham one day during the blood evidence portion of the prosecution. After days of listening to the DNA evidence, I was beginning to feel like I was going to explode. No matter how hard I tried, I couldn't explain it all away. For the first time in the whole process, a question had forced its way into my consciousness: what if he's guilty? What if he actually committed those murders? It was an overwhelmingly painful question, a question made even more painful by the fact that I couldn't voice it to anyone. I needed real answers, not just the word games the attorneys were all playing. I was angry at the world by then, and when my mother lectured me on supporting Uncle O.J. that day in the car, I just lost control. My dad was driving my car, and I was in the front seat next to him. My mom was sitting in the back. Suddenly I couldn't stand it any longer, and I burst out, "Why don't we ever ask him anything? Did you ever think maybe he really did do it? What about all the DNA? Did you ever think maybe he really did kill these two people? Why can't I be part of this family and love him unconditionally, but not be convinced he's innocent?

My mother's reaction to those words was as instantaneous as it was violent. In what I can only describe as a primal outburst, she flew over the seat at me with her fists flying and began beating me. I went numb with shock. My mom hadn't even slapped me in years. It was as if she'd reverted back to the ghetto teanager I never knew.

Dad was appalled. He quickly pulled over to the curb and tried to calm her down. The moment the car stopped, I jumped out into the street and began screaming at my mother. "You can't hit! I'm not a child anymore, I'm an adult! You can't tell me what to think." I was sobbing and shaking, completely out of control.

Then my father hollered that I was acting crazy and that if I didn't get back in car, he'd have me committed. Hearing those words, I realized that nothing I could say would ever make them understand. So, I got back into the car and we drove back to the house in silence.

Nobody said a word about what had just happened, then or ever. It was a moment of truth for me that had been a long time coming.

* * *

Robin Cotton was on the stand for eight excruciating days, and was followed by Gary Sims, a DNA expert from the state of California's crime laboratory. Rock Harmon, another prosecution attorney, questioned him. What he had to say was disturbing. Three of the blood samples recovered from Uncle O.J.'s Bronco matched the blood of Nicole, Ron, and Uncle O.J. himself. This was the first we had heard of Ron Goldman's blood being found in the Bronco. *How could this have happened?* I thought. I couldn't come up with any innnocent explanation of why Ron's blood would have been there. *Even if they did carry around a vial of Uncle O.J.'s blood,* I thought, *how would they have planted Ron's? They didn't carry his around.* It didn't make sense. At least it didn't if Uncle O.J. was innocent.

Sims was on the stand for several days. After Harmon got through with the prosecution's questions, Barry did the cross-examination. He treated Sims with a lot more respect than he had Dennis Fung. Sims was an old pro and was not the least bit intimidated by Barry's aggressive style. The two of them acted more like colleagues than adversaries. But the testimony was so boring. I got completely lost—and so did everybody else. It was obvious that by then the jury, the press, even Uncle O.J.'s other lawyers, had tuned out. But when the prosecution had the jury actually walk past the charts, I knew they were as confused as I was. It was clear to me that we'd reached an important turning point in the trial. I slipped Uncle O.J. a note that said, "These people are as lost as I am. You're coming home."

The only interesting testimony concerned the issue— implied by Barry's questions—of whether blood had been planted on Uncle O.J.'s socks by LAPD. LAPD said they had missed the blood drops when they collected the socks for evidence. Only later did they notice the blood—much later. It raised the question of why no one had noticed the drops, even though the socks had been inspected three times and a note had been made saying, "blood search, none obvious." Uncle O.J.'s lawyers were trying to imply that the blood had been planted on the socks. Barry made a pretty powerful argument. He took the socks, walked over to the jury, and showed them to them. The bloodstains were pretty obvious. How could anyone miss them, much less a trained professional?

I had my own doubts about the socks evidence as soon as I saw the evidence photo. This picture had the socks thrown at the end of the bed, in the middle of the floor. Everyone who knew Uncle O.J. knew that he was so fastidious that he would never leave his socks or any clothing haphazardly laying around.

After weeks of blood testimony, on June 2, the prosecution finally ended its DNA phase and called the Los Angeles County coroner, Dr. Lakshmanan Sathyavagiswaran. His name was completely unpronounceable; even Judge Ito couldn't get it right. Dr. Sathyavagiswaran testified for several days, explaining in detail every aspect of Nicole's and Ron's deaths. His descriptions were graphic, and sometimes chilling, but bearable. But on June 6, it became unbearable. On this day, the autopsy photos were going to be shown. Uncle O.J. was visibly uncomfortable. At one point he leaned over to Bob Kardashian and asked him to lean forward and block the TV camera from zooming in on his face. The prosecution brought in a whole collection of photos, arranged on big display boards. Some members of the jury looked as though they might get sick. Uncle

O.J.'s lawyers had asked Judge Ito to position the charts so that they couldn't be seen by the audience. *Thank God*, I thought. I didn't want to see them.

Dr. Sathyavagiswaran used the photos to describe in graphic detail how Nicole had died. He described how her neck had been cut from left to right, severing her carotid arteries. Brian Kelberg was handling the prosecution's questions. At this point he said, "Would you demonstrate how, in your opinion, the wound was inflicted?" Kelberg handed him a ruler to stand in for the murder weapon. He pulled Kelberg's head back by the hair, and then pulled the ruler across his neck. It was an incredibly dramatic gesture. It made me sick inside. But not as sick as some of the autopsy photos. In addition to the network camera above the jury box, there was a closed-circuit camera that was used for exhibits. Occasionally it would pick up one of the autopsy photos, which would then appear on the TV monitor, on a table to my right. I tried to look away, but I couldn't. My dad would say to me often, "Don't look." But it was always too late. The photos haunted me, especially the one of Ron. I couldn't get them out of my mind.

On June 15 I took the day off and watched the trial on the three TVs at Rockingham. The coroner had finally finished his testimony, and the prosecution was bringing in a buyer from Bloomingdale's and a representative from the Isotoner glove company. The prosecution wanted to establish that the bloody gloves belonged to Uncle O.J. They had entered into evidence a receipt proving that Nicole had bought two pairs of Isotoner gloves, one of which was identical to the ones found at the crime scene and at Rockingham. They wanted to prove that Nicole had given Uncle O.J. the gloves that they believed he'd worn when he murdered her. If they could prove it, it would be an ironic twist worthy of a crime novel.

Toward the end of the day, after several heated sidebars, Chris Darden asked Uncle O.J. to stand up, approach the jury, and try on the gloves. What followed, no one will ever forget. The lawyers, the press, even people on the street, immediately began debating what had happened then. Like most other people, I thought, *That glove obviously doesn't fit.* Then I had second thoughts. *If I had a latex glove on, and tried to put another glove on top of that, it probably wouldn't fit either.* But the science of the issue wasn't that important to me. I wondered how Uncle O.J. could even bear to try putting those gloves on. I couldn't have done it. For me it wasn't a matter of whether they fit or not. I don't think I could have dealt with the emotional trauma of it.

I remembered when they'd brought out the gloves earlier and passed them around. It had been emotional for me just to see them. This was the glove that had grasped Nicole's hair, that she had bled on. Some of her hair was still embedded in it. This was the glove the murderer had worn. Everyone was talking about the fact that the gloves didn't fit. But why wasn't anyone wondering about Uncle O.J.'s demeanor? Putting the gloves on didn't seem to bother him. Uncle O.J. didn't seem emotionally connected to what those gloves were, or what they symbolized. For him, there was no apparent emotion attached to doing it. Was his detachment a defense? Was survival his main goal now? I couldn't understand.

The prosecution was almost done with its case. I heard testimony about Bruno Magli shoes from William Bodziak. He was a good witness. I was hoping F. Lee Bailey would discredit him, but his cross-examination was based on a scenario so far-fetched that I thought it could hurt Uncle O.J.'s case. But, they weren't going to convict a man on the basis of a disputed pair of shoes.

Then two days later the prosecution called a representative from Uncle O.J.'s cell-phone company, and a lawyer for the Mirage Hotel in Las Vegas. They wanted to imply that Uncle O.J. was angry at Paula Barbieri, that he knew she was sleeping with Michael Bolton that night. If Uncle O.J. had known, it could be seen as more fuel for his anger, or so the prosecution wanted to imply. I knew Paula well enough to believe she probably had slept with Bolton at one time or another. I'd heard her talk enough about her sexual needs. She wasn't exactly a virgin flower. But Johnnie decided not to deal with it. There was no good place to go with this testimony, so they skimmmed over it as though it was of no consequence.

The only witness that stood out to me during this period of the trial was the last one to be called by the prosecution: Douglas Deedrick, an FBI agent. Deedrick was a hair-and-fiber expert. He was prepared to testify that the carpet fiber from Uncle O.J.'s Bronco was rare, and not likely to be found in any other type of carpet. This same rare fiber had been found at the Bundy crime scene, on the bloody glove, and on the knit cap left there by the murderer.

It was very damaging evidence. But there was a problem. Deedrick had prepared a report that the prosecution had not passed on to the defense. Johnnie immediately objected. In a heated sidebar discussion, Johnnie and Marcia Clark debated whether the evidence was admissible. When the argument was over, Judge Ito took the bench and ruled that all of the fiber evidence would be precluded—it couldn't even be mentioned. And so for the next three days, I sat through agent Deedrick's testimony about other matters. He never mentioned the fibers once.

I was so tired by that point that I didn't think much about the fiber evidence. Like the DNA, it seemed pretty damaging. How did the fiber get there? Where did those fibers come from? It was very lucky for the defense that the prosecution had screwed up badly again, I thought, or the defense might have had a hard time explaining the fibers away. I asked Uncle O.J. about the fibers later. He didn't have an answer. He was only interested in talking about how the prosecution had withheld the report. Privately, I was thinking, *I don't care about the rules of evidence; I only want to know the truth. The prosecution made a mistake, maybe a deliberate mistake, but it doesn't change the fact that those fibers were found.* Uncle O.J.'s lawyers had done a masterful job of systematically casting doubt on almost every piece of evidence. But this was different. I could see that Johnnie was relieved that he didn't have to deal with it.

A little over one year after the murders, the prosecution rested. As far as I was concerned, "rested" was the right term. After more than 150 days in court, I was exhausted. We were all holding on by our fingernails by then. Aside from the physical and emotional strain of the long days in court, we were all wearing down in other ways as well. My mother's employer wouldn't hold her job any longer, so she'd had to resign. That meant both my parents were now surviving on Dad's monthly check alone. It was a scary situation.

My employer was willing to hold my job until the trial was over, but my disability allowance had run out, and I was nearly out of money, too. To survive, I'd relied on my friend Jerry's contacts and got regular work as an extra on "Melrose Place." Working as an extra usually only requires a commitment of a day or two at a time, and it pays fairly decently, so I began taking one or two days a week off from the trial to work as an extra on various shows and movies like *Fresh Prince,* and *The Great White Hype.* I tried only to take work in the middle of the week, so I could be there on Mondays and Fridays when my parents or Aunt Como had to be gone. The financial strain had also forced us to change our eating habits. We'd already been grabbing coffee and rolls at Rockingham when we met there in the morning to go to court, and now we were also relying on Gigi to put out bread and sandwich materials as well. We'd pack sandwiches and snacks and then brown-bag it to the courthouse. The advantage was that we didn't have to waste money on overpriced lunches.

We'd pretty much given up on trying to deal with the mail by then, and our houses were stacking up with dust and junk until they were practically unlivable. My parents were still commuting home to take care of Grandma three days a week in San Franciso, but she no longer had the time or energy to maintain Grandma's house like she used to. My little apartment, once my pride and joy, had become so cluttered I could hardly walk through it without falling over something.

All in all, it was a very hard time for us. We looked forward almost with desperation to the beginning of the defense case, when we could finally present our side of the story and have some hope that this endless trial would finally draw to a close.

On July 10 the defense presented its first witness, my cousin Arnelle. Johnnie had planned to present a series of family members to vouch for Uncle O.J.'s good character. Grandma had flown down for the occasion. She hadn't been in court since that first day in January, when the trial had begun. My aunt Como, Grandma, and Mother would all testify. Johnnie's main purpose was to discredit Ron Shipp, who had presented himself as an old family friend of Uncle O.J.'s. The testimony was mostly uneventful. Arnelle was nervous, but unmistakably sincere. We were all so proud of her.

Johnnie treated her with the utmost gentleness. He asked her about Ron Shipp. Arnelle testified that he had been drinking the night he was at Rockingham, after Uncle O.J. had returned from Chicago. Johnnie was working hard to destroy Ron's credibility. He didn't want Ron's story about Uncle O.J.'s dream to be believed by the jury. Marcia Clark was also gentle with Arnelle during the cross-examination. However, Clark did succeed in establishing that Arnelle couldn't vouch for her dad's whereabouts the night of the murders. Aunt Como continued the attack on Ron's story, followed by Grandma. Mom would eventually deliver the knockout blow by stating that she and my dad had been with Uncle O.J. all night on the Monday in question—sleeping in his room and following him to the bathroom. So Ron Shipp couldn't possibly have talked to my uncle that night.

Things were starting to move faster. My family's testimony was short and to the point. Johnnie had wanted to move the defense along. He was afraid the jury would get too worn-out to pay attention. The prosecution had taken six months to present its case. It seemed like a lifetime. For the next several days a succession of witnesses tried to rebut the prosecution's time line and call into question many of the details that supported its case. If I was having a hard time paying attention even though O.J. was my own uncle, a man I loved and cared about, how about the jury? *They must be going crazy,* I thought.

All through July and into August Johnnie and the rest

of the team picked away at the prosecution case. Finally, on August 22, Dr. Henry Lee was called to the stand. I had been looking forward to his testimony. I knew that there was some concern about him on the Dream Team. He was their expert, and he had raised some troubling questions for the prosecution, but he was also his own man and wouldn't bend his testimony to fit the defense's agenda. He was known as a consummate professional, with a reputation for complete integrity. But he was no comfort to the prosecution. "Something's wrong," he said on the stand as he talked about the forensic evidence. Since so much of the case was still a puzzle for me, his doubts only served to reinforce mine. There were too many mishaps, loose ends, and cover-ups, I thought once again. What was going on? I clung tightly to my hope that it could still all be explained away.

Then on August 29 Johnnie dropped his bombshell. Laura Hart McKinney was called to the stand. McKinney, it turned out, was a screenwriter who had interviewed Mark Fuhrman years earlier about a script. The defense had been working hard behind the scenes for weeks to get access to the audiotapes she had made of her conversations with Fuhrman. It had taken a trip to court in North Carolina to force McKinney to release them. She wasn't anxious to help the defense—she thought Uncle O.J. was probably guilty—and she didn't want to compromise the commercial value of the script she was hoping to sell. But Johnnie had prevailed, acquired copies of the tapes, and subpoenaed McKinney to testify. For the last several days the entire defense team had been working to produce a transcript of the tapes. When it was finally finished, the contents had shocked everyone who read them. A tight lid had been ordered on them by Judge Ito, but excerpts had leaked. Her testimony was going to be a turning point in the trial.

By the morning of the twenty-ninth, the media was buzzing with stories about Fuhrman and the tapes.

After a few preliminaries Gerald Uelmen, our civil-rights specialist, began to question McKinney. She had interviewed Fuhrman from 1985 all the way up to 1994. Some of this stuff was recent. "Did Officer Fuhrman ever use the word *nigger*?" Uelmen asked.

"Yes," she replied. Uelmen had prepared a videotape of the transcript, which he played on the closed-circuit monitors. The words were shockingly racist. Earlier I'd thought, *Why bother with this guy? So what if he'd used the 'N' word ten years ago? If there was a frame-up, he was just one player in a larger conspiracy.* But when I saw the transcripts, I changed my mind. This was much more than I'd expected. I had laughed at F. Lee Bailey for asking the question at the time. In my opinion, he didn't live up to his larger than life reputation. But he had been brilliant with Fuhrman. I could see it now. He had set him up perfectly. He'd made Fuhrman perjure himself. When he had pushed him so hard way back in March, I didn't understand what difference it made. Now I understood. Nothing Fuhrman had said could be trusted.

We were near the end of the defense's case, and Uncle O.J. had still not testified. There was a lot of talk about it in the press. Some commentators were saying that Uncle O.J. didn't want to testify, and that this was a sign of guilt. I knew that wasn't true; I knew that he wanted to testify. He talked about it all the time. Uncle O.J. believed he could get the jury to believe him. But his attorneys were skeptical. Johnnie had said to him that he didn't think it was a good idea. Uncle O.J. had a tendency to go off on tangents, and everyone was afraid he might say something that would hurt his defense. They were ahead, Johnnie insisted, so why take a chance? But Uncle O.J. was insistent.

Early in July, I had heard that Johnnie had arranged for two out-of-town attorneys to cross-examine Uncle O.J. in jail. They were going to play the role of prosecutors and see how Uncle O.J. held up. Word came back that the mock examination didn't go well. Later on I learned that it had been a disaster. Uncle O.J. tried to talk his way through a series of tough questions, and in the process only came across as insincere. Johnnie, ever the diplomat, tried to smooth it over for Uncle O.J. He couldn't come right out and tell him there was no way in hell they'd let him get on the stand. They just strung him along. But because they hadn't given him a firm "no," he told everyone who would listen. "I want to testify," was his constant refrain. But his attorneys worked hard to make sure he didn't. It would not, they believed, be in his own best interest. As I realized much later at the civil trial, they were right.

On Thursday, September 21, the defense rested. Uncle O.J. stood up and made a short statement waiving his rights to speak as a defendant. That was all Johnnie would allow him to say.

The prosecution offered a few rebuttal witnesses, none of whom had anything new to add. Finally, on Tuesday, September 26, the prosecution began its closing arguments. "This isn't going to be anything new, either," I thought to myself. I was more than ready for the trial to be over. But I was a little curious, too. Johnnie had made a lot of promises in his opening statement that he hadn't delivered on. It bothered me. I didn't only want Uncle O.J. to win the trial; I wanted him to clear his name, for all our sakes, and for my own peace of mind. Would the prosecution make the most out of Johnnie's omissions?

Marcia Clark and Chris Darden would each present part of the prosecution's closing arguments. Clark led off. She looked exhausted. As much as I disliked her, I could identify with her fatigue. Everyone was tired, tired to the bone. As she began her statement, I was surprised. She didn't mention Johnnie's broken promises. Instead she started off by apologizing for Mark Fuhrman. She was obviously worried that no one on that jury would hear a thing she had to say if she didn't get him out of the way first. After making her apologies, she went on to summarize the case, making good use of visual displays. She talked all morning and then resumed in the afternoon, after the lunch recess. Late in the afternoon she finished and sat down, a look of obvious relief on her face.

Chris Darden was next. The day was almost over, but Judge Ito let him go ahead. Darden talked on into the evening and then resumed the next morning. His theme was simple: domestic abuse. Uncle O.J. was a batterer, he argued, which also makes him a murderer. *This is the same old stuff,* I thought to myself, still unwilling to make the connection between domestic violence and murder. I repeated the comforting words I had been holding on to since the beginning of the trial: just because a guy hit a woman doesn't mean that he killed her. I was in a sullen mood. *This guy's wasting my time,* I thought. Darden was emotional. He obviously believed in his heart that Uncle O.J. had committed murder. But I didn't like Darden. I'd resented his being brought on to the case in the first place, since his investigation of A.C. before the trial was an obvious conflict of interest. I'd resented it even more when everybody from the D.A.'s office pretended that Chris Darden's being black was just a huge coincidence, that it had nothing to do with the largely black jury. Yeah, right. Besides, he was so melodramtic. Something about his soft voice and the way he constantly bobbed his head turned me off, made me angry. The more he argued, the more I tuned him out.

On Wednesday afternoon, September 27, Johnnie began the closing statement for the defense. The little family bench was full to overflowing. Jason and Arnelle were there, and Larry Schiller decided to come, too. I watched it on TV at my house with a friend. I didn't like being excluded. I had been there almost every day, all through the tedious, never-ending testimony. I wondered if Uncle O.J. had even noticed.

Johnnie was much more comfortable in front of people than Clark or Darden had been. He had real presence. He continued for the rest of the day, summarizing the defense position. He knew how to appeal to the jurors. He began to quote scripture, talking about "deceivers" and "liars." And then he moved on to Mark Fuhrman. Mark Fuhrman was going to be his whipping boy. He called him a "perjurer," a "racist," and a "genocidal racist." He was really getting warmed up. *Where's he going with this?* I wondered. Pretty soon he said, "There was another man not long ago in the world who had these same views." Pausing briefly for maximum effect, he said, "People said he was just crazy . . . they didn't do anything about it." And then with great intensity he said, "This man, this scourge, became one of the worst people in the history of the world, Adolph Hitler, because people didn't care, or didn't try to stop him." Fuhrman as Hitler? "Yes!" I said. "Go Johnnie."

Johnnie's closing statement caused a furor. If you were black, Johnny's words made a lot of sense. The historic injustices against black people enabled all of us to identify with the kinds of social and political oppression that the Holocaust represented. But not everyone agreed. Some

CHAPTER 12

HOMECOMING

Thank God, I'd thought as I left the court after Johnnie's statement. A few days off. Nobody, least of all us, thought the jury would spend less than a week reviewing the evidence. In fact, we'd gotten together a little "pool" with my family, Gigi, and the security guards at the gates at Rockingham, taking bets among ourselves on which day the jury would come back. Nobody bet on less than a week. That meant I'd finally have some desperately needed downtime. I spent the weekend trying to relax. The VCR at my apartment was broken, so I went over to Rockingham and watched movies there. I just wanted to keep myself entertained and not think much. When I wasn't watching movies, I drank beer and slept. There wasn't much else to do. I hadn't talked to my friends for months. The trial had isolated me from everyone outside the family. So I didn't have anyone else to spend time with. Mom, Dad, and Grandma had flown home to San Francisco. Jason and

Arnelle had their own lives. It was mostly Kathy, Gigi, and me at Rockingham. A few other people came in and out, but it was mostly an uneventful time. It was as though time had stood still. I tried not to think about the verdict.

The jury had rested over the weekend, too, we were told, but by Monday they were in formal deliberations. That Monday my mother and father were still in San Francisco, the Dream Team was spread all over the state, and I was still stretched out on the couch at Rockingham. The attorneys were taking turns hanging out at the courthouse; Carl Douglas was on duty today. Uncle O.J. was back in jail, waiting. Right after lunch, a TV commentator noted that the jury had asked to see a portion of the transcript, the part where Alan Park had testified. Everyone assumed they were just working away, and nowhere near a verdict.

But then, about an hour and half later, another reporter broke in. Something was happening. A few minutes later, the reporter announced that a verdict had been reached. I couldn't believe it. *Already!* I thought. After an eight-month trial, they'd deliberated less than one day. I called Mom and Dad. They had already heard the news and were booking a flight with the rest of the family. The verdict would be read in court tomorrow morning. Frantic calls went out everywhere. Johnnie was in San Francisco, too. Gerry Uelman was in Santa Clara. No one had expected this to happen. I didn't know what to think. I was apprehensive.

As usual it was my job to pick people up at the airport. This time the whole family would be coming down, so we managed to round up three cars, and we went to meet them at the airport. They were all coming in on the same flight. As I stood at the gate waiting for them to come down the tunnel that leads off the plane, media were beginning to swarm around me. The word had gotten out that O.J.'s family was coming in on that flight. When they finally appeared, I was shocked at the immediate response from the reporters. As they hurried toward me, everyone looked as tired as I felt. Benny and Panzy were there, along with my sisters and their children. Grandma was in her wheelchair, and my sisters Tracy and Toni were pushing my baby niece and nephew in their strollers. As the reporters surged toward them, and the camera lights began flashing, the babies were frightened and started to cry. For a moment I was terrified that someone would accidentally hurt the children in all the chaos. I vividly remember standing there, feeling absolutely vulnerable. My loved ones looked so helpless at that moment, surrounded by the frenzied reporters, and I couldn't do anything to help them. *My God*, I thought. *If it's like this now, what will it be like tomorrow?*

Our cars were pulled up to the curb at the departure area, waiting, and for a few minutes we were overwhelmed just with the logistics of fitting in the strollers, the wheelchair, the various pieces of luggage, and the small crowd of family who'd come down to support each other. Nobody had known what to bring since they didn't know how long they'd need to stay. That would depend on the verdict. We caravaned back to Rockingham and unloaded everyone there. It was like a rerun of that day a year and a half before when we'd rushed down to help Uncle O.J. right after the murders. Once inside we tried to get the children settled and figure out where everyone was going to sleep. I'd take a couple of my sisters back to my place with me, but it would still be crowded. The house itself was pretty much of a mess. Various friends of Uncle O.J. had been camping there on and off along with my parents and Aunt Como, and with everything that had been going on, Gigi hadn't kept the place up to its usual standards. *Oh Lord*, I thought, glancing around. *This place is a wreck. What if Uncle O.J. comes home tomorrow? He'll have a fit when he sees this.*

Even at a time like that, I couldn't help realizing that my neatnik uncle would be horrified by the mess we'd all made in his home.

While Gigi tried to throw together some snacks, everyone around me was analyzing the situation. As more and more people arrived, the place buzzed with speculation. "Did the jury have time to fill out all those forms?" someone asked. *I give him a fifty-fifty chance,* I thought. Finally we all joined together for prayer, and as we all held hands, we seemed to share a common wish: let it be, Lord, let it be. Whatever happens tomorrow, let it be for your glory and Uncle O.J.'s soul. Give us strength to accept whatever comes, to comfort my uncle, and to love each other. Standing there, I felt a sense of peace overwhelm me for the first time in many days. It would be all right. Whatever happened tomorrow, it would be all right. I drove my brother and sister-in-law back to my place, and we all fell asleep. Morning would be there soon enough.

Somehow we all managed to get dressed and make our way to the courthouse in time the next day. I knew I wouldn't be in court for the verdict; with Jason and Arnelle and Grandma there, there was simply no way I or my siblings could fit on that bench. But we all wanted to be there in person when the verdict was announced, whichever way it went, so we pushed our way through the crowds and followed my parents into the courthouse—for the last time, we prayed.

It was even worse than usual that day. Tee-shirt vendors were offering shirts saying either "Guilty" or "Innocent," buyer's choice, and with little time left to make the shirts marketable, they were holding a last-minute clearance sale. Some of the shirts were going for as little as a dollar as the street hustlers yelled over the crowd, "Tee shirts! Get your tee shirts! Last chance for an O.J. tee shirt!'' They'd expected a few more shopping days, too.

Even when we made it through the carnival and through the courthouse doors, there was little improvement. As the chosen few in our family showed their passes to take their assigned seats in the courtroom, the rest of us went looking for a television monitor. The only place we could find one was in the media lounge, so we had no choice but to make our way directly into the lion's den. As we pushed our way through the crowds of reporters toward one of the monitors, microphones were being shoved in our faces right and left as people asked, ''Which way do you think the verdict is going to go?'' I barely remember what I said—something about ''hoping for the best.'' My mind was focused on finding a clear monitor and then planning an escape route for the moment the verdict came in.

By the time we made it through the crush, it was time for the verdict to be read. I knew that police throughout Los Angeles were on full tactical alert; everyone feared a public reaction like the one following the Rodney King verdict, and Police Chief Williams was taking no chances. I'd seen the lines of police cars as we'd approached the courthouse. When the moment finally came for which we'd waited eighteen grueling months to hear, I saw it on television with the rest of America. I didn't see my mother go flying over the railing and throw her arms around my uncle. As a matter of fact, the only thing I remember is an overpowering sense of relief as my brother and sisters and I burst into tears, and kept repeating, ''Thank you, Jesus. Thank you, God.'' We immediately joined hands and prayed while the press unsuccessfully tried to get our first impressions.

I know we somehow made our way out of that crowd and found our way to the courtroom downstairs that had been reserved for the press conference following the trial. The rest is a blur. The next thing I remember is sitting in the jury box in a nearby courtroom with my family while they asked us how we felt about the verdict. It was one of the stranger moments in that long, strange year. I could look down and see the attorneys being interviewed at their tables, and the press corps sitting in the same place I'd been sitting all that time. It wasn't the same courtroom, but otherwise everything was the same. Things looked different from the jury box, I thought. It was odd how just sitting there gave me a completely different perspective.

At last the press conference ended, and we were able to go home. The adrenaline was wearing off, and we were almost too exhausted to think. We managed to get back to our cars and make the long journey to Rockingham safely. Most of the conversation along the way was about the same thing: When will they finish releasing Uncle O.J.? When will we get to see him? Where should we meet him?

That question was answered for us much sooner than we'd expected—as soon, in fact, as we drove through the Rockingham gates. As we all started to pile out of our cars, the front door opened, and there stood Uncle O.J. One of the deputies had driven him home while we were all in the press conference. We couldn't believe he was standing there. For a minute it was like seeing a ghost. But then Mom and Aunt Como screamed with joy and went running to greet him. We all did. One after another we threw ourselves into his arms to congratulate him and tell him how much we loved him. It was pretty comical, really; my mother isn't a small woman, but she'd run and jumped on her brother like they were both still little kids. As I took my turn putting my arms around him, I couldn't help but notice that he didn't quite seem to be taking it all in. He was pleasant, but he seemed almost detached, more like he was going through the motions of a homecoming than really feeling the moment. Somebody said, "Isn't it wonderful to be home, O.J.?" and he looked at them with a blank expression.

Once inside, the party began. It wasn't much of a party compared to the old days at Rockingham, but it was a joyous occasion nonetheless.

When the verdict was read and we fell to our knees to thank God, we hoped it would be the beginning of a new, wonderful life for my uncle O.J. God had saved him, snatched him back from the edge of the pit. It was God's will, we told each other, God's will that he go through this terrible trial and be vindicated. If God wanted to teach him a lesson during his incarceration, Uncle O.J. seemed to be a slow learner.

From the day my uncle returned home from jail, the gates at Rockingham were thronged with female groupies I nicknamed "yard rats." Uncle O.J. had always attracted women like flies, and his incarceration had only increased his appeal to the young girls who spent their days at Rockingham. Celebrity prisoners are notorious for attracting groupies; Lyle Menendez and Richard Ramirez are only two famous examples of men who became more attractive behind bars. So when Uncle O.J. returned home after sixteen months in prison, there was no shortage of volunteers to meet his personal needs.

After a brief celebration interlude with Paula, he turned to the wider selection of women clustered literally on his front lawn. I use the word "women" loosely; most of them were little more than girls, barely over the legal limit. They would just show up in front of the gates at Rockingham, hang around, and make themselves available. They'd chat with the security guards Uncle O.J. had hired, and if they were cute enough, the guards would go inside and tell Uncle O.J. they had a good prospect for him. It was like Elvis at Graceland, sending his assistants out to the gate for the pick of the litter among the coeds gathered there. The chosen ones would be taken into the house to meet my uncle.

I wasn't certain what happened once they got inside, but I could guess. It didn't take a genius to figure out what was going on, and God knows, the girls were more than willing. If they all had something in common, it was a tight body and an empty head. They flirted outrageously with Uncle O.J., even in front of my parents. If it was a weekend, and my parents were with Grandma in San Francisco, the guards would meet me outside and tell me that Uncle O.J. didn't want to be disturbed. The house was "private" for the weekend. I'd think, *Here we go again*.

And where was Paula in all this? I wasn't entirely sure. As far as I remember, nobody saw her at Rockingham after he was released. It quickly became clear that she wasn't going to be a permanent fixture in Uncle O.J.'s life. For one thing, Uncle O.J.'s incarceration had been good for Paula's career. Her televised strolls past the jailhouse media hadn't gone unnoticed. As a matter of fact, her career had undergone a recent boom; she'd had three films released that year: a film from the series of erotic thrillers entitled *Red Shoe Diaries 5: Weekend Pass* and two "unrated films" entitled *Night Eyes 4: Fatal Passion* and *The Dangerous*. I wondered who held her Bible between shoots. What a woman. How she rationalized her dual lives I couldn't imagine.

Most of the yard rats who hung around Rockingham were merely irritating, but one of them began to worry me. I'll call her Alison. She was about twenty years old, with a botched bleach job. She did have a nice body and a very willing attitude, both of which seemed to be prerequisites for Uncle O.J. And she was white. What a surprise. A rumor had gotten to the family that Alison had some connection with Marcus Allen—that she used to work for him, or sleep with him, or both. I did know that she came from the same city Marcus Allen lived in and had only come to Los Angeles recently. All of this made me nervous. She didn't seem to be just another postteen from L.A. with nothing better to do than hang around Rockingham; there seemed to be some method in her madness.

One day I found myself alone in the kitchen with her and decided to see if I could get some information in the form of a friendly chat. So I said, "Well, Alison, how long have you lived in L.A.?" She mumbled something vague. Then I asked her, "So, what are you doing? Are you working? Or are you out here going to school?"

She said, "Oh, well, I'm thinking about doing both of them. I mean, I'm not really sure."

The rest of her answers were equally vague. Apparently she'd just turned up in Los Angeles with no job, no plans for school, no relatives or friends, no apparent reason for coming here, and happened to turn up at the gates of Rockingham. I said to my mother and father later that night, "Does Uncle O.J. have any idea that this chick didn't just happen in off the street? That she came to L.A. to meet him?" She was spending more time at Rockingham as the weeks went by. She seemed to be very uncomfortable at the house. Nobody was even sure who she was. Then I found out that her mother had come to town and met Uncle O.J. I thought, *Oh boy. Is he just too stupid to see that they're working him?*

It had already become clear to me that it would only take another little white blond girl with a good body for the whole cycle to start again. It was Nicole all over. But at least Nicole had had some substance, a willingness to work hard at contributing something to his life besides her body. I suggested to my dad that someone should try to talk to Uncle O.J. about what was going on with Alison, but that idea was quickly abandoned. My parents didn't want to interfere in his personal life, and I knew he wasn't interested in my opinion. He never had been. We knew from experience that once Uncle O.J. got involved with someone, accepting her was the price we had to pay if we wanted to be part of his life. He seemed to be slipping back into his old pattern.

All through the trial, we had discussed getting together to go on a vacation to celebrate as a family. But it never happened. Instead, Uncle O.J. chartered a plane so he could fly his buddies to Florida for a round of golf.

But, even if we'd actually made the trip we'd planned as a family, I couldn't help but wonder what it would have been like. The emergency caused by his arrest had drawn us together, but now that the crisis was over, what did we really have in common except blood? Uncle O.J.'s lifestyle and values were so different from my family's. My brother Bennie pointed out that it probably wasn't realistic to expect we could bridge a twenty year gap with Uncle O.J. in a few months. We'd been apart for nearly two decades. You don't make up for that kind of loss overnight.

CHAPTER 13

FALL FROM GRACE

When my mother exploded in fury at my suggestion that Uncle O.J. might be guilty, it was only the climax of a long, agonizing process of doubt for me. The violence that greeted my words that night in the car made very clear to me how high the price would be if I broke the family code. I could lose everything, everyone I knew and loved. The thought terrified me. So I shoved my doubts and my anger deep into my subconscious, and I tried to smother the voice crying to be heard in the depths of my heart. I must not listen to that voice, I told myself. I must find a way to silence it.

I found a way.

I'd rarely taken a drink before Nicole was murdered. It was easy enough to avoid. I didn't like the taste of alcohol, so it was no real temptation to me. I knew that there'd been some problem drinkers among my relatives, but since it never seemed to affect our lives, I hadn't paid much attention to it. It wasn't that I avoided alcohol, really; it was just that alcohol made me fall asleep. So, it was a nonissue for me.

One of the results of that indifference was that I had never really educated myself on the process of alcohol addiction. I'd never heard the term "self-medicate," so when I began to use alcohol to dull my own pain I didn't recognize what I was doing. Not that I would have paid attention at that point, anyway. I was too far out of touch with my own feelings to have any awareness of what was happening to me.

As with most alcoholics, my problem began gradually. At first it was just a glass of wine or beer in the evening to help me sleep. Once Uncle O.J. was incarcerated, the pressures of work and trial preparation had left me perennially exhausted and tense. It was hard to go to sleep at the end of the long days, and since my system wasn't used to alcohol, it was a highly effective sedative. A small amount would almost guarantee me a decent night's sleep. I soon began to depend on it to doze off in the evenings.

But as the months wore on and the pressures intensified, the internal pressure building up in me became unmanageable. I couldn't talk about my feelings to my family. I couldn't talk to my friends for fear of the press. I couldn't even admit them to myself, so I instinctively turned to chemical relief. As the holidays approached and jury selection wound to an end, the combined pressures drove me to the bottle more and more often. It was so much easier to shut out the pain with alcohol than to face it sober and alone. And as so often happens, I had a friend who was happy to help me do it.

I'd known Mary for a couple of years. She was a kind, motherly divorcee who lived in the neighborhood with her eight-year-old son. I'd stop at her house occasionally on the way home after visiting Uncle O.J. in jail, and she'd cook me a great meal and let me unwind. It was wonderfully comforting. With my parents still in San Francisco most of the time, and family pressures on me increasing, Mary offered me a safe place to be, a home of sorts and a sympathetic ear. Even though she was only a few years older than me, she was a mother figure in many ways. She had a real house, a set schedule with home-cooked meals, and a son. For me, it was the closest thing to home I could find.

The catch was that Mary drank. She'd been doing it as long as I'd known her, and on some level I thought she was an alcoholic. But it was easy to ignore that fact because I wanted to ignore it. At first I'd just have a couple of glasses of wine with her in the evening, but then it started growing. After a while I'd drink so much of her bottle that she'd feel deprived, and one of us would go out and buy another one. Pretty soon we were buying a second bottle every night, or I'd pick one up on the way over and bring it with me. I knew I was drinking more and more, but I rationalized that since I still didn't drink as much as Mary, it was all right. Every time the voice in my head gave me a warning, I'd say to myself, *But look at Mary. And it doesn't really affect her life. She goes to work, cleans house, takes care of her son, even plays on a softball team.* I'd play mind games with myself: as long as I don't drink as much as Mary does tonight, it's okay.

One night we drank two oversized bottles of wine in one evening, and when I woke up the next morning, I was too sick to function. After vomiting most of the morning, I told myself I'd never drink that much again. But of course, I did. Soon I was at Mary's house every night after court and on the weekends. She was my drinking buddy, and since I didn't want to go home, where I'd have to be alone,

I was soon sleeping at Mary's house much of the time. I was going home less and less. I completely lost interest in my own home. The dust piled up around the unopened mailbags, and my apartment gradually became almost uninhabitable.

Meanwhile the trial ended, and it was time for me to return to my so-called normal life, the life I had led before the murders. But I couldn't do it. I tried. I went back to my old job, which they'd held for me while I was on leave, and I tried to go back to being the old Terri. The problem was, that Terri no longer existed. Somewhere along the line I'd stopped being Terri Baker and become O.J. Simpson's niece.

Uncle O.J.'s name was still on the news nearly every night as the custody dispute with the Browns over Justin and Sydney went into full swing and the backlash that followed the criminal trial descended with hurricane force. It was clear that the trial wasn't over for anyone in America. Outrage over Uncle O.J.'s acquittal poured from everyone's mouth. An economic boycott was launched against him, and pressure put on the networks to keep him from speaking out on television. Clearly, whatever the jury had said, he'd been judged and found guilty in the eyes of the American public. The Goldmans, and then the Browns, followed through on their threat to sue him in civil court.

Trying to function in a competitive work environment under the circumstances became more and more difficult. The buzz about Uncle O.J. was in the air all around me. My boss was getting frustrated with my deteriorating work performance, and with every week that went by, I felt more desperate. I was breaking down, and I didn't know how to stop the process.

The signs I was disintegrating were everywhere. My health was going rapidly downhill. I started getting bruises, huge bruises all over my body, as the iron level in my blood dropped. Then the nausea started. At first the nausea would come from drinking too much and not having enough food. After a while I'd just drink all evening and never eat at all. Eventually I had trouble keeping food down, period. I was going to the doctor more and more often for various complaints, but they didn't realize what was going on, so they just gave me something for the nausea and assumed I had the flu. My resistance was so poor, I was vulnerable to every flu bug that came along anyway.

Then one night I injured myself more seriously. I'd been sitting in a chair at my house watching TV and drinking all evening, with one leg propped up on the back of the couch. At some point I fell asleep, or more likely passed out. There was a floor heater under my leg, and it was cold that night, so I'd turned it on and wrapped up in a blanket before I sat down. By the time I woke up the next morning, with the television and heater still going full blast, the heater had burned huge blisters on the back of my right leg. I'd sat there all night with the flesh on my leg burning and not even felt it.

I patched my leg up as best I could by myself. It was very painful, but I couldn't think of a plausible explanation for letting my leg burn all night, so I wanted to cover up what had happened. The blisters took a long time to heal, though, and eventually my family noticed, and said, "What happened to your leg?" I tried to explain, but they looked at me so strangely that I knew they were puzzled. I still have deep scars on that leg that have never faded.

For a long time I used Mary's house as an escape and an excuse to drink. But, I was gradually getting to the point where any human contact was too much for me. All I wanted was to be alone, to lie on the couch and watch TV, and not have to deal with anybody. So I started going home again after work and on the weekends, but now I was stopping at the 7-Eleven on the way home every night to buy a six-pack of beer. Once I got home, I could tune out everybody and just curl up in front of the TV and drink until my mind was a blank. Pretty soon I stopped seeing Mary. I still made it to work most of the time, but it was getting harder and harder to get up in the morning as time went on. My family knew something was wrong, but they didn't know what. My drinking was still a closely guarded secret. And then I started having real trouble. I was beginning to have blackouts, and when they were over, I had no idea what I had said or done. I was frightened for myself.

It all came to a head with my family one night not long after the trial ended. I'd come home, taken off my work clothes, and started drinking in front of the television when my mother called me. That night I had a bottle of hard liquor, and when my mother called me to complain about something, she caught me at the wrong time. I lost my temper and began yelling at her. At some point in the argument, I blacked out. The last thing I remember is standing there partially dressed, screaming into the receiver at my mother.

Apparently I was incoherent by then, so my mother hung up and called my sister Tracy and said, "Call Terri. There's something wrong with her. She doesn't sound right." When I didn't answer the phone, my parents really panicked. They were in San Francisco at the time, so they called my best friend Jerry, who lives in Glendale, and said they were really worried about me.

By that time it was 2:00 A.M., but Jerry threw on some clothes and drove over to my house to see if I was all right. Meanwhile, Mom had called my cousin Jason in L.A. to tell him what was going on. Jerry and Jason got there about the same time and started knocking on my door, but I didn't answer, and they couldn't get in because the door was locked. My car was sitting outside, so they knew I must be in there. My neighbor from across the street, saw all the commotion and came running over to find out what was going on. Finally, when they couldn't rouse me, they went upstairs to my upstairs neighbor, who knew where I kept an extra key. Once they got in, they found me wandering aimlessly around my apartment in my underwear, talking nonsense, unaware that anything was wrong. My only memory of that evening is a flashback of bright lights in my little apartment, and of me standing in the living room in my bra and panties looking at all of them asking, "What are you doing here?"

Amazingly enough, they still didn't realize what was wrong with me. A little while later I fell sound asleep, and my neighbor slept on the couch nearby so I wouldn't be alone. Either Jerry or Jason called my family, and my sister Gyne took the next flight out of San Francisco and was at my house by 7:30 the next morning, before I even woke up. When I finally did wake up, I had no memory of the night before, but I did manage to concoct an excuse to explain my behavior. It's incredible how good I'd gotten by then at covering my drinking. I told them I'd accidentally taken too much medication, and I must have had a bad reaction. I'd seen a psychiatrist a while back for the posttraumatic stress, and she had prescribed an antidepressant and a sedative to help me sleep. But since I was drinking by then, I was too afraid to take the pills because I knew mixing them with alcohol could be deadly. Still, it made a great excuse. I don't know what Gyne thought, but she stayed two or three days to take care of me; and the whole time she was there, I was sneaking sips from a bottle I'd hidden under a slipcover. As soon as she left, I started drinking all over again.

Looking back on it, I'm amazed that I kept working in the middle of it all. I desperately wanted out of there by then, but I didn't know where to go. I kept thinking, if I stop working for Polo, what am I going to do? How will I survive? The worse my work performance got, the more the tension built, and the more I drank. The more I drank, the worse my work performance got. And so on. I was caught in a downward spiral.

My friend Alexa who knew I was unhappy at work asked, "What do you want to do? You can do anything you want." But the problem was, I didn't want to do anything. I had lost all interest in life. All my life I'd been such a high achiever. I had an exciting job; I'd lived in Europe; I'd started my own business. Now nothing interested me. Nothing seemed important. Certainly not myself. I had been torn away from my old life the day my mother called me in Las Vegas to say Nicole was dead, and I couldn't readjust. Even the trial ending had given me no real relief, just a different set of problems. At least with the trial I'd had a purpose, a reason to get up in the morning. Now there was nothing.

In the constant state of emergency I'd lived in for the last year and a half, I had never had the luxury of emotionally processing what I was experiencing, much less recovering from the trauma. In a ten-day period the previous June, I'd gone from living a relatively sheltered life to a relentless series of horrific events. Within a week I had stood in the middle of a gruesome double-murder scene, attended Nicole's open-casket wake, gone to the funeral and burial service, watched as my uncle threatened suicide for several hours, been ejected from a family home by a SWAT team, and sat in maximum security at County Jail while my celebrity uncle was led out to us in shackles, accused of murdering my aunt. And all of this had happened while helicopters and telephoto lenses ripped my family's privacy from our hands. The grueling months of jail visits and the trial had depleted my physical and psychological resources. I longed to cry, but the tears would not come.

The day came when I couldn't go to work anymore. I didn't see Mary anymore. I didn't see anyone. I quit taking care of my hair, and after a while I even quit bathing. When life becomes intolerable, you find a way to end it. I didn't put a gun to my head, but I was killing myself nonetheless. Liquor is a powerful weapon, and I was using it to destroy myself. I'd drink until I passed out, and when I woke up again in the middle of the night, I'd drink until I passed out again. And each time I'd think, *Maybe I'll just close my eyes this time, and I won't wake up again.*

I pulled the drapes shut, and I unplugged the phone, and I quit eating. There was so much junk on the floor I could hardly walk. I couldn't handle the simplest task. Even getting up for another drink was too much trouble. I filled up an ice chest and put it by my bed so all I would have to do was just reach over and grab another beer. Then I didn't have to get out of bed at all. I could just stay there forever.

Talk about hitting bottom. All those months I'd lived in fear, hiding my drinking from the people around me, terrified everyone would say, "Oh, look at her. She's crazy. She's an alcoholic." One night early in April, 1996, I woke up from an alcohol haze, and thought, *I don't care what they think anymore. If someone doesn't help me, I'm going to die.* I hadn't gotten out of bed or eaten for days. I'd reached a level of absolute desperation. So I picked up a phone in the middle of the night, and called my brother Benny. He understood and suggested I call my parents. I said, "You know all the things about me that have been happening to me that you can't figure out? Well, I've been drinking. I drink every day. I'm an alcoholic. I don't want to live anymore. I just want to die." And I meant it.

"What do you mean, you've been drinking?" my mother asked me. Although my parents didn't really understand, they were concerned for me. "Do whatever you have to do to get well," they said, sounding relieved. "We'll help you." By the next morning my sister Tracy was already looking for a place to take me. She called Betty Ford first, but they said it would be a two- or three-week waiting period, and I knew I couldn't wait. I had good health insurance, so two days later we found a place in Orange County that said they could take me right away. A short while later someone from the rehab clinic called and told me someone would come to pick me up in the morning. My friend Richard came over to wait with me until they came.

The following day, a driver from Orange County Community Hospital pulled up in a black Continental, helped me make the long journey from my bed to the driveway, and put me in the backseat of the car. I stretched out on the cool leather and slept all the way to the clinic. When we arrived an hour or so later, he woke me up and took me inside to start my new life.

CHAPTER 14

THROUGH THE LOOKING GLASS

Orange County Community Hospital is an unremarkable structure near the Santa Ana Freeway, in a quaint little community just miles from Disneyland. The flat, one-story building is divided into clinics designed to serve two different segments of the population. As you enter the building, those who go to the right find themselves in a clinic designed to treat various kinds of chemical addiction. If you go to the left, you enter an AIDS clinic serving those in the advanced stages of AIDS who either suffer from addiction problems or who are at the point of death. I was taken to the right-hand wing. When I felt a tendency to despair those first weeks there, I would catch a glimpse of the AIDS patients who were quarantined behind the windows across the courtyard. Somehow, it gave me hope.

Rehab is a strange place, a place most of us never expect to be. As I was taken in that first day, everything and everyone around me seemed strange, foreign. What was I doing in a place like this? *They look so weird*, I thought as I looked at the other patients around me; and then I thought, *Who am I kidding? I probably look stranger than they do at this point*. The staff was kind and professional. I met Dave Patterpoff, the director of the center, a very sweet man.

After being processed in, I was taken to a doctor for a physical exam and some lab tests, assigned a counselor and a psychiatrist named Dr. Heffner to administer medication, and then assigned to the room I would be living in for the next few weeks. The room was plain: two twin beds, two desks, and two side tables. Everyone had a roommate. The doctor gave me a sedative, and I immediately fell asleep. I went in on a Thursday and slept most of Friday, Saturday, and Sunday. I remember very little about those days. I dimly remember being wakened for meals and meetings. From the beginning my days there were very regimented: meals, meetings, bedtime, activities of all kinds were carefully regulated for each of us. I accepted it all passively, without thought or protest. I felt like a little child again. I just wanted somebody to take care of me and would have done pretty much anything they'd told me. I had no will of my own anymore. I'd given up.

Several times a day I went to group sessions and to one-on-one sessions with my counselor and psychiatrist. Their analysis of my condition was that my lethargy and despair were connected to deep anger that had turned inward and begun destroying me in the form of depression. Because I couldn't face my anger at those around me, I had turned it against myself. Not only was I mad at my uncle, they said; I was deeply angry with my mother. I had to deal with the anger, they advised me, or the depression and the alcohol addiction would continue.

I found their analysis baffling, incomprehensible. What

did they mean, pent-up anger? I wasn't mad at anyone, especially my mom. I was just tired and sad, I told myself. After I'd been there about a week, they finally took me into a weight room, put boxing gloves and a shield on themselves, and tried to get me to hit them. They egged me on, by insulting me. But I wouldn't fight back. Eventually they even hit me with the gloves, but I still wouldn't fight back. I just stood there. After a while I laughed at them and said, "You'll have to do a lot more than that to get me mad!"

Finally they gave up the boxing idea and had me write letters. The letters weren't the kind you actually send to people; they were therapeutic letters where I could pour out all my feelings without fear of what the person I wrote to might say. It was then, as I wrote those letters, that the anger started coming up. The first letter I wrote was to Uncle O.J., then one to my mother, and one to Grandma. I was astonished by how much pain, anger, and frustration were in those letters.

All the feelings I'd been storing up over the years came pouring out. I was angry at my family for taking me for granted and not respecting any of my thoughts or feelings that differed from their own. I was just supposed to go along with the family and keep my mouth shut. I remembered the rage I'd felt the day during the trial when I'd raised the possibility that Uncle O.J. had committed the murders, and my mother's violent reaction. All the opinions I wasn't allowed to express, all the questions I wasn't supposed to ask. Then I went back in my mind ten years, to the day my theft of Carla's money was discovered; I remembered the humiliation of that moment, and how Uncle O.J. had stood silent after Nicole and her sisters had searched my apartment. I could see Nicole's face as she called me a thief, and her sisters' faces years later as they repeated the insult on the day Uncle O.J. almost killed himself. I remembered the nude photos I'd done, the shame and humiliation of its publication, and my mother's voice saying, "Why do you need to see a therapist?" We never talked about that, either. It was another shame that had to remain unspoken.

And for the first time in my life, I saw clearly that the sense of inferiority I felt in those moments had been with me all my life. On the outside I had been an achiever, the one who made my parents proud; but on the inside I had absorbed a deep sense of "not good enough," never fitting in with the people I loved the most. Uncle O.J.'s trial had simply brought to the surface a pain I'd been feeling for most of my life. It was the catalyst that brought out the symptoms of my hidden disease; alcohol had been my "pain reliever."

A few days after I entered the Orange County facility, my parents came to visit me. I had mixed feelings about their coming; I wanted their support, but I was embarrassed to have them see me there. My oldest sister Cindy came with them, and I was relieved to have her there. She served as a kind of buffer, lessening the awkwardness of the situation. My counselor talked with them, giving them the results of my medical tests, and suggesting to them that I stay in an inpatient sober-living environment for a while when I left. I was adamantly against it at the time.

The counselor also suggested that my parents come back and do some family sessions with me, to help me work through some issues. My hopes rose at this idea. But, they were noncommittal, and it was clear they didn't want to be involved in the therapy process. They would visit me while I was there, but that would be the extent of it. I was disappointed; if nothing else, I just wanted them to listen to me.

They did go to a meeting with me later on, and I remember how impressed everybody was with them. Nobody recognized them from the trial, but everybody loved them and kept commenting on what great parents I had. After the meeting people kept coming up to me and saying things like, "God, your dad is so cool and your mom is so great. You're so lucky—your parents are the best." It was confusing; I felt consumed by guilt all over again. If my parents were so perfect, why was I so mad at them? *There is something wrong with me,* I thought for the thousandth time. *My parents shouldn't even have to see me in a place like this.*

Mom and Dad tried to support me in their own way, but it was hard for them. They went through the motions, doing what they thought was right, but emotionally they kept their distance. During the three months I spent in rehabilitation, they visited me three times. I couldn't help but contrast it with the way they'd visited Uncle O.J. in jail; they were there every day they could manage it. True, I had chosen to be where I was, unlike my uncle, but the contrast troubled and sometimes angered me. We'd always been there for other family members with illnesses or operations, taking shifts at the hospital when necessary. But now, when I needed their participation the most, they backed away. Everyone in my family thought I'd be all right if I just got ahold of myself and went back to work. I couldn't go back yet. My family was distrustful of the recovery process, and they didn't know how to deal with the reality of my alcoholism. To this day they're uncomfortable with the fact that I'm an alcoholic, even a recovering one.

I can understand their hesitation; it was hard for me to grasp, too.

Maybe I'm not really an alcoholic, I thought at first. But as I worked through what I was learning, two things stood out for me. First, even though I hadn't started drinking until later in life, the emotions that led to it had been going on throughout my teens and twenties. The trial had been the catalyst, but not the cause. The moment I took that first drink to numb the pain, the compulsion was triggered in my body. Second, I'd had at least two black outs, something that never happens to simply social drinkers. I couldn't remember certain periods of time because my mind had never recorded them in the first place. This was another sign of the alcoholism. As I listened and thought about what I heard in the meetings, I gradually came to understand what had happened to me.

One of the things I learned during recovery, is that honest communication is a healing factor. In my family we don't confront issues in an honest dialogue, we just live with them. Uncle O.J.'s trial was just the most obvious example. From the day we got the call telling us Nicole was dead, nobody ever asked even the simplest, most obvious questions. It was as if the problems would just go away if nobody talked about them. I thought about my own mistakes, and my parents' unwillingness to talk about what had happened to me. Why would their daughter be so ashamed to ask for money that she would stoop to stealing and degrading herself to get it? And I thought of all the other things they were terrified to acknowledge.

I wasn't the first one in my family with an alcohol problem, but no one had ever talked about it. It wouldn't look good for our family. I thought about all the things no one ever said about my uncle such as the rumors about his womanizing and problems with Nicole.

I thought about my grandfather. More than one book about Uncle O.J. had claimed Grandpa was gay. But I never heard anyone in my family talk about it. I have a lot of gay friends and was old enough to recognize my grandfather' lifestyle. I thought back to the days right before Grandpa died, when I'd sat with him at his home during his last days on earth. As I sat next to him watching TV, a program about gay issues came on, and I said with irritation, "Those damned guys! I'm sick of them!" The moment the words slipped out of my mouth, I wanted to take them back. There was a stabbing pain in my heart. I couldn't look at my grandfather. Why had I said it? I didn't even mean it, not really. I loved my grandfather so much; I would never willingly hurt him. A short time later he died. I never got to talk to him about it, to tell him I loved him whatever the truth was. It remains one of my biggest regrets.

In rehab, though, I got to talk. I got to say all the things I'd been storing up for years. Nobody knew or cared that I was O.J. Simpson's niece; I was just Terri, and they accepted me on that basis. After the first few days, I felt more at home with the people there than I'd ever felt with anyone. In the important ways, we were all so much alike. I recognized in them so many of my own feelings: the loneliness, the pain, the sadness, and the anger that had brought me to this place of healing. Our talks together made the other conversations I'd had in my life seem so shallow by comparison. We talked about what mattered to us with an honesty I'd never encountered. None of us had anything to lose; simply being in that place together, struggling to recover, gave us a powerful sense of community and mutual support. There was no false pride, no pressure to keep up a certain image of ourselves. For over a year I'd been unable to cry; I'd drunk to ease the pain. Now for the first time I could cry. Facing and talking about my feelings released them, and without alcohol to stifle them, a wellspring of tears came up. I felt like a crying machine; I'd cry until I was exhausted, and then I'd sleep more deeply than I had since I was a child.

It was healing. And after a while there was fun, too. My new friends and I would sit around the tables in the courtyard in the evenings to tell poignant stories about ourselves and laugh. After an hour or so of Ping-Pong, it felt like summer camp. There was a joyous sense of release to those evenings. The facility was as bare as could be with its white walls and plain furniture, but as the days passed, I became comfortable there. When I'd first arrived, I'd been anxious to get out of there, but now I dreaded leaving. I didn't want to go back to my apartment; I didn't even want to take phone calls from the outside. I didn't want to see or talk to anyone from my old life. That life was filled with pain. This new life gave me hope, promise. The thought of returning to the place I'd come from filled me with terror.

As the alcohol left my system and the sedatives wore off, I began to regain my appetite. At a certain point most alcoholics stop eating, so the place was kept well stocked with nutritious, sometimes fattening food, and the refrigerator was filled with juices. I began eating again with a vengeance—three meals a day plus snacks. I put on a lot of weight, but I didn't care. It was fun, part of the "being at camp" feeling. One day they even had us do "crafts," posters to represent our lives. We sat around together on this old Salvation Army couch and folding chairs and made posters that included images of our lives. I don't remember exactly what mine looked like, but I do remember the insightful comments people made about it. There were images of my family structure and even of the trial. I was startled and intrigued by the process of self-discovery I'd begun to undergo.

I stayed at Orange County Community Hospital for two weeks, until the detoxification portion of my treatment was over, and then I transferred to their daycare program.

Many of the people I'd come to know from Orange County were there, and we continued the therapy and group sessions together. When the time came, I left that program and entered a sober-living facility for a few weeks longer, preparing for my reentry into the "real world." On June 8, two months and one day after that black Lincoln had picked me up and saved my life, I returned home. The old Terri didn't go home that day, though; a new person did. I wasn't quite sure who she was yet, but I was beginning to like her. Like Alice, I had stepped through the looking glass, and there was no going back.

I came home frightened but determined to get on with my life. The months of recovery had left me energized, refreshed. I was frightened, but I was also excited and determined to put into practice all the things I'd learned "inside." Predictably, I was headed for a fall, though not in the way anyone could have predicted. My first few days at home went remarkably well. I continued to attend meetings with a support group every day, and they were my lifeline. Many of the meetings were at clubhouses or elementary schools, public places where we could meet without cost.

About a week after I came home, I went over to Rockingham with a friend. I was a little nervous because I didn't know how much Uncle O.J. knew about what had happened with me. I was afraid Uncle O.J. would say, "Where have you been?" But instead, when I said I could only stay a few minutes because I was on my way to a meeting, he asked, "Is it the one at the church down on San Vicente?" It was his way of letting me know that he understood what was going on.

I was very surprised that he knew the location, so I said,

"Yeah. How did you know about that?" He explained that an old girlfriend of his had gone to meetings there all the time. I was pleasantly surprised that he was open-minded about my going to meetings, that he didn't attach a stigma to it like I'd expected. But it was Uncle O.J.'s assistant, Kathy Randa, who touched me the most. We would sit out front at Rockingham sometimes and talk about all the things that were going on in our lives. She encouraged me so much to continue what I was doing, and to my amazement, she told me she was proud of me. It took a lot of courage, she told me, to do what I did.

I didn't feel very brave. One night as I was sitting in a meeting, the speaker got up at the podium and asked, "How many of you are afraid to die?" A lot of people raised their hands. Then he said, "When I was drinking, I was afraid to *live!*" I immediately identified with him. My life felt overwhelming, unmanageable. I was afraid to open my letters, afraid they'd contain bad news, or bills I couldn't pay, or news that they were coming to arrest me because I hadn't paid them. I looked to Monika for guidance during that difficult time. Monika, the woman who had become my sponsor, was warm and supportive, with a crisp German accent and a straightforward manner. I liked her the minute I met her. She had a calming influence on me. I thought of her as an example of the kind of woman I hope to become: independant, confident with herself and others.

I began the process of gradually stepping back into my family, of finding a place for myself in their midst. Now that there was no alcohol to cloud my judgment, I was objective enough to realize that although some things about my family system were unhealthy, there was little I could do to change it. My family and I had danced around each other for years. We had not confronted issues that affected all of our lives—particularly our relationship with Uncle O.J. We put him on a pedestal and left him there, always concerned about his life, his career, his image, or his money before our own. I realized how unhealthy it was for me and knew I couldn't dance anymore. If I wanted to be respected, I was going to have to stand up for myself and demand it.

When Uncle O.J. had first been incarcerated, my grandmother had said that God would use this experience to work good in Uncle O.J.'s life. But there's another saying about life's trials and tribulations, one that gets printed on bumper stickers and pins: God isn't finished with me yet. As it turned out, God wasn't finished with Uncle O.J. The Browns and the Goldmans had filed a civil suit against Uncle O.J. for the wrongful deaths of Nicole and Ron. This lawsuit could not result in criminal penalties but in financial sanctions if Uncle O.J. was convicted, which seemed entirely possible since a civil conviction only required a numerical majority of the jury, not a unanimous vote. *Not again,* I thought.

CHAPTER 15

CIVIL LIBERTIES

Uncle O.J.'s second trial began on October 23, 1996. So much of it was going to be a repeat of the criminal trial: the constant media pressure, the loss of privacy, the daily inconveniences of attending a trial. But I knew there would also be important differences this time around. The location had changed, the cast of characters was new, and the rules for a civil trial were different. More importantly, I wasn't the same. I wasn't the naive young woman who had accepted whatever the defense had to say. This time I was going in with my eyes and ears wide-open. I was no longer willing just to accept what Uncle O.J. said on faith. I wanted answers.

The days before the civil trial had been full of news about Uncle O.J. and the other players in the new trial. The whole Mark Fuhrman affair had come to a head. Three weeks earlier he had pleaded no contest to a charge of perjury in the criminal trial. He was given a $200 fine and three years probation. A lot of people, including me, thought he got off easy.

Bob Kardashian, arguably Uncle O.J.'s closest friend through the long ordeal of the criminal trial, had recently expressed public doubts about Uncle O.J.'s innocence. Now Bob was being investigated by the State Bar Association for violating professional ethics by expressing those doubts. He wasn't hanging around Rockingham anymore, and he wouldn't be at Uncle O.J.'s side the way he had been for the criminal trial. No one in the family talked about him much. He was the first one in the inner circle of Uncle O.J.'s friends to break rank publicly.

Johnnie's book *Journey to Justice* had just arrived in bookstores. Opinion polls showed that the public was hoping for revenge in the civil trial. Women's rights advocates had taken on Uncle O.J. as a cause; Nicole had become a national symbol of abuse against women, inspiring candlelight vigils and crowds of protesters. And a long list of much less savory people were protesting, too: racists and bigots were finding a sympathetic audience among disgruntled whites.

Uncle O.J. had been making his own contributions to the media circus, too. To say the least, he wasn't being discreet. His purported public flirtations with a variety of women were raising eyebrows and attracting the kind of remarks from journalists and commentators that could damage public opinion and his case in the civil trial. Worse yet, the amount of time he spent on golf courses was the subject of frequent media sarcasm. He didn't seem to realize that his public image was in desperate need of rehabilitation. And to compound matters, he was making frequent statements to the press that did more harm than good. His attorneys certainly weren't happy about his behavior, but they had little control over him. When he'd been incarcerated during the criminal trial, the Dream Team had been able to carefully monitor his statements. This defense team, however, had to deal with an O.J. who was free to do and say whatever he wanted.

This was no "Dream Team" ready to put up with the whims of a celebrity client. Uncle O.J.'s attorneys for the civil trial were very different from those in the criminal trial. Bob Baker, his son Phil, Bob Blasier, and Dan Leonard were preparing Uncle O.J.'s defense. They were straight-arrow white guys: no flashy suits, no deep suntans, no Hollywood connections. They had no interest in the limelight, no need to promote their careers, and no patience with nonsense. They were hardworking professionals who had nothing to prove and a long list of powerful clients. When they gave instructions they fully expected them to be followed. But, of course, this was impossible with Uncle O.J. He let them know right away that he was in charge, and that he had no intention of letting them dictate what he could or couldn't say in public. It made for some tense moments. Bob Baker had an uphill battle from day one.

Since this was a civil trial, the prosecutors from the district attorney's office had been replaced by a whole team of lawyers acting on the behalf of the plaintiffs. It was no longer the State of California pursuing Uncle O.J., but a bunch of gray-suited private attorneys. The Browns had hired John Kelly; the Goldmans Daniel Petrocelli and Peter Gelblum; and Sharon Rufo, Ron Goldman's biological mother, had hired Michael Brewer. This was a very different group of people from the team headed by Marcia Clark and Chris Darden. This time around the court battle would not be a clash of personalities. There would be no preaching, no pouting, no playing to the camera. This would be a high-stakes legal chess game. I hoped that Bob Baker had the moves—and Uncle O.J. would trust him to do his job.

The venue was a dramatic change as well. The Santa Monica courthouse could hardly have been more different from the one downtown. Downtown L.A. is gritty, densely populated, and surrounded by ethnic communities. The criminal-trial jury represented an ethnic mix not unlike the one where Uncle O.J. grew up in San Francisco. The jury that acquitted him was made up of nine blacks, two whites, and one Hispanic.

The Santa Monica courthouse, however, was a modest, low-rise building two blocks from the beach. Fortunately for me, it was also a much easier drive than the long trek downtown had been. A couple of blocks away from the courthouse was the upscale Third Street Promenade, a trendy shopping street filled with mostly white, affluent people like most of Uncle O.J.'s friends the last twenty years.

The chances of getting a predominantly black jury in Santa Monica were slim. If opinions about Uncle O.J.'s guilt or innocence were divided along ethnic lines—and they certainly were—then the balance of opinion in Santa Monica was strongly tilted in favor of his guilt. This wasn't going to be an easy audience for Uncle O.J. to convince. He was going to have to play it straight and honest with the civil jury. *If he tries to bullshit them,* I thought, *he'll lose.*

The judge assigned to Uncle O.J.'s case was the stern and impassive Hiroshi Fujisaki. It had seemed to me in the criminal trial that the choice of Judge Ito was no coincidence. *He's Asian,* I thought, *neither white nor black.* When Judge Fujisaki was appointed, I thought, *This definitely can't be a coincidence, either.* Although the trial wasn't supposed to be about race, it struck me that an Asian judge, in both trials, was a politically correct, safe decision. And a clever one, too. Judge Ito had been strongly criticized for letting things get out of hand in the criminal trial. He had loved the media and the celebrities, deferred to the attorneys, and allowed the trial to drag on forever.

But Judge Fujisaki, we had heard, would be very different. He had a reputation as a strict disciplinarian. He was expected to move the trial along quickly, and show great impatience with any and all attempts to slow things down. He disliked the media and celebrities, would not allow cameras in the courtroom, and was decisive to the point of being dictatorial. And he didn't care what anybody thought of him. He was retiring right after the trial.

Compared to the criminal trial, jury selection went quickly. Six days before opening statements a twelve-member jury was sworn in, and eight alternates were selected the next day. The civil jury was the mirror-opposite of the criminal jury. It was comprised of seven women and five men. Eight jurors were white, two black, one Hispanic, and one racially mixed. The juror of mixed race described himself as "half-black and half-Asian." The alternates were made up of five men and three women of which five were white, two black, and one Hispanic. Bob Baker made a motion to overrule the plaintiff's challenges to five potential black jurors, arguing that the objections were racially motivated. Judge Fujisaki, setting a tone that would continue throughout the trial, promptly denied it.

On the day of opening statements, my parents were in court in Orange County, with Uncle O.J. where he was battling the Browns for custody of Sydney and Justin. Grandma Simpson and I would be the family representatives for the opening day of the civil trial. Ironically, it was Grandma Simpson's seventy-fifth birthday. But there would no party today. No one was in a party mood, anyway. I loaded Grandma's wheelchair into the back of my car and helped her get in the front seat for the short ride. The front of the place was mobbed with reporters and cameras. Like the criminal trial, there were also crowds of protesters carrying signs both supporting and condemning Uncle O.J. They made me uneasy. I knew Grandma was aware of them. I pulled around to the back of the building and parked. I got Grandma in her chair and wheeled her in through the rear entrance. The scene inside the court-room, however, was very different from what I had experi-enced the year before. There were no cameras, no mobs, no disorder. The familiar faces in the press were quiet and reserved, and when Judge Fujisaki entered, it was clear that things would move along quickly.

Daniel Petrocelli led off for the plaintiffs. O.J. Simpson, he argued, was a murderer. The Goldmans had made a point of referring to Uncle O.J. in public as a murderer as well. It angered me because he had been acquitted in a court of law. Before the trial began, the judge ordered them to stop making public statements. Petrocelli then reviewed a long list of evidence he would introduce to support that allegation. There was going to be a lot of new evidence in this trial, material that had not been allowed in the criminal proceeding. The plaintiffs intended to talk about the slow-speed chase, Uncle O.J.'s suicide note, his lie-detector test, and his interview with LAPD on June 13, 1994. None of this had been introduced by the prosecution in the criminal trial. Petrocelli also made it clear that he was going to review blood evidence that he considered to be conclusive proof of Uncle O.J.'s guilt. *Do they have any-thing new?* I wondered.

It was clear that Petrocelli had taken a look at the evi-dence against Uncle O.J. and reached some conclusions that were at odds with the prosecution in the criminal trial. He announced that he planned to show that the murders took place between 10:35 P.M. and 10:40 P.M., rather than at 10:15 P.M. as Marcia Clark had argued. He said that the testimony of Robert Heidstra would establish this time table. He also planned to introduce a photograph from the *National Enquirer* that reputedly showed Uncle O.J. in a pair of Bruno Magli shoes. In a deposition taken before the trial, Uncle O.J. had denied ever owning such shoes. Uncle O.J. was going to have to testify at this trial. *This is going to be great,* I thought. *He'll finally clear up all the questions.*

Bob Baker got his chance the next day. His strategy was considerably different from Johnnie's. Adopting the approach that the best defense was a good offense, he was planning to discredit the victim. Bob opened with an attack on Nicole. He described her as a woman out of control. Nicole, he said, had a problem with alcohol, drugs, and promiscuity. She had "many boyfriends," and brought "prostitutes and drug users" into her condo. She pursued Uncle O.J. after the divorce, he asserted. Uncle O.J. was angry at Nicole because of her behavior, and in fact, it was Nicole's own "behavior and lifestyle" that led her to have "enemies." Then he argued that the police had acted improperly in their investigation, and said that all the evidence they had gathered was, at best, suspect. He mentioned the testimony of Henry Lee in the criminal trial, and said that something was very wrong with the blood evidence. The *Enquirer* photo, he said, was a fake. In regard to the abuse allegations, he argued, Uncle O.J. hadn't "touched Nicole in anger" since 1989.

Nothing made much of an impression on me for the first two weeks of the trial. It was pretty much the same things I'd heard a dozen times before. But during the third week, on a Wednesday, the plaintiffs introduced evidence of Uncle O.J. wearing a pair of Bruno Magli shoes. A shoe specialist testified about pictures of Uncle O.J. and authenticated the Bruno Magli make and model. Prints of a pair of that same rare type of shoes had been found at the Bundy crime scene. Uncle O.J. had steadfastly maintained that he'd never owned a pair of those "ugly-ass shoes." But here were the pictures. Later on, dozens of other photos would be introduced into evidence by other photographers, photos showing him in those same shoes. I wondered what Uncle O.J. was going to say about it when they put him on the stand.

After a Thanksgiving recess Kato Kaelin took the stand. Kato testified about the mysterious bumps he'd heard outside his bedroom the night of the murder and admitted that he might have heard them as late as 10:50 P.M. Kato also said that on the day of the murders Uncle O.J. was angry at Nicole, and that he had said she was playing "hardball" with him. Nicole was "restricting his access" to Justin and Sydney, Kato said, and Uncle O.J. was thinking of reporting Nicole to the IRS in retaliation. Kato also testified that Uncle O.J. owned a dark sweat suit, the same kind the plaintiffs were claiming he wore to commit the murders. I wondered how his memory could have improved so much after two years. On cross-examination Bob Baker went after Kato's testimony by suggesting that he was trying to sensationalize his testimony to further a book deal. I wondered how much Kato had been certain of in either trial. He didn't exactly have a photographic memory. I doubted he'd put together some elaborate plot to discredit Uncle O.J. But I also knew he'd had plenty of time to absorb all the media theories about what had happened that night. Besides the fact that he'd heard thumps, I was pretty sure his memories of that evening were a haze.

Testimony resumed the next day with FBI Special Agent William Bodziak. Bodziak testified that the shoes Uncle

O.J. had worn in the disputed photo had eighteen distinctive features that positively identified them as Bruno Magli, Lorenzo-style shoes. In his previous deposition Uncle O.J. had no explanation for this. He had said (and he would repeat later in his testimony) that he could positively identify the blazer, shirt, and tie, but wasn't sure about the belt and pants. The shoes were not his, he said. The photo was a fake, he argued, saying that he had seen a picture of himself playing golf with Mark Fuhrman. Uncle O.J. never had an explanation for all the other photos. I thought to myself, *Why doesn't he just say 'I don't remember owning those shoes'?*

Next the limo driver, Alan Park, was called to the stand. Just like he had in the criminal trial, he testified that no one had answered his calls at Rockingham between 10:40 P.M. and 10:52 P.M. At 10:54 P.M. he'd seen a black man in dark clothing walk from the driveway into the front door. I had no doubt his observations were accurate, but this was old news. I'd known from the beginning that the man he'd seen was Uncle O.J. I also knew that the location of the Bronco that night was unusual. It was one of the things that had bothered me at the criminal trial.

What happened next, however, was anything but old news. It was arguably one of the most anticipated moments in American judicial history. Uncle O.J. was going to be called to testify. Few things about the criminal trial had caused more comment than the fact that Uncle O.J. hadn't testified. Numberless commentators had used his failure to appear as proof of his guilt; an innocent man, they insisted, would want to testify. Vincent Bugliosi had made quite a point of this in his indictment of Uncle O.J. What these people didn't realize is that Uncle O.J. was ready to testify; in fact, one of the Dream Team's biggest challenges had been to talk him out of it. He'd scheduled several

TV and radio interviews to talk about it, only to have his attorneys cancel his appearance at the last minute. He'd even gotten so frustrated at his attorneys' gag order that he'd impulsively called a couple of radio talk shows to respond to the latest new reports over the phone.

The general public was dying to hear what he had to say. Those who thought he was guilty wanted him to lie himself into a corner and reveal what they believed was the truth; those who believed in his innocence wanted him to have a chance to vindicate himself. Everybody in America, it seemed, except his attorneys, wanted to hear what O.J. Simpson had to say about his own case.

On Friday, November 22, during the fifth week of the trial, Uncle O.J. took the stand. I was worried. I knew he could ramble. A good witness has to be concise. The more you ramble, the more doors you open for your opponent to go through. I'd been relieved that he hadn't testified in the criminal trial; it was clearly in his own best interest. But in the civil trial, the plaintiffs had the right to call him to the witness stand, and he couldn't refuse. I knew that he would have to come up with some very specific answers to some very specific questions, and that he would have to curb his tendency either to overexplain or avoid issues. On the other hand, I was curious to hear what he had to say.

Uncle O.J.'s testimony surprised me in more than one way. First of all, he was more concise than I had expected. But what he actually said—the content of his testimony—surprised me a great deal. First he denied *ever* hitting Nicole at all. In light of the pictures of Nicole's battered face that I had seen, not to mention all the other evidence, I didn't know how he could claim never to have hit her. It was obvious that he had inflicted the bruises on her face and body somehow. I didn't know what happened, or the circumstances. I could well believe that Nicole had hit him first. But to claim he'd never touched her in anger?

I remembered the night at Rockingham when we'd overheard the fight, and how Uncle O.J. had said he'd shoved her out the door. He'd admitted it after the battery hearing in 1989; even A.C. had admitted taking Nicole to the hospital after one of their fights. It didn't mean that he'd killed her. It would have been so much better if he'd just admitted to their violent arguments, even if it only meant sharing the blame with Nicole for the physical part.

His testimony had so many holes in it, it was inevitable that people would question his sincerity. They all were playing word games. The plaintiffs were asking for a lot of specific information, asking him to remember dates and details. I could understand if he didn't remember some detail about events that had happened years ago, but that was different from denying *everything*. *Big mistake*, I thought.

After questioning Uncle O.J. about the abuse, Daniel Petrocelli moved on to ask him about his home-phone records on the day of the murders. Petrocelli displayed a huge enlargement of the phone bill and started working through it with Uncle O.J., call by call, verifying the calls just before and after the call to his message service.

Petrocelli was particularly interested in this call because he was trying to establish that Paula had called Uncle O.J. and left a message that she was breaking up with him. The prosecution theory was that that message had only added to Uncle O.J.'s anger on the night of the murder: first being pointedly ignored by Nicole after Sydney's dance recital, and then being dumped by Paula right afterward.

At first Uncle O.J. said he didn't remember making the call. But the records clearly indicated that *someone* had. It had already been established that he and Kato were the only ones in the house at that time. Then when pressed by Petrocelli, he conceded that he'd probably made the call, but had not heard the full message because Kato had come into the room and distracted him.

Uncle O.J. was so used to people accepting whatever he said that he'd lost touch with how incredible this sounded. The records spoke for themselves. I thought that no intelligent person would believe him. Didn't he realize that by not conceding on what appeared to be minor points, he jeopardized his credibility on the more important ones?

Next, Petrocelli asked Uncle O.J. if the entries made by Nicole in her diary on June 3, 1994, were accurate. Nicole had written in it that Uncle O.J. came over to her condo, started "raving" because she had hung up on him, called her a bitch and said that she was "going to pay for this." Uncle O.J. had a hard time with the questions, and then under pressure admitted that some parts of it were true.

Petrocelli moved on to the question of the Bronco's location the night of the murders. Why did he park on Rockingham instead of Ashford? Uncle O.J. really didn't have an answer. He mentioned his concern that the dog, Chachi, didn't escape. Then the plaintiffs showed a photo of Chachi lounging on the driveway with the gates wide open. I never heard that Chachi's running out the front gate had ever been an issue; he was old and had arthritis and never ran anywhere, anyway. (Ironically the next day, he did slip through the gate as we were leaving for court.)

The plaintiffs continued questioning him the following day. Petrocelli began by asking questions about the slow-speed chase. Had he said on the cell phone to Detective Lange that he himself was "the only one who deserves" to be hurt? I wondered what he'd meant. Uncle O.J. didn't really have an answer. During the same call he had said to Lange "You've been honest with me from the beginning'' and ''You're doing a good job.'' Uncle O.J. admitted saying those things.

He asked him about the blood evidence next. That had been the hardest part for me in the criminal trial. To rebut it, Bob Baker had made the strong point in his opening statement that the blood evidence was either tainted or planted at the crime scene. Petrocelli pushed Uncle O.J. hard on this point. Could he explain how blood consistent with the victims', and his own, got into his Bronco, his driveway, the foyer of his house, and into his bedroom within hours of the murders? Uncle O.J. said he had no idea. Could he explain the three cuts and seven abrasions his own physician had photographed after the murders, after insisting that he had only one cut when he came back from Chicago? Uncle O.J. testified that he got one of the cuts from a broken glass in his hotel room, and that the other cuts may have resulted from a wrestling match with Justin or when he retrieved his cell phone from the Bronco.

I was relieved when Uncle O.J. finished testifying. Johnnie had been right not to put him on the stand during the criminal trial. I thought some of his responses had been hard to believe. And, if I thought so, the jury might as well. We knew that the jury's reaction to him could make or break this case.

It was incredible to me that after everything he'd been through, Uncle O.J. had failed to shake his image of himself as a celebrity. He didn't realize how angry some segments of the American public were at him and seemed to hold to the thought that everyone still adored him as they once had.

A week after Uncle O.J.'s testimony, A.C. was called to the stand. He clearly didn't want to be there, offering testimony that would be damaging to his oldest friend. He reluctantly contradicted some of Uncle O.J.'s testimony.

Petrocelli pressed him on the abuse issue. Contrary to what Uncle O.J. had said, A.C. testified that there was violence in their relationship. *This is his childhood friend,* I thought. *A.C. had grown up at Grandma's table.* He was in a terrible position. He was torn between his loyalty for Uncle O.J. and his legal obligation to tell the truth. I remembered A.C.'s grief when Nicole died, and the hours he'd spent that week taking care of Sydney and Justin. I respected his close friendship with Uncle O.J., but wondered if he had doubts.

The rest of the trial was a blur. For the most part, it was déjà vu for me. Bob Baker presented a well-organized defense, playing on many of the same themes Johnnie and the Dream Team had used in the criminal trial. But there was no new evidence to help Uncle O.J.'s case, and some of the old evidence wasn't allowed in. Judge Fujisaki was determined to limit what the defense could introduce into evidence or testimony, though he admitted almost everything the plaintiffs wanted. My family knew he was biased. If Judge Ito was guilty of letting the Dream Team run wild, as the prosecution had claimed, Judge Fujisaki was his opposite. He kept a choke hold on the defense by not admitting the crucial evidence surrounding the issues of racism and evidence tampering of LAPD.

Fred Goldman was the last witness the plaintiffs called. What really moved me was the slide presentation of Ron's life with his family. The images of him were full of life and reminded me of the same close relationship that my family shares. As I sat there trying to hold back the tears, a woman sitting next to me whispered, "I don't know about you, but I'm bored." I thought how callous could anyone be. Anyone sitting in that courtroom would have be touched by the emotion of the moment.

Because I was part of the Simpson family, it was inappropriate for me to cry during the presentation, but the feelings were there. As soon as it was over, there was break and I rushed out away from the media because I couldn't hold back the tears any longer. I went to the roof of the building overwhelmed with sadness and empathy. The tears wouldn't stop coming.

On January 16, 1997, both sides rested their cases. There had been only forty-one days of testimony. Compared to the eight months of the criminal trial, forty-one days was nothing. On January 21 Daniel Petrocelli made his closing arguments. He pointed at Uncle O.J. and said, "There's a killer in this courtroom." It was very melodramatic.

The next day Bob Baker presented his closing arguments. He looked at the jury and said, "It's law enforcement versus O.J. Simpson." The jury stared back, impassive. I wondered what they thought. I wasn't very optimistic.

Back at Rockingham we had a betting pool going. No one was sure how long it would take for a verdict, but we were all sure it would take more than the few hours it had taken in the criminal trial. The jury began its deliberations on Thursday, January 23.

On Tuesday, February 4, we got the call. The verdict was in, and we needed to get down to the courthouse right away.

Uncle O.J. was out playing golf. It might sound implausible to people who didn't know him, but it made perfect sense to us. It was his way of coping with the stress of the situation. Mom, Dad, and I were at Rockingham together, but Bob Baker was out of town. Bob Blasier had gone home to Sacramento. So Dan Leonard would represent us in court and drove my parents and me there. Kathy Randa was trying to get ahold of Uncle O.J. on his cell phone as we rushed out the door.

As we drove toward the courthouse, my mother coached "No matter what the verdict," she said, "we will see this through with dignity and come out of that courtroom with our heads held high."

When we arrived in the courtroom, we found out that the rush was unnecessary. The announcement was being postponed until the Browns arrived from Orange County. They were driving up from Laguna in the middle of rush hour. It would be a least an hour more before they could get to court. Kathy had managed to contact Uncle O.J. on the golf course. The delay gave Uncle O.J. time to get there.

When everyone was finally in place, the jury filed in, followed by Judge Fujisaki. I was nervous, but not nearly so much as I was for the criminal trial. The criminal trial was about whether Uncle O.J. would spend the rest of his life in jail. The civil trial was about money. The jury found him liable for the deaths of Ron and Nicole, and awarded the plaintiffs $8.5 million in compensatory damages, with punitive damages to be determined. My heart dropped, and suddenly, all I wanted was to get away from there and be alone with my family.

Meanwhile, a media circus was going on outside. Because cameras weren't allowed in the courtroom this time, the TV stations couldn't carry the reading of the verdict live. To compensate for this, they had come up with a bizarre communication system for the American public. Designated members of the media had made up cardboard signs with numbers indicating the various charges against Uncle O.J., the words "Guilty" and "Not Guilty," and dollar amounts for possible damages. The people with the signs were stationed inside the press room at the courthouse, next to a window, listening to a live feed from the courtroom that they weren't allowed to broadcast. Cameras from all the major networks were fastened on this window, waiting to beam the signals all over the world. As the ruling for each count was read, someone would hold a placard up to the window for the news commentator outside to read aloud. Each time part of the verdict was read, the crowd outside would go crazy.

As the verdicts were read, the Goldmans wept with joy. The Browns were less demonstrative. We filed out as quietly as we could in the midst of the general hysteria. A moment later I found myself hustled out the front entrance with my parents, and Uncle O.J. Lights began to flash from the cameras all around us. The news commentators identified me as Arnelle. My Mom stood as proud and straight as ever behind her brother, but at the precise moment we looked down to negotiate the steps in front of the courthouse, a *Los Angeles Times* photographer took our picture. So much for keeping our heads high. The photo, naturally, would grace the front cover of the next day's paper. We all looked defeated. The media has many ways of making its comments.

Thomas, Uncle O.J.'s bodyguard, was waiting in the Suburban, surrounded by hundreds of media people and hordes of curious onlookers. People were hooting, shouting, and protesting. A barrage of racial epithets came our way. I was glad to get into the safe confines of the car. As we pulled out of the courthouse and onto the Santa Monica Freeway, we all said, "Well, we expected this." We weren't prepared yet to consider the implications of the verdict for Uncle O.J.'s life.

With the now-familiar helicopters buzzing overhead, we made the transition to the 405 Freeway north. We talked about the kids, other events of the day, and whatever else came into our minds. We needed to pretend it was just a normal day for us. As we got off the freeway at Sunset,

Uncle O.J. said, "Let's stop for ice cream." Justin and Sydney were back at Rockingham, and Sydney had wanted Uncle O.J. to bring some home. We pulled over to the Baskin Robbins on Barrington, and Thomas double-parked in the tiny cul-de-sac by the entrance. Tom, Uncle O.J. and my Dad went in while we stayed in the Suburban. *Nicole had stopped for ice cream the night she died. Cookies and cream. Her favorite.* I shook off the thought.

A crowd started to gather outside. However, unlike past crowds who always had something to say, this group was silent. They'd just heard about the verdict and didn't seem to know how to respond.

"I want some ice cream, too," I said to my mother, and started to get out of the car. At first she tried to stop me, but then decided to join me instead. Pretty soon we were all inside, standing at the counter. My dad got a cone with cookies and cream ice cream. The press later reported that Uncle O.J. had ordered it, but it wasn't true.

As we licked our cones in silence, the car wound its way down Sunset and back to Rockingham. The media still hovered all around, though their ranks were beginning to thin out. More than two years ago I had taken my first ride in that strange celebrity caravan, on the way to Nicole's wake. That day I had been so traumatized I could hardly eat. Now the incessant media clamor all around us had become like a buzzing mosquito, irritating but ordinary, blending into the pattern of our everyday lives. The old Terri would have been devastated by the events of the day. This Terri could ignore the roar of the helicopters and focus on her cousins who were home and probably needing help with their homework. For better or worse, the trials of the century—both of them—were finally over, and we had survived. I guess that's all any of us can ask.

IN A MIRROR, DARKLY

I did not write this book either to exonerate or convict my uncle, O.J. Simpson. That is a matter for the courts, and they have made their decisions. Based on the evidence presented to them, I think both juries made the correct decision. As for my personal belief, that answer is much more complicated. My head tells me one thing, and my heart tells me another. It is a painful conflict for me, one I must live with every day.

The idea for this book was born in a series of conversations with my brother Benny, my friends Alexa, Monika and other people who are important in my life. A few weeks after I came out of rehabilitation more than a year ago. I had been home long enough by then to see the problems in my relationship between me my family. For a while I toyed with the idea of writing a letter to Uncle O.J., telling him how I felt about the events of the last few years. I saw my release from rehab as parallel in some ways to his release from jail: we had both been given the chance to start new lives, as better people, and to learn from our past. After the civil trial, I began to write down my thoughts and feelings, which eventually turned into this book.

My family has struggled with my decision to write it. "Do you want to hurt your uncle?" they ask me. No. I get no pleasure from hurting him. I hope he will learn from what I have to say. I hope we will all learn. I hope it will become clear how very much we love Uncle O.J. no matter what has happened in the past. "Do you want to hurt us?" they ask next. No, never. Fearing their pain has been the hardest part of this experience. It would be so much easier for me just to keep silent.

Why did I write this book, then? For many reasons. Because I feel I must honor the truth, for as much as I love my family, my first duty is to God. Because I am tired of hiding what I believe for fear someone won't love me if I say what I am really thinking. And most of all, because I love the new woman I have become, the woman who survived the fires of shame, failure, and rebirth, to tell a story I think is worth telling. That woman deserves her own respect.

There's a chapter in the New Testament that's sometimes referred to as the "love chapter." It's the kind of thing that gets printed on greeting cards and posters because it says a lot of pretty things about human love. But the most compelling part of the apostle Paul's *First Letter to the Corinthians*, Chapter 13, is not what it says about human love, but about God's love. God's love is a great deal stronger and more all-encompassing than human love. It is also a great deal more dangerous, for it requires us to look deeply into the mirror of our own souls. Sometimes we don't like what we see there. But there is an infinite source of comfort in the murky image that flickers before us, for God also tells us that we see our lives "in a mirror, darkly" on earth, but that someday we will know ourselves as God already knows us. And he promises us that in that moment of clear vision, we will find ultimate love and acceptance. That is what this book is about—finding the truth, accepting it, and learning to love it. It isn't easy.

Ron and Nicole weren't the only ones who died that night in June. Sydney and Justin lost their mother and their childhood. They will never get them back. The Goldmans lost their son and brother, and Ron's sister Kim lost her faith in the goodness of life. The Goldmans may never find the justice they seek on earth. And if they search for it too long, they will lose what Ron held most precious—their own lives together. My family lost their privacy, their hard-earned good name, most of their financial resources, and three years of their lives. What else they will lose as we put our lives back together remains to be seen. Americans, black and white, lost even more of the battered remnants of their idealism. My uncle O.J. lost his reputation, a good part of his wealth, and the illusion that he would not be held accountable for his choices. Whatever his part was in the events of that night, he is accountable for a lifetime of choices that have hurt the people who love him. As for the rest, that will be between him and God when he makes the same journey Nicole and Ron made before their time.

And me? My life died that June day, too. I lost my job, my health, and for a while, my sanity. I am no longer the sheltered young girl who grew up in Westborough and dreamed big dreams of a family, a career, and vacations in Italy. That girl would never recognize the alcoholic who was carried out of my Los Angeles apartment two years ago. That girl is gone. So is the woman whose only remaining hope in life was a painless death. For with every death, there is the possibility of new life. I have that chance. I am one of the fortunate ones.

CELEBRITY BIOGRAPHIES

BARBRA STREISAND   (0-7860-0051-1, $4.99/$5.99)
By Nellie Bly

BURT AND ME   (0-7860-0117-8, $5.99/$6.99)
By Elaine Blake Hall

CAPTAIN QUIRK   (0-7860-0185-2, $4.99/$5.99)
By Dennis William Hauck

ELIZABETH: (0-8217-4269-8, $4.99/$5.99)
  THE LIFE OF ELIZABETH TAYLOR
By Alexander Walker

JIMMY STEWART:
  A WONDERFUL LIFE   (0-7860-0506-8, $5.99/$7.50)
By Frank Sanello

MARLON BRANDO:
  LARGER THAN LIFE   (0-7860-0086-4, $4.99/$5.99)
By Nellie Bly

OPRAH!   (0-8217-4613-8, $4.99/$5.99)
  UP CLOSE AND DOWN HOME
By Nellie Bly

RAINBOW'S END:
  THE JUDY GARLAND SHOW   (0-8217-3708-2, $5.99/$6.99)
By Coyne Steven Sanders

THE KENNEDY MEN: (1-57566-015-6, $22.95/$26.95)
  3 GENERATIONS OF SEX, SCANDAL, & SECRETS
By Nellie Bly

TODAY'S BLACK HOLLYWOOD   (0-7860-0104-6, $4.99/$5.99)
By James Robert Parish

Available wherever paperbacks are sold, or order direct from the Publisher. Send cover price plus 50¢ per copy for mailing and handling to Kensington Publishing Corp., Consumer Orders, or call (toll free) 888-345-BOOK, to place your order using Mastercard or Visa. Residents of New York and Tennessee must include sales tax. DO NOT SEND CASH.